Probation and Parole
in America

Probation and Parole in America

Harry E. Allen • Chris W. Eskridge
Edward J. Latessa • Gennaro F. Vito

THE FREE PRESS
A Division of Macmillan, Inc.
NEW YORK

Collier Macmillan Publishers
LONDON

The Free Press
A Division of Macmillan, Inc.
866 Third Avenue, New York, N.Y. 10022

Collier Macmillan Canada, Inc.

Printed in the United States of America

printing number

1 2 3 4 5 6 7 8 9 10

Library of Congress Cataloging in Publication Data

Main entry under title:

Probation and parole in America.

    Includes bibliographies and index.
    1. Probation—United States.   2. Parole—United States.
3. Corrections—United States.   I. Allen, Harry E.
HV9304.P77   1985   364.6'3'0973   85–10093
ISBN 0–02–900440–3

Dedicated to
Cleo, Cherie, Sally, and Mary

Contents

10. The Use of Paraprofessionals and Ex-Offenders   205

11. The Use of Volunteers   223

List of Illustrations

List of Tables

Preface

Probation and Parole in America is a text designed for criminal justice and criminology students in their second or third year of study, and would be for the student's second course in the area of corrections. It explores the broad areas of the system: the procedures, processes, and people that constitute the probation and parole areas of corrections. As such, the text covers a wide range of activities. It reviews the origins of probation and parole, where the fields are currently, where they seem to be going, and what policy issues and questions need resolution in order to arrive at those goals.

It will become apparent that such questions as "What is probation and parole?" and "What strategies are best to handle clients?" are not easily answered. An awareness of this fact should serve to stimulate students to develop and implement reforms in their chosen area, whether probation or parole.

We have tried to give a clear overview of each of the practices and issues that comprise probation and parole, exploring in some depth the crucial questions and presenting contemporary evidence of the current scenes. We present this text to students and educators with the firm hope that it will be an enjoyable as well as an educational process. We offer a textbook that has been organized and written with the goal of making the learning experience as interesting and comprehensive as possible.

Each of the authors brought specific areas of expertise to the efforts of writing this text: correctional (and law enforcement and prosecutorial) practice, research, and administration. We individually wrote from two to four chapters, revised them extensively, and combined our efforts to produce this final version. Allen had primary responsibility for Chapters 5 and 13; Eskridge for 6, 8, and 11; Latessa for 4, 9, 10, and 12; and Vito for 1, 3, and 7. Lawrence F. Travis III (University of Cincinnati) contributed Chapter 2, "The Development of Parole in America," for which we are appreciative and grateful. This has truly been a collaborative—if sometimes painful—effort and therefore we list our names alphabetically.

Organization of the Text

There are thirteen chapters in the text, each of which ends with review questions and key terms to focus the student's learning experience and to help instructors in their teachings roles. Notes have been held to a minimum, and references have been identified in order that students might research a topic more thoroughly. Each chapter ends with recommendations of from two to six additional sources to which the student might turn for more current or extensive data on an issue or topic.

Chapter 1 outlines the roles of probation and parole in the criminal justice system. Chapter 2 studies the development of parole in America, tracing its historical and philosophical antecedents, as well as its rise, in America. Chapter 3 defines probation and traces its development from Judaic law through early English and European precursors. It specifically focuses on the philosophical bases of probation and its implementation as an American innovation.

Chapter 4 defines the functions, use, and objectives of the presentence investigation, including its role in sentencing hearings. Chapter 5 discusses the process of granting and revoking probation, the individualization of sentencing, and conditions of probation. Chapter 6 deals with the process of granting parole, parole board hearings, and factors considered by parole boards in decision making.

Chapter 7 examines the various roles of probation and parole officers, types of styles of supervision, and the treatment-supervision dichotomy. Chapter 8 studies the education and training of supervising officers, including entry-level requirements, standards, and roles of professional organizations.

Chapter 9 examines service delivery strategies, including innovative administrative approaches to traditional casework. Chapter 10 discusses the use of paraprofessionals and ex-offenders in probation and parole, and includes the most recent data on the extent of both programs. Chapter 11 focuses on the use of volunteers, their recruitment, training, services, and cost factors.

Chapter 12 ranges over the major subjects of probation and parole effectiveness in general, and specific types and classes of supervised offenders. Costs, effectiveness, outcomes, and future research agenda needs are examined. Chapter 13 is a futuristic view of the contemporary scene ("at the crossroads"), identifying political philosophy, costs, management issues, and strategies and tactics for expanding and increasing the effectiveness of probation and parole in the next decade. These are the tasks facing the future officers in these areas of the correctional field.

Acknowledgments

We acknowledge the ground-breaking efforts of the National Council on Crime and Delinquency in two important areas of probation and parole: their National Probation Reports (NPR) and Uniform Parole Reports (UPR). Both efforts, funded through grants from the Department of Justice, have provided meaningful, current and national statistics on both sets of clients. Not only are their data significant, the implications inherent in these are salient, and their statistics are included in several chapters of this text.

Special thanks are expressed to Joyce Seltzer, Senior Editor of The Free Press, for her counsel, gentle prodding, and kind support. Her efforts have helped produce this volume and made the task less onerous.

Professors Robert Culbertson, Patricia Hardyman, Dennis Longmire, and Donal E. J. MacNamara reviewed a draft of this text and provided many pertinent comments that subsequently guided the revision of the manuscript.

Finally, we offer a special word of thanks to the Academic and Professional Development Service of the University of Louisville for their efficient and tireless editing and re-editing of several versions of this manuscript, and to Candalyn Fryrear, who offered special help in the preparation of the manuscript for final typing.

1

Probation, Parole, and the Criminal Justice System

The purpose of this text is to explain and examine the process of probation and parole in the United States, and current statistics indicate just how important that role is in the criminal justice process. Fortunately, two statistical reporting systems have recently been developed to give some indication of how many persons are presently involved with probation and parole nationwide. We will get to these, but first we start with an overview of the place and purpose of probation and parole in the criminal justice system.

The Concept of a Criminal Justice System

As indicated by Hudzik and Cordner (1983: 87–90), the idea of a criminal justice system was first presented in President Lyndon Johnson's Crime Commission report, *The Challenge of Crime in a Free Society*. This report included the now-famous diagram (see Figure 1–1) that outlined the basic sequence of events in the criminal justice process. Police, courts, and corrections were thus viewed as elements that were interrelated and interdependent. The idea was to demonstrate the manner in which successful crime prevention was the goal of the entire system.

What is the sequence of events in the criminal justice system?

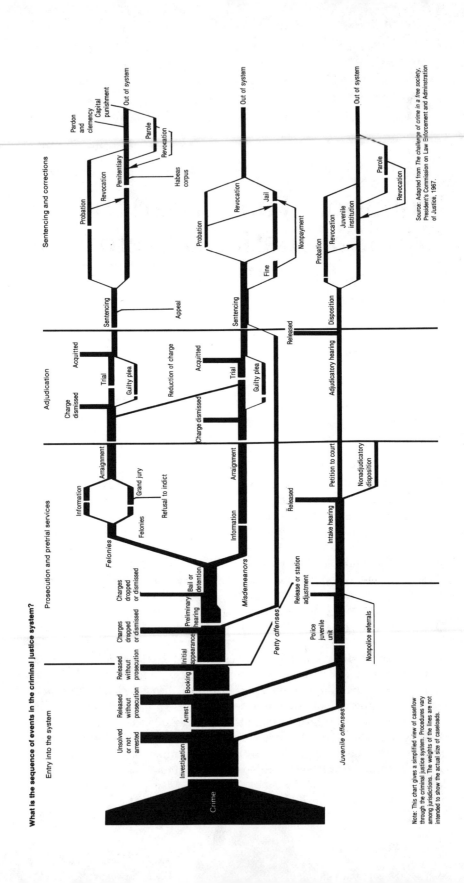

Entry into the system

Prosecution and pretrial services

Adjudication

Sentencing and corrections

Crime

Investigation

Arrest

Booking

Initial appearance

Preliminary hearing

Bail or detention

Unsolved or not arrested

Released without prosecution

Released without prosecution

Charges dropped or dismissed

Charges dropped or dismissed

Felonies

Information

Arraignment

Grand jury

Felonies

Refusal to indict

Misdemeanors

Information

Arraignment

Petty offenses

Released

Charge dismissed

Trial

Acquitted

Guilty plea

Reduction of charge

Charge dismissed

Trial

Acquitted

Guilty plea

Sentencing

Appeal

Probation

Revocation

Penitentiary

Habeas corpus

Pardon and clemency

Capital punishment

Parole

Revocation

Out of system

Sentencing

Probation

Revocation

Fine

Nonpayment

Jail

Out of system

Juvenile offenses

Police juvenile unit

Nonpolice referrals

Release or station adjustment

Intake hearing

Released

Petition to court

Nonadjudicatory disposition

Adjudicatory hearing

Released

Disposition

Probation

Revocation

Juvenile institution

Parole

Revocation

Out of system

Note: This chart gives a simplified view of caseflow through the criminal justice system. Procedures vary among jurisdictions. The weights of the lines are not intended to show the actual size of caseloads.

Source: Adapted from *The challenge of crime in a free society*, President's Commission on Law Enforcement and Administration of Justice, 1967.

In Figure 1-1, it is clear that probation and parole represent outputs from the system, with offenders placed under community supervision. Probationers and parolees can return to the system (recidivate) by either committing a new offense or violating a condition of their release (resulting in a revocation). A brief consideration of the numbers of persons involved at different stages in the process gives some indication of the place of probation and parole in the criminal justice system.

A statistical picture of how the system operates has been published by the Bureau of Justice Statistics (November 1983) based upon its Offender Based Transaction Statistics program (OBTS). Analyzing data collected in four states, OBTS focuses upon the arrested individual as the unit of analysis and traces that offender through the criminal justice process. In short, for every hundred felony arrests, there is clear evidence of what has been termed the "funnel effect." This funnel results from the attrition that occurs at every stage of the criminal justice process. There is a clear and steady reduction in the number of offenders from arrest through imprisonment.

As Table 1-1 reveals, forty-eight out of every hundred felony arrests result in prosecution, thirty-one of these cases are convicted and twelve persons are eventually imprisoned (most for one year or less). Naturally, these figures vary with the severity of the offense, but the funnel effect remains pronounced. Probation and parole, at their respective stages, play a major role in the creation of this funnel effect. For example, the National Probation Reports (1979) states that the percentage of probationers convicted of a felony was 46 percent, showing that a sizeable portion of convicted persons were diverted from the prison population and placed on probation. A close examination of this source of information reveals the impact of probation upon the criminal justice system.

National Probation Reports (NPR)

In 1980, through a grant from the Bureau of Justice Statistics, the National Council on Crime and Delinquency instituted the National Probation Reports, the first attempt to establish a systematic annual census of the nation's probation population. As a result of their efforts, fifty-eight central probation reporting agencies were identified. These fifty-eight agencies were responsible for centralized data collection on probationers in their jurisdiction. Contact with these agencies yielded the following information about probation in the U.S. (see Table 1-2).

In calendar 1982, the adult probation population rose by more than 100,000 persons to 1,335,359—an increase of 9 percent in 1982 alone; forty-eight persons per 10,000 population were placed on probation (since 1979, the probation population has grown 25 percent). The median proba-

Table 1-1
Outcome for Felony Offenders in Four States, by Offense

DISPOSITION	FOUR-STATE TOTAL	PART I PERSONAL	PART I PROPERTY	ALL OTHER FELONIES	PART I PERSONAL OFFENSES				PART I PROPERTY OFFENSES			
					Homicide	Rape	Robbery	Assault	Burglary	Larceny	Auto theft	Arson
For 100 arrests:												
Not prosecuted	52	16	38	70	9	15	11	20	21	51	32	32
Prosecuted	48	84	62	30	91	85	89	80	79	49	68	68
Of those prosecuted:												
Dismissed	15	33	17	8	23	35	31	36	21	13	24	21
Acquitted	1	3	1	1	6	6	3	2	1	1	1	3
Other disposition	1	1	1	1	1	1	1	1	1	1	1	1
Convicted	31	47	43	20	61	43	54	41	56	34	42	43
Of those convicted:												
Not imprisoned	19	24	26	14	18	19	20	29	30	23	25	24
Imprisoned	12	23	17	6	43	24	34	12	26	11	17	19
Of those imprisoned:												
A year or less	7	8	11	4	8	7	10	8	15	8	14	7
More than a year	5	15	6	2	35	17	24	4	11	3	3	12

SOURCE: Bureau of Justice Statistics, *Bulletin: Tracking Offenders*, p. 4 (Rockville, Md.: National Criminal Justice Reference Service, 1983).

Table 1-2
Adults on Probation, 1981–82

	Adult Residents 7/1/82	Probation Population 12/31/81	Entries	Exits	Probation Population 12/31/82	Entries per 10,000 1982
U.S. total	168,740,000	1,225,934	817,042	707,617	1,335,359	48
Federal		46,711	20,329	19,029	48,011	
State total	168,740,000	1,179,223	796,713	688,588	1,287,348	47
Northeast	36,919,000	219,631	139,983	118,095	241,519	38
Maine	824,000	2,978	3,812	3,750	3,040	46
New Hampshire	697,000	2,261	1,726	1,724	2,263	25
Vermont	376,000	3,400	2,400	2,400	3,400	64
Massachusetts	4,366,000	21,633	20,017	19,863	21,787	46
Rhode Island	725,000	6,049	3,633	3,181	6,501	50
Connecticut	2,370,000	24,778	27,226	18,943	33,061	115
New York	13,151,000	69,583	30,991	25,594	74,980	24
New Jersey	5,534,000	35,326	24,663	20,050	39,939	45
Pennsylvania	8,876,000	53,623	25,515	22,590	56,548	29
North Central	42,609,000	234,175	167,581	162,594	239,162	39
Ohio	7,818,000	30,540	16,680	14,785	32,435	21
Indiana	3,926,000	21,404	23,190	23,190	21,404	59
Illinois	8,310,000	65,922	42,402	46,775	61,549	51
Michigan	6,530,000	26,751	10,659	9,893	27,517	16
Wisconsin	3,451,000	20,060	9,635	9,149	20,546	28

5

Table 1-2 (*Continued*)

	Adult Residents 7/1/82	Probation Population 12/31/81	Entries	Exits	Probation Population 12/31/82	Entries per 10,000 1982
Minnesota	2,993,000	19,578	20,812	18,979	21,411	70
Iowa	2,109,000	9,850	11,093	10,318	10,625	53
Missouri	3,629,000	19,149	13,664	11,176	21,637	38
North Dakota	447,000	1,098	695	634	1,159	15
South Dakota	490,000	1,302	767	576	1,493	16
Nebraska	1,145,000	6,759	8,804	7,939	7,624	77
Kansas	1,761,000	11,762	9,180	9,180	11,762	52
South	56,515,000	471,410	338,342	273,607	536,145	60
Delaware	443,000	3,893	3,080	2,347	4,626	70
Maryland	3,154,000	48,068	37,329	32,794	52,603	118
Dist. of Columbia	494,000	7,178	6,663	6,911	6,930	135
Virginia	4,053,000	14,326	6,513	6,179	14,660	16
West Virginia	1,405,000	2,726	1,802	1,782	2,746	13
North Carolina	4,402,000	40,335	23,884	19,945	44,274	54
South Carolina	2,278,000	19,170	9,159	9,376	18,953	40
Georgia	4,011,000	66,473	49,608	39,129	76,952	124
Florida	7,987,000	44,962	43,397	31,285	57,074	54
Kentucky	2,625,000	12,615	3,498	1,597	14,516	13

Tennessee	3,390,000	9,716	8,655	8,270	26
Alabama	2,812,000	13,021	5,563	4,381	20
Mississippi	1,752,000	5,668	2,456	1,820	14
Arkansas	1,642,000	2,262	2,267	1,713	14
Louisiana	3,020,000	15,880	9,083	7,595	30
Oklahoma	2,296,000	13,306	7,148	5,705	31
Texas	10,751,000	151,811	118,237	92,778	110
West	32,697,000	254,007	150,807	134,292	46
Montana	570,000	2,369	869	867	15
Idaho	655,000	2,675	2,362	2,122	36
Wyoming	347,000	1,057	850	643	24
Colorado	2,219,000	13,419	10,019	8,835	45
New Mexico	937,000	3,360	1,999	1,845	21
Arizona	2,049,000	14,289	6,942	5,328	34
Utah	974,000	7,346	6,630	5,371	68
Nevada	651,000	5,671	2,324	1,789	36
Washington	3,105,000	30,759	8,596	4,350	28
Oregon	1,938,000	14,211	7,997	6,492	41
California	18,239,000	152,563	96,952	92,636	53
Alaska	297,000	1,314	850	348	29
Hawaii	716,000	4,974	4,417	3,666	62

Source: Adapted from Bureau of Justice Statistics, *Bulletin: Probation and Parole, 1982* (Rockville, Md.: National Criminal Justice Reference Service, 1983).

7

tion entry rate in 1982 was 38, with the range of rates going from a low of 13 (West Virginia and Kentucky) to a high of 124 (Georgia). The growth in the use of probation was widespread, with only three jurisdictions reporting decreases (Illinois, the District of Columbia, and South Carolina). As a region, the South recorded the largest number of entries, exits, total population, and entries per 10,000 population (Bureau of Justice Statistics, 1983).

In all, it has become clear that a great number of convicted persons are now being placed on probation instead of being incarcerated. In most cases, probation agencies monitor the offender's compliance with the conditions of probation release (i.e., drug/alcohol rehabilitation, payment of fines or restitution, or sentencing to community service). The crucial role that probation plays in the criminal justice process becomes more apparent when institutional and parole population figures are examined.

The U.S. Prison Census

Because the rate of parole in a given state is affected by the size of the prison population, it is necessary to examine the size of the U.S. prison population before considering parole figures. A census of state and federal institutions is conducted each year by the Bureau of Justice Statistics (Gettinger, 1983). Table 1–3 reflects the prison census of 1983.

Overall, the U.S. prison population rose 5.9 percent to an all-time high of 438,830 inmates. The rate of change ranged from an increase of 27.3 percent for North Dakota to a decrease of 17.0 percent for Vermont. However, another key comparison is the number of sentenced prisoners per 100,000 population. This statistic makes it possible to compare rates of incarceration across states of different sizes. Regionally, the South has the greatest rate of incarceration (225/100,000) with the District of Columbia recording the highest number of prisoners per 100,000 population (558). The lowest rate of incarceration was reported by North Dakota (51).

These figures are important to the parole rates because they represent the source of clients for the prison system. Prisoners enter the parole system by a parole board decision or by fulfilling the conditions of mandatory release. Typically, at some time between their minimum and maximum sentences, inmates are released from prison and put on parole by a parole board. Mandatory parolees enter parole supervision automatically at the expiration of their maximum term minus time off for accumulated good time credits. Traditionally, this is the manner in which a parole system operates under the indeterminate sentencing model presently in force in most states. However, a major change in the parole systems occurred during the past decade as several states moved to a determinate sentencing structure.

Table 1–3
Prison Census, 12/31/83

	TOTAL			NUMBER OF SENTENCED PRISONERS PER 100,000 POPULATION
	1983	1982	Percent change	12/31/83
U.S. total	438,830	414,362	5.9	179
Male	419,811	396,439	5.9	352
Female	19,019	17,923	6.1	14
Federal institutions	31,926	29,673	7.6	11
State institutions	406,904	384,689	5.8	167
Northeast	65,680	60,203	9.1	127
Maine	1,049	999	5.0	75
New Hampshire	479	445	7.6	50
Vermont	497	599	− 17.0	72
Massachusetts	4,559	4,623	− 1.4	79
Rhode Island	1,157	1,037	11.6	92
Connecticut	5,474	5,836	− 6.2	114
New York	30,489	27,951	09.1	172
New Jersey	10,209	8,191	24.6	136
Pennsylvania	11,767	10,522	11.8	98
North Central	81,640	78,549	03.9	135
Ohio	17,766	17,317	2.6	155
Indiana	9,360	8,790	6.5	164
Illinois	15,595	14,293	9.1	135
Michigan	14,382	15,224	− 5.5	159
Wisconsin	4,898	4,670	4.9	102
Minnesota	2,156	4,081	3.6	52
Iowa	2,814	2,829	− 0.5	92
Missouri	8,053	7,445	8.2	162
North Dakota	410	322	27.3	51
South Dakota	824	791	4.2	115
Nebraska	1,677	1,709	− 1.9	91
Kansas	3,705	3,078	20.4	152
South	186,373	180,946	3.0	225
Delaware	2,190	2,062	6.2	273
Maryland	12,606	11,012	14.5	277
District of Columbia	4,344	4,081	6.4	558
Virginia	10,093	10,079	0.1	177
West Virginia	1,628	1,729	− 5.8	83
North Carolina	15,395	16,578	− 7.1	233
South Carolina	9,583	9,137	4.9	276
Georgia	15,347	14,416	6.5	259
Florida	26,334	27,830	− 5.4	235
Kentucky	4,738	4,077	16.2	127
Tennessee	8,768	7,869	11.4	187
Alabama	9,856	9,233	6.7	243
Mississippi	5,586	5,484	1.9	211

Table 1–3 (*Continued*)

	TOTAL			NUMBER OF SENTENCED PRISONERS PER 100,000 POPULATION 12/31/83
	1983	*1982*	*Percent change*	
Arkansas	4,183	3,925	6.6	179
Louisiana	12,976	10,935	18.7	290
Oklahoma	7,487	6,350	17.9	212
Texas	35,259	36,149	– 2.5	221
West	73,211	64,991	12.6	152
Montana	850	914	– 7.0	104
Idaho	1,206	1,047	15.2	121
Wyoming	721	702	2.7	138
Colorado	3,450	3,042	13.4	109
New Mexico	2,013	1,718	17.2	142
Arizona	6,889	6,069	13.5	223
Utah	1,275	1,216	4.9	77
Nevada	3,200	2,712	18.0	354
Washington	6,701	6,322	6.0	155
Oregon	4,181	3,867	8.1	157
California	39,360	34,640	13.6	150
Alaska	1,634	1,306	25.1	219
Hawaii	1,731	1,436	20.5	103

SOURCE: Bureau of Justice Statistics, *Prisoners in 1983*, p. 4 (Washington, D.C.: U.S. Department of Justice, 1984).

In nine states (California, Colorado, Connecticut, Illinois, Indiana, Maine, Minnesota, New Mexico, and North Carolina), the parole board no longer has the authority to release prisoners on parole before the expiration of their sentences. The best example of how this type of system operates is California.

The Determinate Sentence in California

The California law (enacted on July 1, 1977) effectively abolished the indeterminate sentence for crimes other than "capital cases," which carry a maximum sentence of life imprisonment and are parolable at a minimum term of seven years (or which carry a death sentence). As Table 1–4 illustrates, all other felony crimes are classified into four categories arranged on a scale that indicates the severity of the crime committed.

In each category, the court has a choice of three definite sentences. The judge is required by law to select the middle term unless mitigating or aggravating circumstances, which would merit the lowest or highest term,

Table 1–4
The Determinate Sentence in California

FELONY CATEGORY	SENTENCING RANGE	EXAMPLES
Class A	5–6–7 years	Murder in the second degree; rape with force or violence; exploding a destructive device to cause bodily harm
Class B	3–4–5 years	Robbery in the first degree by a person armed with a firearm; safecracking; kidnapping; burglary in the first degree
Class C	2–3–4 years	Robbery in the second degree; arson; assault with a deadly weapon; bribery of a public officer
Class D	1⅓–2–3 years	Grand theft; burglary in the second degree; forgery; car theft

SOURCE: Department of Criminal Justice/California State University at Long Beach, *The Impact of Determinate Sentencing Upon Corrections: A Handbook for Decision Makers*, p. 8 (Boulder, Colo.: National Institute of Corrections, 1980).

are present. When the court selects any of the three prison terms, the judge must set forth in writing the reasons for this decision and must inform the defendant of such reasons. In effect, this requirement opens the sentence to appeal by the defendant by making the sentence a part of the trial record.

The code also provides for "enhancements" (additional years) if certain factors are present. The factors that could lead to the use of an enhancement must be pleaded and proven in court. For example, one year can be added for carrying a weapon in the course of a crime, and three years for seriously injuring a victim or for a prior conviction for a violent felony; in addition, the court may impose an additional year for each prior prison term. However, there are certain limitations. For violent crimes, if an individual's prior prison term was followed by ten years without a felony conviction, that prior term cannot serve as the basis for an enhancement. For nonviolent crimes, the postprison period without a felony conviction for which an enhancement cannot be sought is reduced to five years.

Once the sentence is imposed, the length of time served can be reduced by one-third through the use of good time credit. For example, for each eight months served without a disciplinary infraction, an inmate earns three months' credit, and an additional month can be gained every eight months through participation in required work details or in self-improvement programs. Under this formula, an inmate sentenced to three years who maintains good conduct and participates in programs can be released in two years.

Although the statute abolished the parole release function of the California Adult Authority, parole supervision has been retained. Under the original statute, all inmates were required, upon completion of their sentence, to undergo one year of parole supervision. Inmates convicted of a "capital offense" were required to submit to three years of parole supervision. This provision was amended in 1979 and the required period of supervision was extended to three and five years respectively, with the possibility of final release after one year of supervision. If parole is revoked for a technical violation, the maximum term that can be served in prison is six months.[1]

To administer these provisions, the statute established the Community Release Board. This board has several duties. First, since the new code was applied retroactively to include all persons incarcerated at the time of its passage, the board was required to reset the terms of those prisoners. As a result, some inmates were released shortly after the law was enacted. Second, the board conducts hearings and fixes parole release dates for inmates convicted of capital crimes (e.g., Charles Manson and Sirhan Sirhan). Third, the board reviews all prison sentences within the first year of incarceration and recommends resentencing when it finds that sentencing disparity exists. Fourth, the board reviews all actions and procedures affecting the assignment and forfeiture of good time credit. Finally, the Community Release Board has the power to revoke the parole supervision period (Department of Criminal Justice, California State University/Long Beach, 1980).

In short, determinate sentencing laws such as California's affect the parole system in a number of ways. First, they seek to limit or abolish the discretionary power of the parole board over release procedures. Second, while parole supervision is retained, it is often only on the basis of surveillance and societal protection. Systems such as these stress the retributive, deterrent, and incapacitative (rather than the rehabilitative) functions of imprisonment. Finally, determinate sentencing structures give greater emphasis to good time credit provisions since they represent the only way to shorten the term of incarceration (Parisi and Zillo, 1983).

Also, a re-examination of Table 1–3 reveals that determinate sentencing may have some affect on the rate of imprisonment. Of the nine states that operate under a determinate sentencing law, New Mexico (+ 17 percent), Colorado (+ 13 percent), and California (+ 14 percent) registered increases in the prison population above the national average for 1983 (+ 5.9 percent). It appears that determinate sentencing laws that limit the parole release function could bear some relation to the rate of prison overcrowding. In any event, the determinate sentence alters the manner in which parole boards operate. If determinate sentencing spreads across the country, the size of the mandatory release population will increase. In fact, according to the Uniform Parole Reports (UPR), the percentage of mandatory releases has tripled since 1975. A closer look at the UPR gives an indication of the manner in which parole affects the size of the U.S. prison population.

Uniform Parole Reports (UPR)

Beginning in 1978, the National Council on Crime and Delinquency developed, via a Justice Department grant, a mechanism to collect national parole statistics. The Uniform Parole Reports (UPR) contain data on adult parolees from paroling authorities in all fifty states, the federal government, the District of Columbia, Puerto Rico, and the Virgin Islands. The data represents only persons who have been sentenced to at least one year of imprisonment for a felony offense and who have been placed on supervision via discretionary parole or by mandatory release.

Table 1–5 contains information on the number of adults on parole in the United States in 1982. The total number of parolees under state and federal supervision in that year was estimated to be 243,880. This figure represented a 8.1 percent increase over the 1981 estimate of 225,539 parolees. Since 1979, the parole population has increased by 41 percent. The median state parole entry rate was 6, with a range of rates from a low of 1 (Hawaii) to a high of 29 (District of Columbia). Eight persons per 10,000 population were placed on parole in 1982.

Of course, one of the key questions concerning the number of persons who exit from parole supervision is: How many parolees commit new crimes? The UPR for 1979 (NCCD, 1980: 8) contains information on parole removals by type of exit. The report is that, for 1979, the majority of parole removals were for successful completion of the parole term (59.2 percent); 10.3 percent of the parolees were granted an early discharge by the parole board, 4.3 percent were discharged for other reasons, and 1.6 percent died during their parole term. For 1979, the rate of recidivism (recommitted for a new crime or for a violation of the conditions of parole) was 24.8 percent. Thus, in 1979, three-quarters of persons discharged from parole were classified as successful.

In sum, the parole statistics reveal the relationship between the size of the prison population and the number of parolees. These figures indicate that both the prison and parolee populations are dramatically increasing.

Summary

A brief consideration of statistics from the correctional system (probation, prisons, parole) demonstrates their crucial linkage within the criminal justice system. Just imagine what would happen to the size of the prison population if probation and parole were completely abolished and all convicted persons were required to serve a prison term. If this had happened in 1982, the prison population would have hit 1,991,542! Naturally, the prison system is not equipped to handle such a large number of inmates. We do not wish to suggest that all convicted persons can and should be re-

Table 1-5
Adults on Parole, 1981–82

	Adult Residents 7/1/81	Parole Population 12/31/81	Entries	Exits	Parole Population 12/31/82	Parole Population per 100,000 Adult Residents 12/31/82
U.S. total	168,740,000	225,539	142,723	124,382	243,880	144.5
Federal	168,740,000	22,121	8,865	10,956	20,030	NA
State total	168,740,000	203,418	133,858	113,426	223,850	132.3
Northeast	36,919,000	45,311	21,108	18,689	47,730	129.3
Maine	824,000	153	12	16	149	18.1
New Hampshire	697,000	479	181	189	471	67.6
Vermont	376,000	271	201	225	247	65.7
Massachusetts	4,366,000	3,405	2,207	1,812	3,800	87.0
Rhode Island	725,000	244	267	191	320	44.1
Connecticut	2,370,000	1,450	1,198	1,337	1,311	55.3
New York	13,151,000	19,865	9,454	8,383	20,936	159.2
New Jersey	5,534,000	9,706	3,842	3,034	10,514	190.0
Pennsylvania	8,876,000	9,738	3,746	3,502	9,982	112.5
North Central	42,609,000	37,053	32,147	27,505	41,695	97.8
Ohio	7,818,000	8,471	7,500	7,355	8,616	110.2
Indiana	3,926,000	2,317	2,976	2,615	2,678	68.2
Illinois	8,310,000	9,394	8,398	5,926	11,866	142.8
Michigan	6,530,000	6,585	5,106	4,563	7,128	109.2

14

Wisconsin	3,451,000	2,853	2,016	1,567	3,302	95.7
Minnesota	2,993,000	1,633	1,167	1,321	1,479	49.4
Iowa	2,109,000	785	782	517	1,050	49.8
Missouri	3,629,000	2,948	1,830	1,498	3,280	90.4
North Dakota	447,000	129	160	138	151	31.7
South Dakota	490,000	259	317	281	295	30.8
Nebraska	1,145,000	255	385	363	277	24.2
Kansas	1,761,000	1,424	1,510	1,361	1,573	89.3
South	56,515,000	81,281	55,061	45,448	90,894	160.8
Delaware	443,000	624	436	439	621	140.2
Maryland	3,154,000	6,132	3,081	3,189	6,024	191.0
Dist. of Columbia	494,000	3,281	1,419	988	3,712	751.4
Virginia	4,053,000	5,070	5,165	3,748	6,487	160.1
West Virginia	1,405,000	485	406	281	610	43.4
North Carolina	4,402,000	6,875	9,959	9,924	6,910	156.9
South Carolina	2,278,000	3,306	1,308	1,331	3,283	144.1
Georgia	4,011,000	2,652	5,316	3,040	4,928	122.9
Florida	7,987,000	6,620	3,728	4,374	5,974	74.8
Kentucky	2,625,000	9,188	2,134	1,288	10,034	382.2
Tennessee	3,390,000	3,280	3,614	3,325	3,569	105.3
Alabama	2,812,000	2,361	1,584	1,584	2,361	83.4
Mississippi	1,752,000	2,734	1,605	1,425	2,914	166.3
Arkansas	1,642,000	2,793	1,650	1,382	3,061	186.4
Louisiana	3,020,000	1,913	694	649	1,961	64.9
Oklahoma	2,296,000	2,305	923	1,057	2,171	94.6
Texas	10,751,000	21,662	12,039	7,427	26,274	244.4

Table 1-5 (*Continued*)
Adults on Parole, 1981–82

	Adult Residents 7/1/81	Parole Population 12/31/81	Entries	Exits	Parole Population 12/31/82	Parole Population per 100,000 Adult Residents 12/31/82
West	32,697,000	39,773	25,542	21,784	43,531	133.1
Montana	570,000	642	190	174	658	115.4
Idaho	655,000	396	218	205	409	62.4
Wyoming	347,000	227	142	136	233	67.2
Colorado	2,219,000	1,096	1,334	1,228	1,202	54.2
New Mexico	937,000	1,181	601	576	1,206	128.7
Arizona	2,049,000	1,319	1,584	1,376	1,527	74.5
Utah	974,000	773	571	405	939	96.4
Nevada	651,000	1,172	400	574	998	153.3
Washington	3,105,000	15,102	1,706	1,380	15,428	496.9
Oregon	1,938,000	1,269	1,383	1,167	1,485	76.6
California	18,239,000	16,080	17,267	14,435	18,912	103.7
Alaska	297,000	101	60	65	96	32.3
Hawaii	716,000	415	86	63	438	61.2

SOURCE: Adapted from Bureau of Justice Statistics, *Bulletin: Probation and Parole, 1982* (Rockville, Md.: National Criminal Justice Reference Service, 1983).

leased to the community. It is the function of probation and parole to determine how the population of convicted persons can be managed in a fashion consistent with not only the capacity of the prison system but also the goals of societal protection and offender rehabilitation and reintegration.

In short, the examination of the functions of probation and parole is the theme of this text. Utilizing classic and current information on probation and parole, we will consider such key issues as: What are the best methods of supervision? What background, education, and training should probation and parole officers possess? What is the evidence concerning the effectiveness of probation and parole in providing public safety and facilitating offender rehabilitation? How are probation and parole decisions determined? What are the recent innovations in probation and parole? The consideration of these issues will provide the reader with the opportunity to form his or her own opinions and ideas concerning the proper use of probation and parole in the criminal justice system.

Notes

1. Two determinate sentencing states, Maine (1976) and Connecticut (1981), abolished parole supervision as well as discretionary release.

Study Guides

1. How does determinate sentencing operate in California? What are the purposes of such laws and how do they alter the parole system?
2. What do the statistics on probation and parole reveal? Are any patterns present?

Key Terms

criminal justice system   National Probation Reports (NPR)
determinate sentencing   Uniform Parole Reports (UPR)

References

Bureau of Justice Statistics. *Bulletin: The American Response to Crime.* Rockville, Md.: National Criminal Justice Reference Service, 1983.

_____. *Bulletin: Probation and Parole, 1982.* Rockville, Md.: National Criminal Justice Reference Service, 1983.

_____. *Bulletin: Tracking Offenders*. Rockville, Md.: National Criminal Justice Reference Service, 1983.

_____. *Bulletin: Prisoners in 1983*. Rockville, Md.: National Criminal Justice Reference Service, 1984.

Department of Criminal Justice, California State University/Long Beach. *The Impact of Determinate Sentencing Upon Corrections: A Handbook for Decision Makers*. Boulder, Colo.: National Institute of Corrections, 1980.

GETTINGER, STEVEN. "Prison Population Boom: Still No End in Sight," *Corrections Magazine* 9 (June 1983):6–33.

HUDZIK, JOHN K., AND CORDNER, GARY W. *Planning in Criminal Justice Organizations and Systems*. New York: Macmillan, 1983.

National Probation Reports. *Probation in the United States: 1979*. San Francisco: National Council on Crime and Delinquency, 1981.

PARISI, NICOLLETTE, AND ZILLO, JOSEPH. "Good Time: The Forgotten Issue," *Crime and Delinquency* 29 (1983):228–37.

Uniform Parole Reports. *Parole in the United States, 1979*. San Francisco: National Council on Crime and Delinquency, 1980.

Recommended Readings

National Probation Reports. *Probation in the United States, 1979* (San Francisco: National Council on Crime and Delinquency, 1981). A pioneering attempt to collect nationwide information on the subject of probation. This report will serve as the basis of a continuing effort to develop yearly compilations of probation data.

Uniform Parole Reports. *Parole in the United States, 1979* (San Francisco: National Council on Crime and Delinquency, 1980). This report also represents the development of nationwide information on parole practices.

2

The Development of Parole in America

Parole is the most frequently used mechanism by which offenders may be released from a correctional institution after completion of a portion of the sentence. Contemporary parole also includes the concepts of supervision by the state, release on condition of good behavior while in the community, and return to prison for failing to abide by these conditions or for committing a new crime. As we shall see, earlier parole practices did not include all of these elements.

The Roots of American Parole

Parole from prison, like the prison itself, is primarily an American innovation.[1] It emerged from a philosophical revolution and a resulting tradition of penal reform established in the late eighteenth century in the newly formed United States. As with many other new ideas that emerged in early America, parole had its roots in the practices of English and European penal systems.

Early punishments for offenses were most often what Langbein (1976: 35–63) called "blood punishments." Capital and corporal punishment were accepted penal practices in Europe and the United States well into the nineteenth century. This was so, in part, because the technology and economy of these principally rural societies were unable to process and control large inmate populations, and also because these societies had strong traditions of corporal punishment that were rooted in the Old Testament.

In the late seventeenth and early eighteenth centuries, two massive social changes occurred that altered the direction of Western civilization and, consequently, had an impact on criminal law and penalties. The first was the Enlightenment, which gave rise to a conception of the human being as a rational and ultimately perfectable being and, along with this, a belief in basic human equality.[2] Second, urbanization and the earliest movements toward industrialism simultaneously changed the nature of social interactions and created a new social class, the urban working class.

The writings of such thinkers as Locke, Voltaire, Beccaria, and Montesquieu both created and reflected a changing conception of man and the social order. These writers believed that government or society existed because individuals allowed it to exist. In other words, a "social contract" governed society. In order to be secure in their persons and possessions, free and equal individuals banded together and surrendered certain of their freedoms to the government on condition that it protect them from their enemies.

Among those enemies were criminals. The state assumed the responsibility of controlling crime and, by administering justice, punishing offenders. Individuals surrendered their "rights" to seek revenge and to commit "crimes" so that they would be safe from others who might want to commit crimes or avenge themselves. The social contract was the product of rational, free individuals. And since rational and free people had control of their own fates, they could be held responsible for their actions.

A crime was considered a "breach of contract," an offense against all parties to the social contract and not just the injured party. This state of affairs enabled the establishment of a central body of law (such as the Common Law in England), and centralized control of enforcement. Finally, rational individuals, presumed to have prior knowledge of the law and its penalties, were expected to perceive that it was in their own interest not to violate the law and suffer the penalties. Deterrence was the rationale of the criminal law and its sanctions, which were severe so as to enhance the deterrent effect of the law. (In fact, over two hundred offenses carried the death penalty in England at one time. During the reign of Henry VIII, some 72,000 major and minor thieves were sent to the gallows. Under his daughter Elizabeth I, three hundred to four hundred at a time were hanged, attracting large crowds where pickpockets flourished—even though pickpocketing was an offense punishable by death [Rennie, 1978: 6–7].)

Since the criminal law in colonial America developed from the English Common Law, it was also very harsh. Judges and magistrates in the English system had the option to impose a variety of penalties less severe than death, such as brandings, maimings, the stocks, fines, or any combination of these. As a reaction against these cruel punishments, the "benefit of clergy" was developed to mitigate punishment for clerics and the wealthy. Initially designed to separate church and state, the "benefit" was eventually extended to all literate British citizens, even to those who could feign literacy (Clear, 1978: 6–7).

The reluctance of juries to convict and judges to impose sentences that were perceived to be disproportionate to the severity of most offenses did much to detract from the deterrent effect of the law. In addition, the inequity evident in sentencing, coupled with the potential and actual practices of abuses of the power to suspend sentences altogether, led to calls for reform in the English eighteenth-century criminal code, particularly for a reduction in the severity of penalties. A gradual shift in the conception of humankind and concommitant re-evaluation of the effectiveness and severity of punishments contributed significantly to the origins of parole as it exists today (Fogel, 1975: 30–35).

Other writers, however, felt that poverty and lack of education, or heredity and biological inferiority, were the factors that gave rise to crime. The shifting conception of mankind as being at least partly at the mercy of forces beyond their control reduced the degree to which they could be held responsible for criminal actions, and paved the way for a reduction in the severity of many penalties. These changes in the philosophical conception of crime and punishment brought a new factor into the determination of sentences. Instead of imposing uniformly harsh sanctions for nearly all offenders, judges began to mitigate penalties for those "unfortunates" whom they "deemed to be worthy."

In England, orders of transportation were thought to be a severe punishment. In the eighteenth century, banishment, a common penalty for the aristocracy or nobility for centuries, was imposed on the common offender for the first time. The judge would order the common offender transported to the colonies rather than to the gallows or pillory. The criminal would be allowed to go at liberty in the new land, sometimes after a period of indenture, on the condition of not returning to England for a specified time period (such as ten years), if at all (Hawkins, 1971: Chapter 1). The concept of transportation thus avoided the extreme harshness of existing criminal law while at the same time serving the incapacitative purposes of those penalties. The serious felony offender, of course, was still sentenced to death.

While transportation was a partial solution to England's crime problem and, for a time, helped to settle and develop the new lands (the colonies, however, had no similar outlet for their offenders, with the exception of casting them into the wilderness, with usually the same results as the death penalty) it was only a temporary one. As a result of the American Revolution, England was forced to transport her convicts elsewhere, and for a time they were sent to Australia; until, eventually, even Australia closed its doors to English convicts.

Criminologists commonly accept punishment by transportation as the principal forerunner of parole (Hawkins). They argue that transportation was an organized, uniform process by which thousands of convicts were punished in a manner short of execution or corporal punishment, and it was a system wherein offenders eventually obtained their freedom. In addition, transportation did not necessarily involve a period of incarceration.

The Rise of Prison Punishments

The Treaty of Paris in 1783 acknowledged the creation of the first republic in Western civilization since the fall of the Roman Empire. The United States of America, free from the English monarchy and founded on the teachings of the Enlightenment, became a fertile ground for the development of a new system of criminal justice.

While the influence of English Common Law, with its harsh penalties, was strong in the new republic, even stronger were anti-British sentiment and the desire to abandon the oppressive regime of the English king. American reformers moved away from the archaic, tyrannical sanctions of colonial law and toward a more humane and rational penalty of incarceration. It was argued that fair, simple laws, backed by certain and humane punishment, would eradicate crime.

Chief among the reform groups were the Quakers. The Act of 1789 established imprisonment as the penalty for most crimes in Pennsylvania (Edelfonso, 1979: 79). In a nation that had newly acquired independence, what more fitting penalty could be found than the deprivation of liberty? When Patrick Henry uttered his now famous line, "Give me liberty or give me death," little did he know that he had identified the perfect penalty for crime. The prison replaced the penalty of death and yet denied liberty to its inmates.

Much to the dismay of these first reformers, their efforts were not rewarded by a reduction in crime. Rather, the first penal institutions were dismal failures:

> The faith of the 1790s now seemed misplaced; more rational codes had not decreased crime. The roots of deviancy went deeper than the certainty of punishment. Nor were the institutions fulfilling the elementary task of protecting society, since escapes and riots were commonplace occurrences [Rothman, 1971: 62].

The search for the causes of crime continued. The reformers still believed that offenders were rational people who would strive to improve themselves, but the manner in which they could be convinced to obey the law was still unknown. In a time of rapid social change and movement from an agrarian to an industrial society, environmental factors came to be viewed as criminogenic: Cities, poverty, and idleness were believed to be the hotbeds of crime.

The proposed solution that emerged was: Remove the offender from bad environments and teach the benefits of industry and morality. Offenders needed to be shown the error of their ways. Criminal law was required to do more than punish and deter; it should change the prisoner into a productive citizen. Punishment should serve to allow the prisoner to repent, to be trained, and to be reformed into a good citizen. A place to repent was thus needed, and prisons were developed to fulfill that need.

The original basis of the prison was the reformation of the offender, and the ideal of reformation placed high value on discipline and regimentation. In short, in the newly created free society, incarceration itself was punishment, and while incarcerated, the goal was to reform the prisoner. Offenders were expected to obey strict rules of conduct and to work hard at assigned tasks. In this milieu, it was believed, the offender would learn the benefits of discipline and industry.

The founders of the penitentiaries were mindful that the prison was a means to an end; their successors were not (Rothman, 1971: 245–46). Reformation of inmates came to be identified solely with confinement, and custody eventually grew to be the ultimate goal of incarceration (Rothman: 238). Furthermore, inmates posed significant threats to the security of the penitentiaries. Prison officials resorted to severe corporal punishments in order to maintain control within the prison—a penalty the development of prisons was supposed to replace.

This second generation of prison officials also saw another way of keeping the inmates out of trouble. American industry in the middle 1800s was labor-intensive, and prison populations were ideal sources of cheap labor. Inmate labor was expected to generate the money necessary to run the prisons, and prison administrators were thus receptive to offers to hire entire populations. This situation led to grossly underpaid prison labor, antagonism from unemployed free citizens, and the emergence of the labor contractor as a major force in institutional administration. A report from the Massachusetts General Court Special Committee on Contract Convict Labor (1880: 16) illustrates the problems:

> In the State Prison, contracts have been made which have no clause giving the State power to annul them. . . . Such bargains are bad, and, carried out to the fullest extent with large contracts, may naturally be expected to lead to a condition of affairs that has existed in other States giving ground to the popular assertion that contractors, and not the State, control the prison.

Early Parole Practices

Parole in the United States as we know it today developed from earlier penal practices, both abroad and in this country. While contemporary parole differs from the earlier systems in significant ways, it also shares many of the same characteristics.

Early Practices in Other Nations

The first operational system of conditional release was started by the governor of a prison in Spain in 1835. Up to one-third of a prison sentence could be reduced by good behavior and a demonstrated desire to do better (Carter, McGee and Nelson, 1975: 200). A similar system was enacted in Bavaria in the 1830s, and many prison reformers in France in the 1840s advocated the adoption of similar conditional release systems. In fact, the term "parole" comes from the French *parole d'honneur*, or "word of honor," which characterized the French efforts to establish parole release. The prisoner would be released after showing good behavior and industry in the prison, and on his word of honor that he would obey the law.

Despite the fact that these efforts predate those of Alexander Maconochie, it is he who is usually given credit as being the father of parole. In 1840, Captain Maconochie was put in charge of the English penal colony in New South Wales at Norfolk Island, about a thousand miles off the coast of Australia. To this colony were sent the criminals who were "twice condemned." They had been shipped from England to Australia, and then from Australia to Norfolk (Allen and Simonsen, 1981: 44). Conditions were allegedly so bad at Norfolk Island that men reprieved from the death penalty wept and those who were to die thanked God (Barry, 1957: 5). It was under these conditions that Maconochie devised an elaborate method of granting conditional release.

Maconochie's plan was based on five basic principles (Barnes and Teeters, 1959: 419):

1. Release should not be based on the completing of a sentence for a set period of time, but on the completion of a determined and specified quantity of labor. In brief, time sentences should be abolished, and task sentences substituted.

2. The quantity of labor a prisoner must perform should be expressed in a number of "marks" which he must earn, by improvement of conduct, frugality of living, and habits of industry, before he can be released.

3. While in prison he should earn everything he receives. All sustenance and indulgences should be added to his debt of marks.

4. When qualified by discipline to do so, he should work in association with a small number of other prisoners, forming a group of six or seven, and the whole group should be answerable for the conduct and labor of each member.

5. In the final stage, a prisoner, while still obliged to earn his daily tally of marks, should be given a proprietary interest in his own labor and be subject to a less rigorous discipline, to prepare him for release into society.

Under his plan, prisoners were awarded marks and moved through stages of custody until finally granted release. His system involved *indeterminate sentencing*, with release based upon the number of marks earned by prisoners for good conduct, labor, and study. The five stages, based upon the accumulation of marks, each carried increased responsibility and freedom, leading to a ticket of leave or parole resulting in a conditional pardon and, finally, to full restoration of liberty.

To fulfill the labor requirement, it was common practice to put convicts to work on public projects, or to rent them out to private persons or businesses, and newly arrived prisoners were often assigned to work for conditionally pardoned prisoners. Unfortunately, this system led to a great many abuses and was eventually discontinued.[3]

Sir Walter Crofton, director of the Irish prison system in the 1850s, built upon the foundations laid by Maconochie. He decided that a transitional stage between prison and full release was needed, and developed a classification scheme based upon a system in which the prisoner progressed through three stages of treatment. The first was segregated confinement with work and training provided to the prisoner. This was followed by a transition period from confinement to freedom, during which the prisoner was set to work on public projects with little control being exercised over him. If he performed successfully in this phase, he was released on "license" (Clare and Kramer, 1976: 69–70).

Release on license was constrained by certain conditions, violations of which would result in reimprisonment. While on license, prisoners were required to submit monthly reports and were warned against idleness and associating with other criminals. Prisoners on license, then, had to report, could be reimprisoned for violating the conditions of release, and had not been pardoned. These distinctions from earlier systems of release were large steps toward modern parole.

Early American Practices

Convicts sentenced to prison in America in the early 1800s received definite terms; a sentence of five years meant the offender would serve five years in prison. This strict sentencing structure led to overcrowded prisons and widespread problems in the institutions. It was not uncommon for a governor to grant pardons to large numbers of inmates in order to control the size of prison populations. In some states, this pardoning power was even delegated to prison wardens (Serrill, 1977: 5).

This method of rewarding well-behaved prisoners with reductions in sentence was first formalized in 1817 by the New York State legislature. In that year, the first "good time" law was passed. This law authorized a 25 percent reduction in length of term for those inmates serving five years or more who were well behaved and demonstrated industry in their prison work. By 1869, twenty-three states had good time laws, and prison administrators supported the concept as a method of keeping order and controlling the population size (Serrill: 6).

The liberal use of the pardoning power was continued in those states that did not have good time laws, and the mass pardon was not uncommon even in those states that already allowed sentence reductions for good behavior. These developments are important because they represent the first large-scale exercise of sentencing power by the executive branch of government, the branch in which parole boards would eventually be located.

Another philosophical base for American parole was the indenture system established by the New York House of Refuge. Although not called parole, for all intents and purposes a parole system was already operational for juveniles committed to the House of Refuge in New York. The House of Refuge had developed a system of indenture whereby youths were released from custody as indentured servants of private citizens. Unfortunately, this system permitted corruption.[4]

To combat these abuses, the New York House of Refuge developed a system of supervising the indentured. A committee was formed that selected youths for indenture, defined the conditions under which they served their indentureships, and established rules both for the superintendent of the House of Refuge and for the persons to whom youths were indentured.

There was no formal mechanism for releasing the youths from custody, but they were able to work off their contracts and thus obtain their freedom. Their masters could break the contract and return the youths to the House of Refuge at any time. In essence, a parole system was operating.

In addition to these forms of release from custody before the expiration of the maximum term, the concept of supervising released offenders had also been operationalized. It is important to note, however, that supervision of released prisoners prior to the creation of parole in America only required providing assistance and not crime control duties.[5]

In 1845, the Massachusetts legislature appointed a state agent for discharged convicts and appropriated funds for him to use in assisting ex-prisoners in securing employment, tools, clothes, and transportation.

Other states followed this example and appointed agents of their own. As early as 1776, however, charitable organizations, such as the Philadelphia Association for the Alleviation of Prisoners' Miseries, were already providing aid to released convicts (Sellin, 1970: 13). By the late 1860s, dissatisfaction with prisons was widespread and a concerted effort to establish a formal parole release and supervision system began. In 1867, two prison reformers (Enoch Wines and Louis Dwight) reported that "There is not a state prison in America in which the reformation of the convicts is the one supreme object of the discipline, to which everything else is made to bend" (Rothman, 1971: 240–43).

In 1870, the first meeting of the American Prison Association was held in Cincinnati, Ohio. Reform was the battle cry of the day, and the meeting took on an almost evangelical fervor (Fogel, 1975: 30–31). Both Sir Walter Crofton and American warden F. B. Sanborn advocated the Irish system (Lindsey, 1925: 20).

Armed with the success of this meeting, the focus of prison reformers shifted from incarceration as the answer to crime and, instead, concentrated on the return of offenders to society. Prisons remained central, but they were now seen almost as a necessary evil, not as an end in themselves. Prison reformers everywhere began to advocate adoption and expansion of good time laws, assistance to released prisoners, the adoption of the ticket of leave system, and parole. In 1869, the New York State legislature passed an act creating the Elmira Reformatory and an indeterminate sentence ". . . until reformation, not exceeding five years."

This law created the reformatory as a separate institution for young offenders, expressly designed to be an intermediate step between conviction and return to a law-abiding life. The administrators of the reformatory were empowered to release inmates upon demonstration of their reformation. Such release was conditional, and released offenders were to be supervised by a state agent (Lindsey: 21–23).

With the passage of this law, parole in the United States became a reality. It soon spread to other jurisdictions, and by 1944, every jurisdiction in the nation had a parole authority (Hawkins: 64). The rapid growth of parole, however, was fraught with difficulties and criticism.

The Spread of Parole

Parole release was adopted by the various state jurisdictions much more rapidly than was the indeterminate sentence. By 1900, some twenty states had adopted parole; by 1944, every jurisdiction had a parole system. (See Table 2–1.) The expansion of parole has been characterized as being a process of imitation (Lindsey: 71), yet a great deal of variation in the structure and use of parole was observed.[6]

Table 2–1
Significant Developments in Parole

Date	Development
1776	Colonies reject English Common Code and begin to draft their own codes.
1840	Maconochie devises mark system for release of prisoners in Australian penal colony, a forerunner of parole.
1854	Crofton establishes ticket-of-leave program in Ireland.
1869	New York State legislature passes enabling legislation and establishes indeterminate sentencing.
1870	American Prison Association endorses expanded use of parole.
1876	Parole release adopted at Elmira Reformatory, New York.
1931	Wickersham Commission criticizes laxity in early parole practice.
1944	Last state passes enabling legislation for parole.

The growth and expansion of modern parole was assisted by a number of factors. One of the most important was the tremendous amount of support and publicity that prison reformers gave the concept at the National Congress on Penitentiary and Reformatory Discipline. Its inclusion in the congress's Declaration of Principles, coupled with the publicity of Alexander Maconochie's work in New South Wales, provided the necessary endorsement of correctional experts.

In addition, it was quickly recognized that a discretionary release system solved many of the problems of prison administration. A major factor in favor of parole was that it supported prison discipline. A number of writers pointed out that by placing release in the inmate's own hands, the inmate would be motivated both to reform and to comply with the rules and regulations of the prison.[7] Finally, parole provided a safety valve to reduce prison populations, which were generally overcrowded (Wilcox, 1929: 345–54).

A third contributory factor was that the power to pardon was being liberally exercised in a number of states. The effect of liberal pardoning policies was to initiate parole even though it was not yet authorized by law.

These early parole systems were controlled by state legislatures that, in general, rigidly defined which prisoners could be paroled. Most legislation authorizing parole release restricted it to first offenders convicted of less serious crimes. Through the passage of time and a gradual acceptance of the idea of discretionary early release, the privilege was eventually extended to serious offenders.

Early parole systems were primarily operated by persons with a direct interest in the administration of prisons. So the decisions on parole release and those who acted as parole officers were institution-based. Eligibility was strictly limited, at the inception of parole, and only gradually expanded to include more serious offenders. Supervision of released inmates was nominal, and the seeds of corruption and maladministration were present.

Early Public Sentiments

The decade between 1925 and 1935 was a turbulent time, including both the economic boom (and the Prohibition Era) as well as the Great Depression. Crime—particularly as sensationalized in the mass media—appeared to be rampant. As crime rates increased—a trend even more pronounced today—the public felt more and more that crime was "public enemy number one." This period also saw the rise of attempts by the federal government to stem interstate crimes, particularly kidnapping, bootlegging, bank robbery, and a host of newly enacted legislation that considerably widened the net of crime the government would seek to prevent and prosecute. Two significant events, reflecting public concern about crime, were the establishment of the maximum security federal prison on Alcatraz, and a crusade headed by J. Edgar Hoover, chief of the Federal Bureau of Investigation, against interstate crime. His pronouncements assumed a political nature, as he strongly advocated neoclassical responses to crime: long-term prison sentences, abolition of parole, increased incarceration of offenders, etc.

Both the releasing and supervision functions of parole were sharply and roundly criticized. The major concern of these criticisms was the failure of parole to protect the public safety. The Report of the Advisory Commission on Penal Institutions, Probation and Parole to the Wickersham Commission in 1931 summarized the problems with parole stating:

Parole is defective in three main respects:

1. In the chasm existing between parole and preceding institutional treatment
2. In the manner in which persons are selected for parole
3. In the quality of supervision given to persons on parole

In short, parole was seen as failing to be effective in attaining the promised and lofty goals. The primary arguments were that convicted criminals were being set loose on society, inadequately supervised, and unreformed. The concept of parole and the general ideology of reform were not yet under attack; it was the means and not the ends that were being criticized.

The decade of the 1930s saw the publication of two documents concerning parole, the 1931 Wickersham Commission Report, noted above, and, in 1939, the Attorney General's Survey of Release Procedures (Hawkins: 47). As with the reports of Wines and Dwight and the International Prison Congress of over fifty years earlier, the 1931 and 1939 documents pointed to flaws in the operation of American corrections and advocated reforms to improve both prisons and parole services.[8]

Simultaneously, the correctional medical model was on the rise. This criminogenic approach was based on a belief that human beings are basically moral, and that crime is deviation from humankind's basic behavior inclinations. Unlike the earlier views that humans were, at heart, bestial, but restrained their primitive drives because reason informed them that by doing so they would be safe, the idea that humans are basically good led to the inevitable conclusion that there must be something fundamentally wrong with those who were bad. The job of corrections should then be to diagnose the problems, prepare and administer the treatment programs, and make offenders well again. Offenders committed crimes when social, personal, or psychological forces and factors overwhelmed them. Hence, the instillation of new habits, the threat of deterrent sanctions, and the giving of religious instruction dealt only with the *symptoms* of a deeper disorder. The *real* causes of crime remained deep within the personality structure of the offender. If the prisons were to be hospitals, the parole board was to release the patient when "well"—that is, when able to deal with all phases of everyday life. This development had significant implications for parole.

Between the adoption of parole release at Elmira in 1876, and the enactment of enabling legislation for parole in Mississippi in 1944, the concept of parole faced two critical challenges. The first involved the issue of legality of executive control over sentencing and indeterminate sentences. The second centered on the administration of parole systems. Toward the end of the first quarter of the twentieth century, a new behavioral technology came into its own and grew to be the predominant goal of corrections and sentencing. The rehabilitative ideal gave new legitimacy to parole, endorsing discretion.

Legal Challenges to Parole

The basic legal challenge raised against parole was that the placing of control over sentence length and criminal penalties in the hands of a parole board was unconstitutional. The specific arguments varied across individual lawsuits, but they were basically of two types. First, the questions of infringement on the principle of the separation of powers clauses of the federal and state constitutions were raised in several states (Lindsey: 40–52).

These suits claimed that parole release was an impairment of judicial sentencing power, an improper delegation of legislative authority to set penalties, and usurpation of the executive branch's power of clemency (Hawkins: 47). For the most part, parole authorities emerged victorious from these court battles, and those constitutional questions of parole were laid to rest.

The second rationale behind challenges to the constitutionality of parole release were based on the Eighth Amendment prohibition against cruel and unusual punishment. These suits argued that the uncertainty of sentence length involved in a parole system constituted cruel and unusual punishment. Although the issue was weighty, most criminal penalties were limited by legislatively set maximum terms. The most common judicial response to these arguments was that indeterminate sentences would be interpreted as sentences that would not extend the maximum terms as set by the legislature or judge, thereby rending moot the issue of cruelty by virtue of uncertainty (Hawkins: 49).

Administrative Challenges

We have seen that, in the late nineteenth and early twentieth centuries, parole practices were criticized for failing to protect the public. The basic arguments were that parole authorities were not following procedures that would lead to the release of only deserving inmates, and that the lack of subsequent parole supervision placed the community in danger. Such were the complaints reflected by the Wickersham Commission and the Attorney General's Survey. These were not the only critical voices.[9]

One salient argument, supported by ample evidence, was that parole had become a commonplace method of reducing prison populations. In several states, most inmates were released immediately upon expiration of their minimum terms. Only those inmates whose conduct records within prison showed a failure to conform were held longer. The problem was defined as inadequate or improper release decision making.

Blanket release policies were felt to be inappropriate for several reasons. First, because parole boards failed to consider risk, and parole supervision was inadequate, such wholesale release practices were felt to endanger public safety. Second, since most parole boards were dominated by prison officials, it was believed that too much weight was attached to prison conduct and the needs of the prison administration. Finally, failure to consider reformation efforts of the inmate, or the prison, worked to hamper the success of prisons in reforming criminals.

Proposed solutions were varied and involved beefing-up parole supervision staffs and increasing postrelease surveillance of parolees. It was believed that these actions could enhance public protection. Additionally, there were calls for professional parole boards comprised of trained, salaried, full-time decision-makers who would be removed from the pressures of day-to-day prison administration and its needs, and were skilled in identifying those inmates who were reformed.

These proposals arose at about the same time behavioral sciences expanded into the world of public policy. Psychology and sociology were beginning to develop practical components in addition to their traditional theoretical bases. The new professions of clinical psychologist, social worker, and criminologist were developing. An ability to predict, change, and control undesirable human behavior was promised. Corrections and parole seemed ideal places in which these professions could have their most positive impact. The dawn of the rehabilitative model was at hand, and this model caused radical changes in the practice and organization of the American parole system, as will be seen in the next chapter.

Summary

Although the early beginnings of parole can be traced to Europe and Australia, the process as it is known today is almost exclusively an American invention. Once embraced by early reformers, parole quickly spread and, by 1944, every state jurisdiction had a parole system. In spite of the growth, parole was not without its detractors. Early criticisms of parole included a suspicion of the way in which prisoners were selected for release, concern over a lack of community supervision, and extensive abuse by prison authorities. Many of the criticisms leveled at parole continue today, and these issues will be discussed in greater detail in later chapters.

Notes

1. Various forms of conditional release from incarceration were developed in other countries before an American state adopted a parole system. However, the core elements of a parole system—an administrative board making release decisions and granting conditional, supervised release with the authority to revoke it— were first created by legislation in New York State (1869).
2. For an excellent reading of the movement as it relates to the study of crime, see: Ysabel Rennie, *The Search for Criminal Man* (Lexington, Mass.: Lexington Books, D. C. Heath, 1978).
3. The abuses were common to those encountered in the post-Civil War South. See Harry E. Allen and Clifford E. Simonsen, *Corrections in America: An Introduction*, 3rd edition (New York: Macmillan, 1981), 48–49.
4. It was not uncommon for juveniles to be indentured without a careful investigation of those who would hold the indenture contracts. Thus, juveniles were sometimes indentured to criminals, and the conditions of their indentureships went virtually uncontrolled.

5. The first legislatively authorized "parole officer" position was established in 1837 in Massachusetts. That officer was charged with assisting released convicts to obtain shelter, tools, and work. The legislation made no mention of any surveillance duties.

6. See Edward Lindsey, "Historical Sketch of the Indeterminate Sentence and Parole System," *Journal of Criminal Law and Criminology* 16 (1925). Lindsey writes, "There has been considerable modification and variation in various phases of the system as it has spread from one state to another. Methods of administration are also widely different."

7. Perhaps chief among these were E. C. Wines and T. W. Dwight who, in 1867, published a report to the New York Prison Association that was entitled, "Prisons and Reformatories of the United States and Canada" (Albany, N.Y.: 1867). Other state committees echoed the call for a parole system. See "Report of the Massachusetts General Court Joint Special Committee on Contract Convict Labor" (Boston: 1880).

8. The authors of those reports were joined by others. Reformers wanted full-time, paid parole authorities who had to meet certain qualifications and who were as far removed as possible from political patronage. See D. Colvin, "What Authority Should Grant Paroles? If a Board, How Should It be Composed?," *Journal of Criminal Law and Criminology* 12 (1922):547.

9. See H. E. Field, "The Attitudes of Prisoners as a Factor in Rehabilitation," *The Annals* 157 (1931):162.

Study Guides

1. Prior to the advent of the prison, what were the ways in which criminals were punished?

2. Where did the ideas of parole originate? Briefly trace its development outside of the United States.

3. What were the early customs of parole in the United States?

4. Beginning with the Congress of 1870, why did parole gain such popularity in the United States?

5. Define parole.

6. What philosophical developments created the atmosphere conducive to the development of parole?

7. Why did the American Revolution lead to the acceptance of a new approach to the treatment of law breakers?

8. What criticisms were leveled at the system of parole from 1876 to 1944?

Key Terms

American Prison Association
conditional release

Enlightenment
good time

mark systems   reformatory
pardon   ticket of leave
Quakers

References

ALLEN, HARRY E., AND SIMONSEN, CLIFFORD E. *Corrections in America: An Introduction.* New York: Macmillan, 1981.

BARNES, HARRY E., AND TEETERS, NEGLEY D. *New Horizons in Criminology.* Englewood Cliffs, N.J.: Prentice-Hall, 1959.

BARRY, JOHN V. "Captain Alexander Maconochie," *The Victorian Historical Magazine* 27 (June 1957):1–18.

BECCARIA, CESARE. *On Crimes and Punishment.* Translated by H. Paulucci. Indianapolis, Ind.: Bobbs-Merrill, 1963.

CARTER, ROBERT M.; McGEE, RICHARD A.; AND NELSON, KIM E. *Corrections in America.* Philadelphia: J. B. Lippincott, 1975.

CLARE, PAUL K., AND KRAMER, JOHN H. *Introduction to American Corrections.* Boston: Holbrook Press, 1976.

CLEAR, TODD R. *A Model for Supervising the Offender in the Community.* Washington, D.C.: National Institute of Corrections, 1978.

EDELFONSO, EDWARD, ED. "Development of Modern Correctional Concepts and Standards." In *Issues in Corrections.* Beverly Hills, Calif.: Glencoe, 1974.

FOGEL, DAVID. *We Are the Living Proof . . .* Cincinnati, Ohio: W. H. Anderson, 1975.

HAWKINS, KEITH O. *Parole Selection: The American Experience.* Unpublished doctoral dissertation: University of Cambridge, 1971.

LANGBEIN, JOHN H. "The Historical Origins of the Sanction of Imprisonment for Serious Crime," *Journal of Legal Studies* 5 (1976):35–63.

LINDSEY, EDWARD. "Historical Sketch of the Indeterminate Sentence and Parole System," *Journal of Criminal Law and Criminology* 16 (1925):9–126.

National Commission on Law Observance and Enforcement, George W. Wickersham, Chairman. *Report on Penal Institutions, Probation and Parole.* Washington, D.C.: Government Printing Office, 1939.

RENNIE, YSABEL. *The Search for Criminal Man.* Lexington, Mass.: D. C. Heath, 1978.

Report of the Commissioners to Examine the Various Systems of Prison Discipline, and Propose an Improved Plan, cited in Harry E. Barnes's *A History of the Penal, Reformatory and Correctional Institutions of the State of New Jersey—Analytical and Documentary* (n.d.).

Report of the Massachusetts General Court Joint Special Committee on Contract Convict Labor. Boston: 1880.

ROTHMAN, DAVID J. *The Discovery of the Asylum: Social Order and Disorder in the New Republic.* Boston: Little, Brown, 1971.

SELLIN, THORSTEN. "The Origin of the 'Pennsylvania System of Prison Discipline'" *The Prison Journal* 50 (Spring-Summer 1970):13.

SERRILL, MICHAEL S. "Determinate Sentencing: History, Theory, Debate" *Corrections Magazine* 3 (September 1977):3.

WILCOX, CHARLES. "Parole: Principles and Practice" *Journal of Criminal Law and Criminology* 20 (1929):345–54.

Recommended Readings

Dressler, David. *Practice and Theory of Probation and Parole* (New York: Columbia University Press, 1962). A well-developed and documented analysis of the history of parole.

Rothman, David J. *The Discovery of the Asylum: Social Order and Disorder in the New Republic* (Boston: Little, Brown, 1971). This book presents an excellent history of the use of punishments and corrections in early colonial America.

_____. *Conscience and Convenience: The Asylum and Its Alternatives in Progressive America* (Boston: Little, Brown, 1980). An excellent discussion of the modern effort to reform the programs that have dominated criminal justice in the twentieth century.

3

History of Probation

Probation represents one of the unique developments within the criminal justice system. The development of this method of minimizing offender penetration into the correctional system was a crucial aspect of the rise of the rehabilitation model in this country. Any study of probation must begin with an analysis of its predecessors. This historical review will reveal how probation—both for adults and juveniles—developed into their current forms and practices.

Definition of Probation: Adults

A sentence not involving confinement which imposes conditions and retains authority in the sentencing court to modify the conditions of sentence or to re-sentence the offender if the offender violates the conditions. Such a sentence should not involve or require suspension of the imposition or execution of any other sentence.

Therefore, probation is a *conditional sentence* that avoids incarceration of the offender—it is an alternative disposition available to the court. While probation is an outcome of the offender's conviction in a criminal court, it neither confines him or her in an institution nor allows the offender's release from court authority. Supervision by a probation officer is almost always a condition of release.

As indicated by the National Advisory Commission on Criminal Justice Standards and Goals (1976: 115–17), probation can also refer to other functions, activities, and services. It is a *status*, given to the convicted offender, which falls somewhere between that of free citizen and incarcerated felon. As a *subsystem* of criminal justice, it refers to the agency or organization that administers the probation process. As a *process*, it refers to those activities that include the preparation of reports for the court, the supervision of probationers, and the providing of services for those probationers. These activities are undertaken by the probation officer as a part of his or her regular duty. Finally, as Finn (1984) notes, probation can serve to lower prison populations.

The rationale for the use of probation has been clearly stated by Dressler (1962: 26):

> . . . the assumption that certain offenders are reasonably safe risks in society by the time they appear in court; it would not facilitate their adjustment to remove them to institutions, and the move might well have the opposite effect. Meantime, the community would have to provide for their dependents. And the effect of such incarceration upon the prisoner's family would be incalculable. If, then, the community would not be jeopardized by a defendant's presence, and if he gave evidence of ability to change to a law-abiding life, it served both society and the individual to give him the chance, conditionally, under supervision and guidance.

Probation is thus clearly tied to the correctional goals of rehabilitation and reintegration, providing potential benefits to the offender as well as the community.

Precursors of Probation

The use of probation dates back to the mid-nineteenth century, and while its precursors bear some resemblance to their modern-day counterparts, they did not possess all the attributes that are currently associated with probation. Indeed, crucial elements were absent in *all* predecessors!

Benefit of Clergy

A common association with the term probation is forgiveness. After all, the word *probation* derives from Latin, its root meaning "a period of proving or trial" (Dressler, 1962: 6). Upon cursory examination, some of these precursors would appear to be farfetched. Barnes and Teeters (1959: 552) cite the early *right to sanctuary* as one of these early but questionable forms.

Under this procedure, cities or places were set aside to which the accused might flee and escape punishment for his or her crime. Another earlier predecessor was the *benefit of clergy* (United Nations 1976a: 82–83; Dressler, 1962: 7–8). This special plea was a part of the feudal power struggle between Church and State in England as Henry II sought to expand his power over the Church by subjecting clerics to the King's Court. The benefit of clergy was a mechanism through which Church functionaries escaped potential persecution. Ordained clerks, monks, and nuns accused of crimes could claim the benefit and have their case transferred to the Bishop's Court.

Dressler (1962: 7) describes the process in greater detail:

> When a member of the cloth, suspected of a crime, was brought into King's Court, his bishop could claim the dispensation for him. Thereupon, the charge was read to the cleric, but no evidence was presented against him. Instead, he gave his own version of the alleged offense and brought in witnesses to corroborate his testimony. With all the evidence against the accused expunged and only favorable witnesses testifying, it is hardly astounding that most cases ended in acquittal.

By the fourteenth century, the benefit was extended to nonclerics, providing they were literate. A passage from the Psalms ("Have mercy upon me, O God, according to thy loving kindness, according to the multitude of thy tender mercies blot out my transgressions") was utilized as a literacy test. Since the benefit of clergy was most often used to avoid capital punishment and gain access to the more lenient Bishop's Court, this Psalm became known as the "neck verse." As Dressler indicates (1962: 8), the benefit of clergy deteriorated to the point that it became "a clumsy set of rules which operated in favor of all criminals to mitigate in certain cases the severity of the criminal law." It was abolished for commoners in 1827 and for peers in 1841; the American colonies did not use the plea until after the Revolution. Thus, although the benefit of clergy was very unlike probation in terms of actual practice, it can be viewed as a predecessor. As we shall see, opponents of probation have often complained that it is also "too lenient," and that the offender is avoiding a harsher punishment so richly deserved.[1]

Judicial Reprieve

Of course, other predecessors bear a much closer resemblance to probation. The English courts utilized *judicial reprieve*—a temporary suspension by the court of either the imposition or execution of a sentence—which was often used to permit the convicted person to apply for a pardon. While designed to suspend the sentence temporarily, it sometimes led to the abandonment of prosecution (United Nations, 1976a: 83). Although the defendant remained in the community until a final disposition of the case, judicial reprieve did not involve certain practices of probation, particularly the conditions of release and the supervision by an agent of the court (Dressler, 1962: 8).

Recognizance

More aspects of contemporary probation appear in the practice of *recognizance*. This practice, also called "binding over," involves the use of "a bond or obligation entered into by a defendant, who thus is bound to refrain from doing, or to do, something for a stipulated period, and to appear in court on a specified date for trial or for final disposition of the case" (Dressler, 1962: 9). In England, it was frequently used with petty offenders. If the offender violated the terms of the agreement, the bond would be claimed by the state and the defaulting offender might also be incarcerated.

For this reason, recognizance has been described as containing the "germs of supervision": the suspension of sentence, conditional freedom, and possible revocation. However, unlike probation, recognizance did not provide official supervision by an agent of the court. Therefore, although recognizance (bail) is one method of assuring a defendant's appearance at trial, it also played an important role as a precursor of probation (Eskridge, 1983).

Filing of Cases

This practice, unique to Massachusetts, involved suspension of the imposition of sentence when: "After [a] verdict of guilty, in a criminal case . . . the court is satisfied that, by reason of extenuating circumstances, or of a question of law in a like case before a higher court, or other sufficient reason, public justice does not require an immediate sentence" (United Nations, 1976a: 86). With the consent of both defendant and prosecutor, the judge filed the case and made the offender subject to certain conditions set by the court. But, as Dressler indicates (1962: 11), the filing of a case did not constitute final action. The court could later take further action, and could order imprisonment.

Therefore, the filing of cases also contained some aspects of probation: the suspension of sentence, conditional release, and provisions for revocation. Again, supervision by an officer of the court was the crucial omission in comparison to probation. With these precursors in mind, let us now look at the major historical creators of probation.

Founders of Probation

John Augustus of Boston is commonly recognized as the originator of probation, but there were other contributors to its development both before and after his unique contribution.

Dressler (1962: 12–13) cites the 1841 activities of Matthew Davenport Hill of Birmingham, England. In Warwickshire, Hill observed that, in the case of youthful offenders, magistrates often imposed token sentences of one day with the special condition that the defendant remain under the supervision of a guardian. This experiment represented a mitigation of the punishment; no other conditions were imposed and there was no provision for revocation. When Hill became a Recorder, he modified this procedure; he suspended the sentence and placed the offender under the supervision of a guardian, under the assumption that "there would be better hope of amendment under such guardians than in the [jail] of the county." Hill's program has some of the same elements as Augustus's method: selected cases, suspended sentences, and if the defendant got into trouble again, no sanctions were levied. Hill, however, took action against repeaters: "That the punishment should be such as to show that it was from no weakness, from no mistaken indulgence, from no want to resolution on the part of the court to perform its duty" that the previous sentence had been suspended. Hill also demonstrated his concern for the safety of the community by requesting that the superintendent of police investigate the conduct of persons placed under a guardian's supervision.

This program was an example of the practice of "binding over," discussed earlier. In this country, one of its foremost proponents was Judge Peter Oxenbridge Thatcher of Boston. By 1836, Massachusetts passed legislation promoting the practice of releasing petty offenders upon their recognizance with sureties[2] at any stage of the proceedings.

However, it was a volunteer to the court, John Augustus, who is most often given credit for the establishment of probation in the United States. Augustus first appeared in police court in Boston when he stood bail for a man charged with drunkenness and then helped the offender find a job. The court ordered the defendant to return in three weeks, at which time he demonstrated great improvement. Instead of incarcerating this individual, the judge imposed a one-cent fine and ordered the defendant to pay costs.

From this modest beginning, Augustus proceeded to bail out numerous offenders, supervising them and offering guidance until they were sentenced. Over an eighteen-year period (from 1841 until his death in 1859), Augustus "bailed on probation" 1,152 men and 794 women (Barnes and Teeters, 1959: 554). He was motivated by his belief that "the object of the law is to reform criminals and to prevent crime and not to punish maliciously or from a spirit of revenge" (Dressler, 1962: 17). Augustus obviously selected his candidates carefully, offering assistance "mainly to those who were indicted for their first offense, and whose hearts were not wholly depraved, but gave promise of better things." He also considered the "previous character of the person, his age and influences by which he would in future be likely to be surrounded and, although these points were not rigidly adhered to, still they were the circumstances which usually determined my action" (United Nations, 1976a: 90). In addition, Augustus provided his charges with aid in obtaining employment, an education, or a place to live, and also made an impartial report to the court. The task was not without its frustrations, as Augustus noted (Barnes and Teeters, 1959: 554):

> While it saves the county and state hundreds and I might say thousands of dollars, it drains my pockets instead of enriching me. To attempt to make money by bailing poor people would prove an impossibility. The first two years of my labor I received nothing from anyone except what I earned by my daily labor.

His records on the first 1,100 individuals which he bailed out revealed that only one forfeited bond (Dressler, 1962: 18). When Augustus died in 1859, he was destitute—an unfitting end for a humanitarian visionary!

Philosophical Bases of Probation

Probation emerged in the United States during the nineteenth century, a period of considerable social turmoil and conflict. It was a development widely influenced by certain thoughts, arguments, and debates in Europe. In a larger sense, probation is an extension of the Western European philosophical arguments about the functions of criminal law and how offenders should be handled and punished. The punishment philosophy generally advocated by the kings, emperors, and other rulers of Europe focused on the crime, and attempted to treat all crimes equally. They viewed the purposes of criminal law as to punish, to deter others, and to seek revenge and vengeance for violations of the "king's peace." Widespread use of the death penalty, torture, banishment, public humiliations, and mass executions resulted from "disturbing the king's peace."

In the eighteenth century, French philosophers created a controversy by focusing on liberty, equality, and justice. Famous French philosophers and lawyers attempted to redefine the purpose of criminal law in an effort to find some way to make the criminal justice system of their time more attuned to the humanitarian ethos of the Age of Enlightenment. A major figure of the time was Cesare Beccaria, a mildly disturbed Italian genius who only left his country once—when invited to visit Paris to debate the French philosophers.

When Beccaria published is famous *Essay on Crime and Punishment* (1764), he established the "Classical School" of criminology, which attempted to reorient the law toward more humanistic goals. This would include: no torturing of the accused in order to extract confessions, no secret indictments and trials, the right to defense at a trial, improvement of the conditions of imprisonment, and so on. His work attracted the attention of Catherine the Great, the Russian empress, who invited Beccaria to revise Russian criminal law.

The philosophical ferment of the period quickly spread to England and, from there, to the colonies. When the United States emerged from the Revolutionary War, the remaining vestiges of the harsher English penal codes were resoundedly abandoned. What emerged was a constitutional system that incorporated the major components of the humanitarian philosophy, along with a populace embued with the belief in the inherent goodness of humankind and the ability of all persons to rise to their optimal level of perfectability.

The differences between the earlier approach to handling offenders (harsh punishments openly administered, and corporal and capital punishments) and the emerging reformation emphasis of the last decade of the eighteenth century, were primarily in (1) the way offenders were viewed and (2) the focus and intent of the criminal law. Prior to the Revolutionary War, offenders were seen as inherently evil, deserving punishment so that they might "get right with God." After the Civil War, Americans had generally recognized that humankind was not basically evil. The focus shifted to dealing with individual offenders, rather than focusing on the crime that had been committed. The Civil War further added to the movement toward democracy, the rise of the reformation movement, and to the further individualization of treatment and punishment. Eventually the question arose: Do all offenders need to be imprisoned in order for them to repent and stop their criminal behavior? It was in this philosophical environment that Massachusetts began to answer the question, and the concern was juvenile probation.

Juvenile Probation

As is the case with adult offenders, the development of community corrections has led to probation—currently, the most frequently used disposition for juveniles. In the United States, almost 60 percent of the cases that reach the juvenile court dispositional stage result in probation.[3]

As it relates to juvenile offenders, probation is defined as a legal status created by a court of juvenile jurisdiction. It usually involves:

(1) a judicial finding that the behavior of the child has been such to bring him within the purview of the court, (2) the imposition of conditions upon his con-

tinued freedom, and (3) the provision of means for helping him meet those conditions and for determining the degree to which he needs them. Probation thus implies much more than indiscriminately giving the child "another chance." Its central thrust is to give him positive assistance in adjustment in the free community.[4]

Historical Background

The historical antecedents of juvenile probation are generally outlined above. The legal underpinnings of modern juvenile probation were laid down in the early Middle Ages, when English kings enunciated the principle of *parens patriae*: "the King, being father of His country, must protect the welfare of the children."

As with probation for adult offenders, John Augustus is viewed as the "father of juvenile probation" since he began to speak for and assist juvenile girls in trouble with the law by supervising, guiding, and counseling them. His efforts led to the establishment of the first visiting probation agent system in Massachusetts (1869), as well as passage of the first enabling legislation for the creation of probation (1878), also in Massachusetts. In the interim, the Society for the Prevention of Cruelty to Children (1875) was established. Their proposed policies and advocacy set the stage for the first juvenile court in America specifically set up to address the needs of juvenile offenders: the Cook County (Chicago), Illinois, juvenile court, 1899 (see Table 3–1).

The first juvenile court emerged from the concerns of a group of wealthy, humanitarian, and compassionate women in Chicago who wished each child to receive such care, custody, and treatment as their natural parents ought to have provided. The juvenile court was devised to attain these objectives. The means to these ends required *individualized* treatment, based on an extensive *diagnosis* of the child's needs and personality, with the judge serving as a *counselor* to the patient (juvenile). It was believed that the juvenile court would safeguard presumed *superconstitutional* rights (the child would receive more than his or her just deserts) and avoid the stigma of criminal conviction through *informal court proceedings* focused on understanding the juvenile, humanitarian intervention, solicitous care, regenerative treatment, and benevolent attention. To attain these objectives, the procedural safeguards guaranteed under the U.S. Constitution were believed unnecessary; the focus was on the child, not the deed.

Juvenile court proceedings were informal, closed to the public, conducted in the absence of legal counsel, and individualized in outcome and guidance. Records were confidential, further reflecting the efforts of the court and decision-makers to provide and protect the "best interests of the child." Legal challenges were rare.

Juvenile courts were rapidly established throughout the various states, federal government, and Puerto Rico. By 1927, all but two states had passed enabling legislation to establish both juvenile courts and juvenile probation. The juvenile probation that emerged was predicated on the basic assumption that providing guidance, supervision, resources, and counseling would, with little danger to society, assist low-risk juveniles, in adapting to constructive living, and thus avoid the need for institutionalization.

The primary goal of probation, therefore, was to assist juveniles in dealing with their social environments and problems. By resolving causes of the youthful offenders' problems, reintegration into the community would be brought about. Probation should be the disposition of choice, rather than incarceration, because:

1. Probation provides for community safety while permitting the youthful offender to remain in the community for reintegration purposes.
2. Institutionalization leads to prisonization, the process of learning the norms and culture of institutional living.[5] This decreases the

Table 3–1
Significant Events in the Development of Probation

DATE	EVENTS
Middle Ages	*Parens patriae* established to protect the welfare of the child in England.
1841	John Augustus becomes the "father of probation."
1869	Massachusetts develops the visiting probation agent system.
1875	Society for the Prevention of Cruelty to Children established in New York, paving the way for the juvenile court.
1878	Massachusetts passes first juvenile probation law.
1899	The first juvenile court in the United States is established in Cook County (Chicago), Illinois.
1925	Congress authorizes probation at the federal level.
1927	All states but Wyoming have juvenile probation laws.
1954	Last state enacts juvenile probation law.
1956	Mississippi becomes the last state to pass authorizing legislation to establish adult probation.
1967	*In re Gault* decided by the U.S. Supreme Court.
1973	National Advisory Commission on Criminal Justice Standards and Goals endorses more extensive use of probation.
1980	American Bar Association Institute issues restrictive guidelines to limit use of preadjudication detention.
1982	Mulvey and Saunders develop prototype criteria for limiting preadjudication detention, with feedback loops for comparing outcomes.

ability of the juvenile to function as a law-abiding citizen when released, and thus leads to further involvement as an adult offender.[6]

3. The stigma of incarceration is avoided.

4. The negative labeling effects of being treated as a criminal would be avoided.[7]

5. Reintegration is more likely if existing community resources are used and the youth continues to engage in social and familial support systems (family, school, peers, extracurricular activities, employment, friends, etc.).

6. Probation is less expensive than incarceration, arguably more humanitarian, and is at least as effective in reducing further delinquent behavior as is institutionalization.[8]

One can see the "child saving" movement implicit in the development of the juvenile court. The procedures for handling juveniles are less visible.

Functions of Juvenile Probation

The four major functions that contemporary probation departments provide to juveniles are: intake and screening, investigation, supervision, and service delivery (Kuhl and Allen, 1983).

Intake and Screening

The major function of intake and screening is to decide if those juveniles referred to juvenile court fall under the jurisdiction of the court. This entails screening each case to determine if the petition falls under the enabling statutes, or if the case is under the appropriate jurisdiction of other community agencies. This requires a preliminary investigation.

The probation officer (or court official) usually confers with the referral agency (usually the juvenile bureau officer), the child, and the child's parents or guardian. The juvenile and parents are informed of the nature of the petition ("charge"), their legal rights, and procedures that may follow. The crucial decision is whether to continue the case or screen the child into an informal disposition or status, such as reprimand and release; place the child on informal probation; divert the juvenile to alternative social agencies; refer to community psychological service units; dismiss the petition; or continue to full investigation. The ensuing crucial decision made at this level is to admit, continue, or remove the child from prehearing detention prior to final case disposition. Good screening officers and procedures are important because wrong decisions and inappropriate referrals can do harm to the child and pose a threat to the safety of the community.

Investigation

Should the screening and intake officer decide to schedule a formal hearing in juvenile court (because of the nature of the act, prior appearances before the court, court philosophy, and so on),[9] a comprehensive investigation of the history of each youth is required. This diagnostic study has implications for alternative case dispositions, ranging from return to family up to commitment to a training school for many years.

Such a study involves the awesome task of predicting human behavior. The focal concern is the probable nature of the child's response to the necessary demands of society: Will he or will he not be able to refrain from offending again if permitted to reside in the free community? An even more complicated question is: What will be his adjustment under the various possible conditions of treatment (i.e., if he is returned home without further intervention, or if he is provided differing sorts of community supervision and service, or if he is confined in an institution)? Only by illuminating such questions can the social study be of value to the court's dispositional decision.[10]

The investigating officer faces the task of preparing the diagnostic study (a presentence investigation report) for juvenile court disposition or adjudicational hearing. Described more extensively in Chapter 4, the presentence investigation report would include such factors as nature of the petition and delinquent act; the juvenile's version; information on school, family, or employment stability and history; prior juvenile involvements and dispositions; psychological and physical conditions;[11] needs and risk assessments; recommendations; and treatment plans.

Supervision and Service Delivery

If the child is formally adjudicated a delinquent at the adjudicatory hearing, the juvenile court may request further information, sometimes psychological in nature. The dispositional hearing, held at a later time, would determine the order to be made for the delinquent child. The order could be for probation, placement in a residential child-care facility or foster home, commitment to a training school, or even return to parents. If the child is placed under probation supervision, three major factors will be involved: surveillance, casework service, and counseling or guidance.

Surveillance, intended to keep the probation officer informed of the delinquent's progress, behavior, problems, and reactions to the treatment plan, involves the officer's keeping in touch with the delinquent, parents, school, and any social agency involved with the case. Casework service, derived from the social work model, requires the officer to diagnose, treat, and handle the juvenile and related case matters through home visits, conducting interviews, working with the school, discussions with parents, and making referrals to treatment-delivery agencies. Counseling and guidance focus on helping the child and parents understand the problems that produced the delinquent act, as well as their relative contributions to the delinquency. Solutions are the major concern here, and both parents and the delinquent child are encouraged to become actively involved in the problem-solving process.

Finally, probation officers serve ancillary functions, especially in larger jurisdictions that administer in-house agency services, including foster-care, drug treatment centers and programs, day attendance centers, group homes, camps, and so on. The probation officer manages the case, using treatment modalities, supervision, and other approaches deemed necessary for the individual case.

The Legal Rights of Juveniles

It should be obvious that the juvenile court, developing over a century, dealt with juvenile offenders with *civil* rather than *criminal* procedures (civil suits deal with individual wrongs, whereas criminal prosecutions involve public wrongs). The greatest thrust of the juvenile court, until the last two decades, was directed at creating a separate court system for dependent, neglected, and delinquent children. Under the doctrine of *parens patriae*, the juvenile court system largely ignored the legal rights of the juvenile that are constitutionally guaranteed to all citizens: the right to trial by jury, to a speedy trial, bail, to confront one's accusers, right against self-incrimination, and other rights. These were believed unnecessary for juveniles, as the court would consider the best interests of the child in a civil setting. Some juvenile judges sensed inequity and, somewhat like salmon swimming upstream, attempted to provide constitutional safeguards. In the 1960s, the U.S. Supreme Court was called upon to examine juvenile court proceedings and the constitutionally guaranteed rights of juveniles. Tremendous aftereffects can be seen. No historical review of probation is complete without a review of the import of those decisions on juvenile probation.

Kent v. the United States

In 1966, the U.S. Supreme Court was asked to rule on the issue of the transfer of a juvenile to the criminal justice system. The legislative nature of the juvenile court procedures was called into question. The Court stated:

> There is much evidence that some juvenile courts, including that of the District of Columbia, lack the personnel, facilities, and techniques to perform adequately as representatives of the State in a *parens patriae* capacity, at least with respect to children charged with law violation. There is evidence, in fact, that there may be grounds for concern that the child receives the worst of both worlds: that he gets neither the protections accorded to adults nor the solicitous care and regenerative treatment postulated for children.[12]

This case presaged more important issues, and pronouncements were not long in forthcoming.

In re Gault

In 1967, the Court rendered its first major decision in the area of juvenile court procedures. In Arizona, Gerald Gault, aged sixteen, allegedly made a telephone call to a neighborhood woman, during which he used obscene words and phrases. The use of obscene language over the telephone violated an Arizona statute. Gerald Gault was adjudicated a juvenile delinquent after a proceeding in which he was denied basic procedural safeguards that he would have enjoyed if he were charged as an adult. This landmark decision[13] categorically granted all juveniles charged with delinquent acts that might result in their commitment to a correctional institution ("grievous harm") the following:

1. Right to know the nature of the charges against them, to prepare for trial
2. Right to counsel
3. Right against self-incrimination, at least in court
4. Right to confront and cross-examine accusers and witnesses

The *Gault* decision ended the presumption that the juvenile court was beyond the scope and purview of due process protections.

In re Winship

This 1970 decision further enlarged these rights. Proof used in a court finding of delinquency must show "beyond a reasonable doubt" that the juvenile committed the alleged delinquent act; this is the same standard used for adults in criminal trials. The Court found unpersuasive the argument that juvenile proceedings were noncriminal and intended to benefit the child.[14] Currently, juveniles do not have the right to trial by jury.[15]

These three major decisions by the U.S. Supreme Court have created a second and nascent model for the juvenile court: the due process model. Juvenile probation, as seen in court proceedings and used in juvenile courts, is currently vacillating between these two models, and major changes are occurring.

Critics of the Juvenile Court and *Parens Patriae*

Disenchantment with and criticisms of the *parens patriae* juvenile court and its procedures have been voiced by such groups as voluntary organizations,[16] private nonprofit organizations,[17] the judiciary[18] and the bar,[19] practitioners,[20] researchers,[21] and the federal government,[22] among others. Such efforts, coupled with decisions by the U.S. Supreme Court, have focused on four major areas of concern:

1. Diversion of juveniles
2. Status offenders
3. Decriminalization
4. Decarceration

It is with diversion and decarceration that juvenile probation is most concerned.

Diversion of Juveniles

The due process model noted above was developed from the *Gault, Winship*, and *Kent* cases by defining those constitutionally guaranteed rights that must be accorded every citizen, whether adult or juvenile. This model requires adherence to minimally guaranteed legal procedures, a voluntary and helping relationship, the least restrictive environments necessary to treat the juvenile, and a requirement for a demonstrated need for detention and, absent this, a mandatory *non*commitment to an institution (del Carmen, 1984).

The question of whether incarcerated juveniles have a mandatory right to treatment if confined has been addressed in several federal cases, the most significant of which was *Nelson v. Heyne*,[23] which upheld a categorical right to treatment for juveniles under the due process clause of the Fourteenth Amendment.[24] The appellate court stated that the *parens patriae* principle of the juvenile court could be justified only if treatment were available for committed delinquent youth:

> . . . the right to treatment includes the right to minimum acceptable standards of care and treatment for juveniles and the right to *individualized* care

and treatment. Because children differ in their need for rehabilitation individual need for treatment will differ. When a state assumes the place of a juvenile's parents, it assumes as well the parental duties, and its treatments of its juveniles should, so far as can be reasonably required, be what proper parental care would provide. Without a program of individual treatment the result may be that the juveniles will not be rehabilitated, but warehoused.[25]

The due process model and the *Nelson* requirements have significantly contributed toward the diversion process of juveniles. Cost is another factor; The American Correctional Association (1984) reports the cost of juvenile institutions as $20,384 and $22,365 for Alabama and California, respectively.[26] Allen and Simonsen (1981) define diversion as:

> The official halting or suspension, at any legally prescribed processing point after a recorded justice system entry, of formal juvenile justice proceedings against an alleged offender, and referral of that person to a treatment or care program administered by a nonjustice agency or to a private agency, or no referral.[27]

Diversion programs function to divert juveniles out of the juvenile justice system, encourage the use of existing correctional facilities and agencies for such offenders, and avoid formal contact with the juvenile court. These programs include remedial education programs,[28] foster homes, group homes, and local counseling facilities and centers. The effectiveness of such programs are not yet definitively demonstrated, but Rausch and Logan (1982) have summarized existing studies and concluded:

> One common component to all rationales for diversion seems to be that *less* intervention is better than *more* intervention. Thus, whatever else it involves, diversion necessarily implies an attempt to make the form of social control more limited in scope. Studies of diversion programs, however, indicate that instead of limiting the scope of the system, diversion programs often broaden it. They do this either by intensifying services or by taking in more cases. The latter is referred to as a "widening of the net" effect. Police and court intake personnel are often reluctant to subject youths to the juvenile justice system; at the same time, they may be reluctant to simply ignore them or turn them loose. When provided with a formal channel for diversion, police and court intake officers have been directing to this channel many individuals who otherwise would have been left alone or released at the intake stage.[29]

Decarceration

The concept of decarceration is recent; 1969 is considered its birthdate. In that year, Jerome Miller was appointed youth commissioner in Massachusetts.[30] He asserted that the era of the confinement of children in large correctional institutions was over; that an age of more humane, decent, and community-based care for delinquents had begun. Over a few short years, he closed the major juvenile institutions in Massachusetts and placed his charges in small group homes,[31] using other, already existing community-based correctional services and facilities to handle delinquents in the state.

Critics of the movement became ascerbic. Miller's peers, Massachusetts juvenile correctional personnel, unions, and the media[32] expressed first concern and then dismay. Program evaluators, after years of study, found the community-based juvenile group did worse (in terms of recidivism[33]) than earlier juveniles processed through the correctional units. Proponents of the decarceration movement argued that the community programs were overwhelmed with clients, services were lacking, and community support systems were weak. The debate continues.[34]

The Future of Juvenile Probation

Several conclusions are evident from this review of current trends. It is obvious that juvenile probation is in a period of rapid change, and that the juvenile courts in America are vacillating between the old *parens patriae* and the newer due process models. Further, the roles of the juvenile probation officer are being sharply revised as the various courts and jurisdictions move toward diversion, transfer of "dangerous" juvenile offenders into the criminal justice system, removal of the status offenders from the jurisdiction of the juvenile court, and even the decarceration of juveniles. In addition, faced with the legal constraints, requirements for treatment of incarcerated delinquent youths, and the high costs of juvenile institutions, probation officers are facing divergent and different demands. Finally, to divert and refer juveniles to social services there must be community and private service agencies to provide services to juveniles.

Currently, juvenile probation services are dependent on the philosophy of the juvenile court and referral agencies, as well as on court administrators. What is emerging is a patchwork of temporizing procedures, responses, and programs. There is no panacea for the quandry of juvenile probation and corrections, and we end by pointing out that certain new demands will emerge: specialized training for probation officers, new technology for probation services,[35] expansion of screening and intake services into twenty-four-hour agencies, coordination of referral and community services, and eventual unification of probation services on local and, in some jurisdictions, state levels. These issues will be explored in the following chapters.

The Growth of Probation

Buoyed by Augustus's example, Massachusetts quickly moved to the forefront of probation development. An experiment in providing services for children (resembling probation) was inaugurated in 1869, under the auspices of the Massachusetts State Board of Health, Lunacy, and Charity (Johnson, 1928: 7). A statute enacted in that year provided that, when complaints were made in court against a juvenile under seventeen years of age, a written notice must be furnished to the state. The state agent was then given an opportunity to investigate, attend the trial, and to safeguard the interests of the child.

Probation on the Federal Level

Although probation quickly became almost universal in the juvenile justice system, no early specific provision for probation was made for federal offenders, either juvenile or adult. As a substitute, the federal courts suspended sentence in instances where imprisonment imposed special hardships. However, this practice was quickly called into question by several sources.

The major question was a legal one: Did federal judges have the constitutional authority to suspend a sentence indefinitely, or did this practice represent an encroachment upon the executive prerogative of pardon and reprieve and was it, as such, an infringement upon the doctrine of separation of powers? This issue was resolved by the U.S. Supreme Court in the *Killits* decisions (Ex parte U.S. 242 U.S. 27–53, 1916). In a case from the northern district of Ohio, John M. Killits suspended the five-year sentence of a man who was convicted of embezzling $4,700 from a Toledo bank. The defendant was a first offender with an otherwise good background and reputation, who made full restitution for this offense. The bank officers did not wish to prosecute. The government contended that such action was beyond the powers of the court. A unanimous opinion, delivered by Chief Justice Edward D. White, held that the federal courts had no inherent power to suspend sentence indefinitely and that there was no reason "to continue a practice which is inconsistent with the Constitution, since its exercise in the very nature of things amounts to a refusal by the judicial power to perform a duty resting upon it and as a consequence thereof, to an interference with both the legislative and executive authority as fixed by the Constitution." However, instead of abolishing this probationary practice, the *Killits* decision actually sponsored its further development. Interested parties interpreted the reversal of the "doctrine of inherent power to suspend sentences indefinitely" to mean that enabling legislation should be passed that specifically granted this power to the judiciary.

At the federal level, the National Probation Association (then headed by Charles Lionel Chute) carried on a determined educational campaign and lobbied for federal legislation. These efforts did not go unopposed, however. For example, prohibitionists feared that the growth of probation would take the sting out of the provisions of the Volstead Act.[36] As Evjen (1975: 5) has demonstrated, letters from judges to Chute clearly denounced the practice of probation.

> What we need in this court is not a movement such as you advocate, to create new officials with resulting expense, but a movement to make the enforcement of our criminal laws more certain and swift. . . .
>
> In this country, due to the efforts of people like yourselves, the murderer has a cell bedecked with flowers and is surrounded with a lot of silly people. The criminal should understand when he violates the law that he is going to a penal institution and is going to stay there. Just such efforts as your organization is making are largely responsible for the crime wave that is passing over the country today and threatening to engulf our institutions.

Objections also arose from the Justice Department. For example, Attorney General Harry M. Daugherty wrote that he hoped "that no such mushy policy will be indulged in as Congress turning courts into maudlin reform associations . . . the place to do reforming is inside the walls and not with lawbreakers running loose in society." A memorandum from the Justice Department further revealed this sentiment against probation: "It is all a part of a wave of maudlin rot of misplaced sympathy for criminals that is going over the country. It would be a crime, however, if a probation system is established in the federal courts."

Approximately thirty-four bills to establish a federal probation system were introduced in Congress between 1909 and 1925. Despite such opposition, a bill was passed on its sixth introduction to the House. The bill was sent to President Coolidge who, as former governor of Massachusetts, was familiar with the functioning of probation. He signed the bill into law on March 4, 1925. This action was followed by an appropriation to defray the salaries and expenses of a limited number of probation officers, to be chosen by civil service (see Meeker, 1975; Linder and Savarese, 1984). Comparable historical data on select states can be found in Table 3–2.

Recent Legal Developments

Understanding the development of probation also requires a quick tour through the major and recent cases that deal with adult probation. These concern the nature of probation, revocation, probation conditions, supervision, and remedies.

Nature of Probation and Revocation

Probation is a privilege, not a right (del Carmen, 1984). This was decided in *U.S. v. Birnbaum*, 1970.[37] Once granted, however, the probationer has

Table 3-2
States with Juvenile and Adult Probation Laws: 1923

	YEAR ENACTED	
STATES	Juvenile	Adult
Alabama..	1907	1915
Arizona...	1907	1913
Arkansas...	1911	1923
California..	1903	1903
Colorado	1899	1909
Connecticut.......................................	1903	1903
Delaware	1911	1911
Georgia	1904	1907
Idaho	1905	1915
Illinois	1899	1911
Indiana..	1903	1907
Kansas	1901	1909
Maine	1905	1905
Maryland	1902	1904
Massachusetts	1878	1878
Michigan	1903	1903
Minnesota	1899	1909
Missouri	1901	1897
Montana...	1907	1913
Nebraska	1905	1909
New Jersey	1903	1900
New York	1903	1901
North Carolina	1915	1919
North Dakota......................................	1911	1911
Ohio	1902	1908
Oklahoma	1909	1915
Oregon	1909	1915
Pennsylvania	1903	1909
Rhode Island	1899	1899
Tennessee	1905	1915
Utah	1903	1923
Vermont	1900	1900
Virginia	1910	1910
Washington	1905	1915
Wisconsin	1901	1909

SOURCE: Adapted from Fred R. Johnson, *Probation for Juveniles and Adults*, pp. 12–13. (New York: Century Co., 1928).

an interest in remaining on probation, commonly referred to as an entitlement. The U.S. Supreme Court has ruled that probation cannot be withdrawn (revoked) unless certain basic elements of due process are observed. If a court is considering removing the offender from probation (through a "revocation" hearing), the following rights and procedures must ensue: The probationer must (a) be informed in writing of the charge against him or her, (b) have the written notice in advance of the revocation hearing, and (c) attend the hearing and be able to present evidence on his or her own behalf. The probationer also has a right (d) to challenge those testifying against him or her, (e) to confront witnesses and cross-examine them, and (f) to have legal counsel present if the charges are complicated or the case is so complex that an ordinary person would not be able to comprehend the legal issues. These rights and procedures were enunciated in *Gagnon v. Scarpelli*, 1972.[38]

Probation Conditions

The judge usually imposes the conditions that must be observed by the offender while on probation and has absolute discretion and authority to impose, modify, or reject these conditions. Some examples of conditions a judge might impose are routine blood testing to detect narcotics use and abuse; participation in Alcoholics Anonymous if the probationer has an alcohol problem; restitution to victims of the probationer (but probation may not be revoked if the offender cannot make payments because of unemployment: *Bearden v. Georgia*, 1983);[39] and not leaving the court's jurisdiction without prior approval. Many cases have challenged the conditions that courts might impose, but case law has determined any condition may be imposed if it is constitutional, reasonable, clear, and related to some definable correctional goal, such as rehabilitation or public safety. These are difficult to challenge and leave the court with broad power and tremendous discretion in imposing conditions. Such discretion has contributed to the volume of civil rights suits (del Carmen, 1984).

Supervision

The probation officer is responsible for seeing that the conditions imposed by the court are met, and if not, calling the violations to the attention of the court. As such, the probation officer functions both as a helper and as a supervisor of the probationer. Legal liability is greater for the probation officer than the court; although an agent of the court, the probation officer does not enjoy the absolute immunity from liability that the court enjoys.

Some areas of potential liability for the probation officer include acts taken or protective steps omitted. For example, a probation officer may be liable for failing to disclose a probationer's background to a third party if this results in subsequent serious injury or death. Case decisions have generally held that the probation officer should disclose the past behavior of the probationer if able to reasonably foresee a potential danger to a specific third party. This would include an employer hiring a probationer as an accountant in a bank when the instant crime was embezzlement, or hiring a child molester to work in a grade school position. Insurance for liabilities can be obtained from the American Correctional Association.[40]

As a counselor to probationers, probation officers are often faced with the problem of encouraging their clients to share their problems and needs. Frequently, during the monthly contact, a probationer will reveal involvement in criminal activities. Under these noncustodial circumstances, probation officers are *required* to warn the probationer against self-incrimination though the *Miranda* warnings[41] or the evidence cannot be used in a court of law. Under detention circumstances, when the probationer is in jail, any discussion with him or her *must* be preceded by the *Miranda* warnings. Litigation is so extensive within the probation area that the probation officer must frequently take an active role as a law enforcement officer rather than a helper, a sad development from the original role John Augustus initiated and correctional personnel usually pursue!

Remedies

While legal remedies are discussed later in this text, we should point out that probationers can seek redress from violation of their rights through civil suits (tort cases) entered in state courts or, should the issue concern whether their incarceration were legal, through state courts over habeas corpus suits (questioning the legality of their current incarceration from revocation procedures). An increasing avenue for seeking of redress is Section 1983 of Chapter 42 United States Code:

> Every person who under color of any statute, ordinance, regulation, custom, or usage of Any State or Territory, subjects or causes to be subjected, any citizen of the United States or any other person within the jurisdiction thereof to the deprivation of any rights, privileges, or immunities secured by the Constitution and laws, shall be liable to the party injured in an action at law, suit in equity, or other proper proceeding for redress. The important issue here is the general trend toward an increased use of legal avenues to standardize the probation service, to remove capricious and discriminatory activities, and to broaden the rights of probationers. The field is in flux, and widespread changes are in progress. What will eventually emerge from the litigation and current turmoil will probably be more clearly defined procedures and policies, increased preservice and in-service training of probation officers, refinement of agency procedures and practices, written policies governing supervision and probationer control, and increased innovation in probation. These will be welcome changes in probation practice.

Summary

This chapter has traced the historical, philosophical, and legal developments in the field of probation over the last two centuries. Major changes are occurring, and probation services will undoubtedly emerge stronger and fairer. The next chapter addresses the start of the probation process: the presentence investigation.

Notes

1. No doubt much of this frustration toward the leniency of probation stems from the fact that probation "lacks the drama of sending a man to a penal institution" (Barnes and Teeters, 1959: 555).

2. Sureties refers to cash, property, or bond posted by an offender, to be forfeited if he or she fails to conform to such conditions as to appear in court for trial, or to avoid further criminal behavior over a specified time period. It can also refer to a pledge by another responsible person to assure that the accused will appear or behave properly.

3. National Center for Juvenile Justice, U.S. Department of Health, Education and Welfare, *Juvenile Court Statistics* (Washington, D.C.: Government Printing Office, 1970).

4. President's Commission on Law Enforcement and Administration of Justice, *Corrections*, p. 130 (Washington, D.C.: Government Printing Office, 1967).

5. Donald Clemmer, *The Prison Community* (New York: Rinehart and Company, 1940), p. 8.

6. The perceived relationship between juvenile delinquency and adult criminality has been seriously challenged by recent research. Arguing that evidence is not sufficient to permit accurate predictions about whether juvenile delinquents will eventually become adult offenders, Lyle Shannon also found that the relationship that does exist can in large part be explained by the effects of processes within the juvenile and criminal justice systems, as well as by the continued delinquent behavior of the juvenile. Lyle W. Shannon, *Assessing the Relationship of Adult Career Criminals to Juvenile Careers* (Washington, D.C.: Government Printing Office, 1982).

7. Edwin Schur, *Labeling Deviant Behavior: Its Sociological Implications* (New York: Harper and Row, 1971).

8. See Solomon Kobrin and Malcolm Klein, *National Evaluation of the Deinstitutionalization of Status Offender Programs* (Washington, D.C.: Office of Juvenile Justice and Delinquency Prevention, U.S. Department of Justice, 1983).

9. An excellent review of the studies of criteria used in making decisions to detain juveniles before their case dispositions can be found in Edward Mulvey and J. Terry Saunders, "Juvenile Detention Criteria: State of the Art and Guidelines for Change," *Criminal Justice Abstracts* 14 (June 1982):261–89.

10. President's Commission, *Corrections*, p. 132.

11. Glenn Collins, "Research Links Violent Behavior to Abuse," *Justice Assistance News* 3 (November 1982):1–2.

12. *Kent v. United States*, 383 U.S. 54 (1966).

13. *In re Gault*, 387 U.S. 1 (1967).

14. *In re Winship*, 397 U.S. 358 (1970).

15. *McKeiver v. Pennsylvania*, 403 U.S. 528 (1971).

16. National Council on Crime and Delinquency, *Standards and Guides for the Detention of Children and Youth* (New York: National Council on Crime and Delinquency, 1961). The address for the National Council on Crime and Delinquency is 411 Hackensack Avenue, Hackensack, NJ 07601.

17. Citizens Committee for Children, *Lost Opportunities: A Study of the Promise and Practices of the [New York City] Department of Probation's Family Court* (New York: Citizens Committee for Children, 1982). The address for the Citizens Committee for Children is 105 East Twenty-second Street, New York, NY 10010.

18. Walter G. Whitlack, "Practical Aspects of Reducing Detention Home Population," *Juvenile Justice* 24 (1973): 17–29. See also Monrad Paulsen and Charles Whitebread, *Juvenile Law and Procedure* (Reno, Nev.: National Council of Juvenile Court Judges, 1974).

19. Institute of Judicial Administration, American Bar Association, *Standards Relating to Interim Status: Release, Control and Detention of Accused Juvenile Offenders Between Arrest and Disposition* (Cambridge, Mass.: Ballinger, 1980). The address for the American Bar Association is 1155 East Sixtieth Street, Chicago, IL 60637.

20. American Correctional Association Commission on Accreditation for Corrections, *Manual of Standards for Juvenile Detention Facilities and Services* (Rockville, Md.: American Correctional Association, 1979). The address of the American Correctional Association is 4321 Hartwick Road, Suite L-208, College Park, MD 20740.

21. See Anthony Platt, *The Child Savers* (Chicago: University of Chicago Press, 1969); Rosemary Saari, *Under Lock and Key: Juveniles in Jails and Detention* (Ann Arbor, Mich.: National Assessment of Juvenile Corrections, 1974); and Charles Fenwick, "Juvenile Court Intake Decision Making; The Importance of Family Affiliation," *Journal of Criminal Justice* 10 (1982):469–80.

22. President's Commission on Law Enforcement and Administration of Justice, *Juvenile Delinquency and Youth Crime* (Washington, D.C.: Government Printing Office, 1967); National Advisory Commission on Criminal Justice Standards and Goals, *Corrections* (Washington, D.C.: Government Printing Office, 1973). Congress passed the Juvenile Justice and Delinquency Prevention Act in 1974, establishing the Federal Office of Juvenile Justice and Delinquency Prevention, charged with creating a comprehensive and unified approach for improving the nation's juvenile justice system.

23. *Nelson v. Heyne*, 491 F. 2nd 352 (7th Cir., 1974).

24. The relevant clause is: "nor shall any State deprive any person of life, liberty, or property, without due process of law. . . ."

25. *Nelson v. Heyne*, supra note 23.

26. American Correctional Association, *Directory of Juvenile and Adult Correctional Departments, Institutions, Agencies, and Paroling Authorities* (College Park, Md.: American Correctional Association, 1984), pp. 7 and 37.

27. Harry E. Allen and Clifford E. Simonsen, *Corrections in America* (New York: Macmillan, 1981), p. 503.

28. An example of this is project READS, San Jose State University, San Jose, CA 95192.

29. Sharla P. Rausch and Charles H. Logan, "Diversion from Juvenile Court: Panacea or Pandora's Box?," paper presented at the Annual Meeting of the American Society of Criminology, Toronto, Canada, November 6, 1982.

30. Michael Sherrill, "Jerome Miller: Does He Have the Answers . . . ?," *Corrections Magazine* 2 (November 1975):24–28.

31. Michael Sherrill, "Juvenile Corrections in Massachusetts," *Corrections Magazine* 2 (November 1975):3–12.

32. Michael Sherrill, "Harvard Recidivism Study," *Corrections Magazine* 2 (November 1975):21–23.

33. The repetition of criminal behavior; habitual criminality.

34. Clifford E. Simonsen and Marshall Gordon, *Juvenile Justice in America* (New York: Macmillan, 1982), pp. 42–46.

35. Franklin H. Marshall and Gennaro F. Vito, "Not Without the Tools: The Task of Probation in the Eighties," *Federal Probation* 46 (1982):37–40.

36. The Volstead Act authorized the enforcement of antialcohol legislation—the "Great Experiment" of the Thirteenth Amendment to the U.S. Constitution.

37. 421 F. 2nd 993, cert. denied 397 U.S. 1044 (1970).

38. 411 U.S. 778, 93 S. Ct. 1756 (1972).

39. 33 CrL 3103 (1983).

40. The current mailing address for the American Correctional Association is 4321 Hartwick Road, Suite L-208, College Park, MD 20740.

41. *Miranda* warnings: "You have a right to remain silent. Any statement you make may be used as evidence against you in a criminal trial. You have the right to consult with counsel and to have counsel present with you during questioning. You may retain counsel at your own expense or counsel will be provided at no expense to you. Even if you decide to answer questions now without having counsel present, you may stop answering questions at any time. Also, you may request counsel at any time during questioning."

Study Guides

1. How did the precursors of probation contribute to its development? Which method was most comparable to probation? Why?

2. Organize a debate between a supporter and an opponent of probation. Which arguments are most persuasive to you? Why?

3. What ideas and movements contributed to the rise of probation?

4. Why was probation established much earlier for juvenile offenders than for adult offenders?

5. Define probation.

6. How is probation related to the reformation and reintegration philosophies?

7. What are the functions of juvenile probation?

8. How did the juvenile court emerge?
9. What steps occur between police referral of a juvenile and commitment to a juvenile institution?
10. What were major legal decisions that have affected juvenile probation?
11. What rights do juveniles have as a result of court decisions in the last twenty years?
12. What factors have led to the increased use of community services for juveniles?
13. What have been the effects of the Massachusetts decarceration effort?
14. What rights does a probationer have in a revocation hearing?
15. What are some conditions that sentencing courts may impose on probationers?
16. Is there a conflict between the counseling and helping role of probation officers and the supervision role they are called on to enforce?
17. What are some avenues that probationers can use to ensure that they have all the rights to which they are entitled?
18. What tactics can be used to keep lawsuits at a minimum?

Key Terms

adjudicatory hearing	judicial reprieve
benefit of clergy	juvenile court
casework service	juvenile probation
counseling	*Killits* decision
decarceration	*parens patriae*
detention	presentence report
diagnostic study	recidivism
filing of cases	recognizance
John Augustus	surveillance

References

American Bar Association Project Standards for Criminal Justice. *Standards Relating to Probation.* New York: Institute of Judicial Administration, 1970.

American Correctional Association. *Directory of Juvenile and Adult Correctional Departments, Institutions, Agencies and Paroling Authorities.* College Park, Md.: ACA, 1984.

BARNES, HARRY E., AND TEETERS, NEGLEY D. *New Horizons in Criminology.* Englewood Cliffs, N.J.: Prentice-Hall, 1959.

DEL CARMEN, ROLANDO. "Legal Issues and Liabilities in Community Corrections." Unpublished paper presented at the annual meeting of the Academy of Criminal Justice Sciences, March 1984, in Chicago.

DRESSLER, DAVID. *Practice and Theory of Probation and Parole.* New York: Columbia University Press, 1962.

ESKRIDGE, CHRIS. *Pretrial Release Programming*. New York: Clark Boardman Company, 1983.

EVJEN, VICTOR H. "The Federal Probation System: The Struggle to Achieve It and Its First 25 Years," *Federal Probation* 39 (1975):3–15.

FINN, PETER. "Prison Crowding: The Response of Probation and Parole," *Crime and Delinquency* 30 (1984):141–53.

FOLKS, HANES. "Juvenile Probation in New York," *Survey* (February 1910):667.

JOHNSON, FRED R. *Probation for Juveniles and Adults*. New York: Century, 1928.

KINDSEY, BEN B. "Colorado's Contribution to the Juvenile Court." In *The Child, the Clinic and the Court*, edited by Herbert Lou, pp. 108–38. New York: World, 1925.

KRAJICK, KEVIN. "Annual Prison Population Survey: The Boom Resumes," *Corrections Magazine* 7 (March 1981):16–20.

KUHL, ANNA, AND ALLEN, HARRY. "Social Policies and Practices in Juvenile Corrections: Issues in Criminological Prediction." Unpublished paper presented at the 9th International Congress on Criminology, September 29, 1983.

LINDNER, CHARLES, AND SAVARESE, MARGARET R. "The Evolution of Probation: Early Salaries, Qualifications and Hiring Practices," *Federal Probation* 47 (1984):3–9.

McKELVEY, BLAKE. *American Prisons: A History of Good Intentions*. Montclair, N.J.: Patterson-Smith, 1977.

MEEKER, BEN S. "The Federal Probation System: The Second 25 Years," *Federal Probation* 39 (1979):16–25.

National Advisory Commission on Criminal Justice Standards and Goals, "Probation: National Standards and Goals." In *Probation, Parole and Community Services*, edited by R. N. Carter and L. T. Wilkins, pp. 115–47. New York: John Wiley and Sons, 1976.

National Criminal Justice Information and Statistics Service. *State and Local Probation and Parole Systems*. Washington, D.C.: Government Printing Office, 1978.

PLATT, ANTHONY M. *The Child Savers*. Chicago: University of Chicago Press, 1969.

President's Commission on Law Enforcement and Administration of Justice, "Probation." In *Probation, Parole and Community Services*, edited by R. N. Carter and L. T. Wilkins, pp. 93–114. New York: John Wiley and Sons, 1976.

ROTHMAN, DAVID J. *Incarceration and Its Alternatives in 20th-Century America*. Washington, D.C.: National Institute of Law Enforcement and Criminal Justice, 1979.

TUCKER, JULIE. "Federal News Clips," *On the Line* 5 (College Park, Md.: American Correctional Association, September 1982).

United Nations. "The Legal Origins of Probation." In *Probation, Parole and Community Services*, edited by R. N. Carter and L. T. Wilkins, pp. 81–88. New York: John Wiley and Sons, 1976a.

———. "The Origin of Probation in the United States." In *Probation, Parole and*

Community Services, edited by R. N. Carter and L. T. Wilkins, pp. 89–92. New York: John Wiley and Sons, 1976b.

Recommended Readings

Bureau of Justice Statistics. *Jail Inmates: 1982* (Washington, D.C.: Department of Justice, 1983). This short report contains a wealth of data and information on jail inmates, as well as juveniles, and is the most recent national picture of jail populations and their characteristics.

Dressler, David. *Practice and Theory of Probation and Parole* (New York: Columbia University Press, 1962). A cogent and well-documented analysis of the historical development of parole.

Evjen, Victor H. "The Federal Probation System: The Struggle to Achieve It and Its First 25 Years," *Federal Probation* 39 (1975):3–15. A very thorough description of the rise of the Federal probation system.

Kobrin, Solomon, and Klein, Malcolm. *National Evaluation of the Deinstitutionalization of Status Offender Programs* (Washington, D.C.: Office of Juvenile Justice and Delinquency Prevention, Department of Justice, 1983). A comprehensive review of the issues that surround status offenders, this report also details the ways in which status offenders are diverted from the juvenile justice system.

Simonsen, Clifford E., and Gordon, Marshall. *Juvenile Justice in America* (New York: Macmillan, 1982). A readable and comprehensive view of the juvenile justice system, its operations and problems. Considerable suggestions will be found for improving the juvenile system.

4

The Presentence
Investigation Report

One of the primary responsibilities of probation agencies is investigation. This includes gathering information about probation and technical violations, facts about arrests, and, most importantly, completing the presentence investigation report for use in sentencing hearings.

The concept of the presentence investigation report (PSI) developed with probation.[1] Judges originally used probation officers to gather background and personal information on offenders to "individualize" punishment. In 1943, the Federal Probation System formalized the presentence investigation report as a required function of the federal probation process. The PSI has tremendous significance in the sentencing process, since 80 to 90 percent of defendants plead guilty and the judge's only contact with the offender is during sentencing (*Georgetown Law Review*, 1970). The judge's knowledge of the defendant is limited to the information contained in the presentence report. The importance of the PSI to a probation agency is illustrated by a Census Bureau survey (U.S. Department of Justice, 1978). The data showed that of the 3,303 responding agencies, 2,540 agencies (77 percent) indicated that they conducted presentence investigations; almost one million (997,514) presentence investigations were performed by these agencies in 1975. In terms of the agency workload, almost one-half (45 percent) of the agencies that conduct presentence investigations reported that more than 25 percent of their workloads were devoted to these reports.

Functions and Objectives

The primary purpose of the PSI is to provide the sentencing court with succinct and precise information upon which to base a rational sentencing decision. Judges usually have a number of options available to them: they may suspend sentence, impose a fine, require restitution, incarcerate, or impose community supervision. The PSI is designed to aid the judge in making the appropriate decision, taking into consideration the needs of the offender as well as the safety of the community.

Over the years, many additional important uses have been found for the presentence report. Basically, these functions include:[2]

1. To aid the court in determining sentence
2. To assist correctional authorities in classification and treatment in release planning
3. To give the parole board useful information pertinent to consideration of parole
4. To aid the probation officer in rehabilitation efforts during probation
5. To serve as a source of information for research

In those jurisdictions in which probation and parole services are in the same agency, the PSI can be used for parole supervision purposes.

A presentence investigation report includes more than the simple facts about the offender, as is seen below. If it is to fulfill its purpose, it must include all objective historical and factual information that is significant to the decision-making process, an assessment of the character and needs of the defendant and the community, and a sound recommendation with supporting rationale that follows logically from the evaluation. A reliable and accurate report is essential, since judges tend to agree with and impose the disposition recommended by the investigator in 85 percent of the cases (Carter and Wilkins, 1967). The officer completing the report should make every effort to ensure that the information contained in the PSI is reliable and valid. Information that has not been validated should be indicated.

Content, Format, and Style

The presentence investigation report is not immune from a lack of consistency across jurisdictions, but there seem to be some common elements that illustrate the uses and content of the PSI. A survey of 147 probation agencies across the nation (Carter, 1976) revealed that the cover sheets contained seventeen pieces of identical information in over 50 percent of the agencies surveyed. The information that appears most often across the various jurisdictions is included in Table 4-1.

The content requirements for the Federal Probation System, as published by the Administrative Office of the United States Courts (1978: 6), consists of five core categories and subsections for the body of the report:

1. Offense (Core)
   Official version
   Defendant's version
   Codefendant information
   Statement of witnesses,
     complainants, and
     victims
2. Prior Record (Core)
   Juvenile adjudications
   Adult record
3. Personal and Family Data
     (Core)
   Defendant
   Parent and siblings

   Marital
   Education
   Employment
   Health
     physical
     mental and emotional
   Military service
   Financial condition
     assets
     liabilities
4. Evaluation (Core)
   Alternative plans
   Sentencing data
5. Recommendations (Core)

Basically, the federal presentence report "core" areas reflect the recommendation of Carter (1976: 9), who states that "In spite of the tradition of 'larger' rather than 'shorter,' there is little evidence that more is better." At a minimum, the PSI should include the five basic areas outlined above. This permits flexibility by allowing for expansion of a subject area and increased detail of circumstances as warranted. On the other hand, a subsection may be summarized in a single narrative statement.

Carter believes it is not necessary to know everything about an offender. Indeed, there is some evidence that in human decision making, the

Table 4-1
Common Elements Contained in Presentence Investigation Reports

1. Name of defendant	10. Plea
2. Name of jurisdiction	11. Date of report
3. Offense	12. Sex
4. Lawyer	13. Custody or detention
5. Docket number	14. Verdict
6. Date of birth	15. Date of disposition
7. Address	16. Marital status
8. Name of sentencing judge	17. Other identifying numbers
9. Age	

capacity of individuals to use information effectively is limited to five or six items of information. Quite apart from the question of the reliability, validity, or even relevance of the information, are the time and workload burdens of collecting and sorting masses of data for decision making. The end result may be information overload and impairment of efficiency.

The PSI contains information related to the present character and behavior of the offender. One has to question the need for detailed information on family members with whom an adult offender has had no contact in many years. On the other hand, this type of information may be crucial to a young defendant who lives at home and has experienced difficulties getting along with other members of the family. The probation officer must use professional judgment in completing and detailing the presentence report. The Federal Probation System has delineated some simple guidelines to be followed in composing the report (Presentence Investigation Report, 1978: 7):

1. *Brevity.* Avoid repetition. For clarity and interest, use short sentences and paragraphs, not, however, at the expense of completeness.

2. *Use of "label" terms.* Generalized terms should be avoided as they have different meanings to different people.

3. *Verbation style.* Use caution in verbation reporting. Use direct quotation only if it gives a better picture of the defendant or situation. Quotation marks are used for the exact words of a person, not an interpretation. Do not take language out of context.

4. *Sources of information.* Verify the facts contained in a presentence report. Clearly label any unverified information. Immeasurable harm may result from unverified information presented as fact.

5. *Technical words and phrases.* Use technical words and phrases only if they have wide usage and a common meaning.

6. *Style and format.* A simple, direct, lucid style is effective. The report need not be elaborate nor seek a dramatic effect.

7. *Writing the report.* Dictate the presentence report at the earliest possible time following the investigation. The longer the delay, the greater the chance of overlooking significant observations.

Figure 4–1, a sample presentence report from the United States District Court, illustrates the style, content, and format followed by the Federal Probation System.

A thorough PSI is not complete without a plan of supervision for those individuals selected for probation. If this type of information is developed while preparing the PSI, supervision can begin on day one, not several weeks into the probation period. During the development of the PSI, special attention is also given to seeking innovative alternatives to traditional sentencing dispositions (jail, fines, prison, or probation).

Figure 4-1 Presentence Report

NAME (Last, First, Middle)				DATE
Long, David H.				August 6, 1977

ADDRESS	LEGAL ADDRESS			DOCKET NO. 77-0084M-02
29 Everett Street Springfield, MA 01104	Same			RACE Caucasian
				CITIZENSHIP U.S.

AGE DATE OF BIRTH	PLACE OF BIRTH	SEX	EDUCATION
19 9-25-57	Springfield, MA	Male	12th grade

MARITAL STATUS	DEPENDENTS	
Single	None	

SOC. SEC. NO.	FBI NO.	OTHER IDENTIFYING NO.
111-22-3333	123 456 A7	

==

OFFENSE

Obstruction of mail, 18 U.S.C. 1701
One Count Information

PENALTY

6 mos. and/or $100
ELIGIBLE FOR YOUTH CORRECTIONS ACT

CUSTODIAL STATUS

Personal recognizance

PLEA

Offered plea of guilty pursuant to Rule 11(e) agreement, 7-18-77

VERDICT

Acceptance deferred

DETAINERS OR CHARGES PENDING

None

OTHER DEFENDANTS

Lawrence Hill, disposition scheduled 8-15-77

ASSISTANT U.S. ATTORNEY	DEFENSE COUNSEL
George Young, Esq.	William Olds, Esq. 112 State Street Springfield, MA (413) 555-1234 (Appointed)

==

DISPOSITION

SENTENCING JUDGE	DATE

SOURCE: *The Presentence Investigation Report* (Administrative Office of the U.S. Courts, 1978).

OFFENSE:

Official Version. On May 1, 1977, postal inspectors received an
anonymous telephone call that Lawrence Hill had sold items stolen from
the mail. Investigation ascertained that Hill worked as a truck driver
for the Pioneer Paper Company of Springfield and was frequently sent to
pick up his employer's mail. It was also learned that David H. Long,
who was employed by Pioneer Paper as a janitor, occasionally accompanied Hill. Postal inspectors instituted surveillance at the post office.
On May 5, 1977, inspectors saw Hill and Long remove two parcels from a
loading dock and place them in their truck. The truck was stopped at
the gate and the packages, containing a woman's coat and a hydraulic
automobile jack, were found inside. These items had a total retail
value of $357. Both defendants admitted that they had taken packages
from the Parcel Post Annex on this and three previous occasions. Total
loss is estimated at less than $750.

On July 18, 1977, Long appeared before Magistrate H.A. Good and
offered a plea of guilty pursuant to an agreement under Rule 11(e) (1)
(C) of the F.R.Crim.P. The agreement proposes that imposition of
sentence be suspended with probation for one year under the Federal
Youth Corrections Act. Acceptance of the plea was deferred pending a
presentence report. The defendant has executed consent forms authorizing the preparation of a presentence report and the court's inspection of the same.

Defendant's Version of the Offense. Mr. Long states he was an
accomplice to codefendant Hill who originally proposed that they take
the packages. The defendant asserts that Hill opened the packages and
sold the contents. After the sales, Hill would give Long $15 or $20 for
his share. Mr. Long said that he went along because it seemed an easy
way to make extra cash.

Codefendant Information. Codefendant Lawrence Hill has also
offered a plea of guilty and Hill admitted to the probation officer that
he was the prime mover in the theft from the loading dock.

PRIOR RECORD:

Juvenile Adjudications.

| 4-28-74 | Dist. the | Springfield, Mass. | 6 mos. |
| Age 16 | Peace | Juvenile Court | prob. |

The defendant was represented by Attorney Robert Parker. Mr. Long and
four other juveniles were arrested for fighting and throwing bottles at
a rock concert. The juvenile probation officer reported that Long performed satisfactorily under supervision.

68

PERSONAL AND FAMILY DATA:

David Long is the younger of two children born to Henry and Ruth Brown Long, with whom he resides. His early years were unremarkable, and he was a happy and outgoing child. However, the family circumstances changed in 1970 when Henry Long suffered a stroke which left him partially paralyzed and unable to work. This event forced Ruth Long to seek employment, and she now works full time in a factory in Springfield. Both parents agree that the necessity of focusing family resources on Henry Long's medical condition had a detrimental effect on David. Since 1970, David has become withdrawn and uncommunicative with his parents. Mr. and Mrs. Long feel responsible for this and regret that Mrs. Long had to find full-time work while David was still in school. The parents feel that part of the blame for David's involvement in the present offense rests with them.

David was educated in the Springfield public school system. He graduated from Vocational High School on June 6, 1976. He completed a general program, and he took specialized courses in radio and television repair. David's high school counselor reports that he seldom came to the attention of school authorities, and he was considered an average student. David's I.Q. was tested twice and each test placed him in the slightly above average range of intelligence.

David was unemployed for 5 months after graduating from high school. On November 4, 1976, he began working as a janitor at the Pioneer Paper Company where he earned $3 an hour. He stayed at this job until he was fired as a result of the present offense.

David was considered a reliable employee who kept largely to himself. He had indicated a willingness to accept additional responsibility. However, the company would not consider re-employing David, who is now dependent on his parents for financial support. He has no substantial assets or liabilities.

David is in good health. He admits to having experimented with marijuana but denies frequent use. He is reluctant to talk about himself, and he expresses no strong feelings on any subject. He indicated no particular personal or career goals.

EVALUATION:

This young man admits participation in the theft of packages from the mail. He was less culpable than his codefendant who instigated the theft. David's expected compensation was small and his involvement in the offense was casual and impulsive. His participation has cost him his job.

David's family is concerned about him but his parents feel power-
less to communicate with him. His father's disability has affected him
deeply but he is unsure of how to handle these feelings. David adopts
an attitude of indifference which has characterized his performance in
school as well as his relations with his family. This attitude results
in a passive approach to life although his job seemed to engage his
interest.

Alternative Plans. David is eligible for YCA treatment or could be
sentenced as an adult if the court makes a "no benefit" finding. If the
court decides on probation, the supervision plan would have two main
features. First, it would address David's need for employment. David
has been referred to the Springfield Regional Skills Center where he was
interviewed and took aptitude tests. The Center is funded under the
Comprehensive Employment and Training Act and will accept David in their
building maintenance program. There he will receive 16 weeks of training
in basic carpentry, plumbing, and electrical work. David has aptitude in
these areas, is willing to participate, and can enroll in 3 weeks. He
will receive a stipend during the training period and he will have good
prospects for employment upon completion.

Second, the supervision plan would involve an attempt to improve
the relationship between David and his parents. David is likely to
continue living at home and his parents can provide important emotional
support if he is willing to accept it. The probation officer has
consulted with a counselor from the Family Service agency, which runs
bimonthly group sessions for disabled people and their families. These
sessions seek to contain the emotional hazards of a disability by educa-
ting people as to what problems may be encountered. Mr. and Mrs. Long
have enthusiastically agreed to participate in these sessions. David is
reluctant but has agreed to attend one meeting.

For the first 4 months of supervision, David would have bimonthly
contact with his probation officer while the details of this plan are
implemented. The skill center would also provide weekly progress reports.
If he progresses well, the level of supervision could subsequently be
reduced.

Sentencing Data. During 1976, disposition of all postal offenses
in this district resulted in probation in 76 percent of the cases. Ten
percent received split sentences and 14 percent were committed. Nationwide, 56.2 percent of defendants sentenced for postal theft were placed
on probation. The only way this case would fall under the jurisdiction
of the U.S. Parole Commission is if the court commits under the Youth
Corrections Act. In that event, we estimate that the Commission would

consider this an offense of "low moderate" severity. David's salient factor score of 9 would result in a parole prognosis of 8 to 12 months.

RECOMMENDATION:

The plea agreement in this case calls upon the court to suspend imposition of sentence and to place the defendant on probation for one year under the Youth Corrections Act. This course of action is reasonable and the Probation Office recommends that the court accept the plea and adopt the proposed disposition. The probation officer would then implement the plan described above.

Respectfully submitted,

Michael Talbot
U.S. Probation Officer

Approved: _____

J. Grant Hogan
Chief U.S. Probation Officer

When to Prepare a PSI

It is best to prepare a presentence report *after* guilt has been determined. This is so for several reasons. First, if the PSI is completed beforehand and the defendant is acquitted, then an invasion of privacy has occurred, and since certain information may come from the defendant, it may be awkward if discussions with a probation officer precede the actual trial. Second, material contained in a PSI is not admissible at trial, but there is always the chance that it may come to the attention of the court before guilt has been determined. This, of course, could bias the outcome and could lead to a mistrial or appeal. Finally, there are economic reasons. A presentence report takes time and resources to complete. It makes little sense to expend resources on a PSI that may never be used. Though there may be exceptions—for example, a defense attorney may believe that having a completed PSI prior to the trial will be in the best interest of his client—the general rule is to complete a PSI only after a determination of guilt.

Carter (1978) believes that a PSI should be prepared in every case in which a sentence of confinement could be a year or longer, where the court has a sentencing option, and in all other cases that the court so requests.

Disclosure and Confidential Nature of Report

Disclosure of the presentence report to defense counsel has been debated for some time. A 1963 survey found that 56.8 percent of the judges in the sample never divulged any information from a PSI to a defendant or defense attorney (Higgins, 1964). Several court cases[3] have resolved much of the debate in favor of disclosure of the report to the defendant. Currently, sixteen jurisdictions mandate disclosure.

The disclosure of the report provides the defendant with the opportunity to identify inaccurate, incomplete, or otherwise misleading information. There is also a fundamental due process consideration. Sentencing is a critical stage in the criminal justice system; due process enables mistakes to be corrected and rights protected.

The arguments against disclosure center around the concern of protecting confidential sources. Rule 32 of the Federal Rules of Criminal Procedures (1978) provides explicit protection for this concern. The Rules state that the court shall, upon request, permit counsel and defendant to read the PSI (exclusive of exempted information and recommendations). The three types of information that the court may exempt are:

1. Diagnostic opinion which, if revealed, might seriously disrupt a program of rehabilitation and treatment. [This could be necessary when the knowledge of psychiatric diagnosis or prognosis might interfere with a defendant's receptivity to treatment.]

2. Sources of information obtained upon a promise of confidentiality. [Not all of the information provided by the confidential sources is protected, but only that information that would in any way reveal the identity of the source.]

3. Any other information which, if disclosed, might result in harm, physical or otherwise, to the defendant or other persons. [Some defendants have had a close relationship with dangerous associates or have had serious family difficulties. If unfavorable information about the defendant or other persons were divulged and there might be a risk of retaliation, such information would also be exempt from disclosure.]

If the court believes that information contained in a presentence report may be harmful to the defendant as well as others, then the court must provide, in writing, a summary of the factual information. As a rule, the presentence report is a confidential document and is not available to anyone without permission of the court. Figure 4–2 is a sample of information excluded from a PSI, and a summary of factual information.

Evaluation and Recommendation

Two of the most important sections of the presentence investigation report are the evaluation and the recommendation. Although the research evidence is mixed, there appears to be a high correlation between the probation officer's recommendation and the judge's decision (Czajkoski, 1973: 9–10). There is also some evidence that the sections most widely read by the judge are the PSI evaluation and recommendation.

The evaluation should contain the probation officer's professional assessment of the objective material contained in the body of the report.

Figure 4-2   Information Excluded from the Presentence Report as Potentially Exempt from Disclosure: Rule 32(c) (3) (A)

<u>Marital</u>. The defendant's ex-wife reported that when he was released
from jail in early 1971, he showed no interest in resuming sexual relations with her. His behavior was unusual in other respects, and he
exhibited great tension and insomnia. Mrs. Hesse began to suspect that
he had some experience in jail that had affected his sexual function.
She questioned him about this on several occasions and he responded with
bitter denials. Mrs. Hesse became convinced that it was impossible to
save the marriage and she filed for divorce. Mrs. Hesse was adamant that
her husband not learn that she provided this information.

Officials of the Hampshire County Jail confirmed that Mr. Hesse was
the victim of a homosexual assault in the jail. He refused to identify
his attackers but he asked to be moved to an isolated cell. This request
was granted.

Officials of the Hampden County Jail, where Mr. Hesse is now lodged,
report that he has displayed acute anxiety during his confinement. They
are not aware of the reasons for this but they note that Mr. Hesse has
requested a transfer to the administrative segregation section. The jail
has not complied with this request because of overcrowding.

<u>Mental and Emotional</u>. The latest psychological report suggests that
Mr. Hesse will continue to experience acute anxiety whenever he is placed
in a situation that threatens recurrence of the homosexual assault. The
psychologist believes that Mr. Hesse is not overtly homosexual but that
his sexual orientation is ambiguous. Since the attack, Mr. Hesse has
reportedly experienced complete sexual dysfunction.

SUMMARY OF WITHHELD FACTUAL INFORMATION

If the court is of the view that the above information is excludable
under Rule 32(c) (3) (A) and if the court intends to rely on that information in determining sentence, a summary of the withheld factual information is provided for disclosure to the defendant or his counsel.

"The court has received information about experiences of the defendant while previously incarcerated which caused him to have serious emotional problems. Subsequent psychological examination confirmed this
existence."

Having gathered all the facts, the probation officer must now consider the
protection of the community and the needs of the defendant.

First, the probation officer should consider the offense. Was it situa-
tional in nature, or indicative of persistent behavior? Was violence used?

Was a weapon involved? Was it a property offense or a personal offense? Was there a motive?

Second, the community must be considered. For example, does the defendant pose a direct threat to the safety and welfare of others? Would a disposition other than prison depreciate the seriousness of the crime? Is probation a sufficient deterrent? What community resources are available?

Finally, the probation officer has to consider the defendant and his or her special problems and needs, if any. What developmental factors were significant in contributing to the defendant's current behavior? Was there a history of antisocial behavior? Does the defendant acknowledge responsibility or remorse? Is the defendant motivated to change? What strengths and weaknesses does the defendant possess? Is the defendant employable or supporting any immediate family? The probation officer should also provide a statement of sentencing alternatives available to the court. This does not constitute a recommendation, but rather informs the court which services are available should the defendant be granted probation.

A sound recommendation is the responsibility of the probation officer. Some of the alternatives may include:

probation	shock probation
work release	halfway house
incarceration	no recommendation
split sentence	

If commitment were recommended, the probation officer would indicate any problems that may need special attention on the part of the institutional staff. In addition, if the defendant were considered a security risk, the investigator would include escape potential, as well as any threats made to or received from the community or other defendants.

Regardless of the recommendation, the probation officer has the responsibility to provide supporting rationale that will assist the court in achieving its sentencing goals.

Psychiatric and Psychological Reports

Occasions arise during a presentence investigation report when a probation officer and mental health professionals interact. While it is not possible to delineate the full range of possible involvements of the mental health professionals with probation officers, Robert Mills (1980) has listed some of the primary relationships as follows:

1. Referral for hospitalization or other treatment as a sentencing alternative. In some cases, the mental condition of the defendant, in relation to his offense(s), warrants a diagnostic evaluation for possible psychiatric treat-

ment. Such an evaluation can be made a condition of probation, or the judge may place the implementation of the referral in the hands of a probation officer without specifying probation.

2. Psychiatric/psychological consultation is requested by the probation officer as a part of the presentence investigation. This is probably the most common use of psychiatric/psychological resources. The probation officer, confronted with a family counseling situation, a sexual perversion, a drug addiction, or some other problem for which referral to a community service agency seems indicated, requests an evaluation for the purpose of verifying diagnostic and treatment recommendations and sometimes providing an intake report to a prescribed agency. In this case, the psychiatric report would be incorporated as a part of his PSI to the court.

3. A sentencing judge desires a prediction of an offender's probable response to incarceration. There are offenders whose adjustment is so precarious that the imposition of a jail sentence may precipitate a negative outcome which exceeds the requirements of justice. For example, a depressed defendant could become a suicidal risk. In another instance, a frail-looking eighteen-year-old was diverted to a halfway house for sentence because of the likelihood of homosexual attack in a jail where adequate safeguards against such attacks were not deemed sufficient.

4. Evaluation of "outside" psychiatric evaluations for the sentencing judge, when such evaluations are offered to the court by defense attorneys. While it may appear presumptuous for a probation officer to get involved in "second guessing" mental health professionals, it is certainly within a judge's discretion to request clarification on psychiatric formulations through consultation with the officers of his court. Where courts maintain their own psychiatric staff, consultation or reexamination of the defendant by the internal staff members would be preferable. However, the probation officer's familiarity with the network of mental health agencies and with treatment methods make him a valuable resource to judges, especially in those instances when the court does not employ its own internal treatment staff.

The Sentencing Hearing

While procedures vary across jurisdictions, most criminal courts will conduct a sentencing hearing independent of the trial or determination of guilt. The role of the defense counsel may be important at this phase of the decision-making process. Some common strategies of defense counsel include having a private presentence investigation conducted at the defendant's expense; filing a sentencing memorandum with the court that points out the strengths and mitigating factors that counsel sees as worthy of the court's attention; advising the defendant on how to interact with the PSI investigator (be cooperative, provide names and addresses of persons who will be able to speak on his or her behalf, give own version of the offense, etc.); and challenging any inaccurate, incomplete, or misleading findings in the court's PSI.

Privately Commissioned Sentencing Reports

Recently, privately commissioned presentence reports have been offered as supplements or alternatives to the probation department's report. As Gitchoff (1980: 1) has pointed out, "the sentencing function performed by judges is the most difficult and distasteful of their judicial role." Indeed, since the vast majority of offenders plead guilty, the most important function of the defense attorney may be at the time of sentencing. The failure of many defense attorneys to adequately prepare for sentencing forces most judges to rely on the probation department's report as the sole source of information on which to base a decision. Because most attorneys are not trained in behavioral science, retaining a "correctional expert" has been suggested as a more plausible approach, and although there are ethical issues involved (Evans and Scott, 1983), it appears that social scientists can serve an important role in the sentencing process.

The private PSI may provide additional information about the offender, but it is more likely to provide a more tailored sentencing alternative. Criminologists who have prepared private PSIs suggest a number of specially designed alternatives including: restitution, counseling, community service, and residential treatment (Rodgers et al., 1979).

In general, private PSIs are expensive and not widespread in practice. Where they are prepared, they tend to be duplicative of much of the information available in the court-ordered PSI; yet they also generally contain a more detailed alternative disposition plan. There are no empirical evaluations of the effects of private PSIs on dispositional outcomes in those cases in which they were available. Anecdotal materials suggest that they have some positive impact on a judge's decision to place the offender on probation.

Factors Related to Sentencing Decisions

As mentioned previously, the PSI involves a great deal of a probation department's time and resources. The presentence report is the primary comprehensive source of information about the defendant that is available to the sentencing judge. Although most judges agree that the PSI is a valuable aid in formulating sentencing decisions, there appears to be some differences of opinion about the value of the recommendation section of the report.[4]

Several studies have attempted to identify those factors that appear to be of primary importance to sentencing judges. Carter's 1976 survey found that the two most significant factors were the defendant's prior criminal record and the current offense. An earlier study by Carter and Wilkins

(1967) found that the most important factors for judges in making a decision to grant probation included the defendant's educational level, average monthly salary, occupational level, residence, stability, participation in church activities, and military record. But, again, when factors were ranked according to their importance in the sentencing decision, the current offense and the defendant's prior record, number of arrests, and number of commitments were ranked most important.

Summary

The presentence investigation report is one of the primary responsibilities of probation agencies. Its importance is highlighted by the fact that the vast majority of defendants plead guilty, and that their only contact with the judge is during sentencing.

Although the presentence report has several functions, its primary purpose is to aid the judge in determining sentence. The five major components of the presentence report include: (1) current offense, (2) prior record, (3) personal history, (4) evaluation, and (5) recommendation.

Preparation of the presentence report is usually made after guilt has been established. Although there may be some exceptions, this is considered to be the dominant practice in the nation.

While some debate remains over disclosure of the presentence report, the federal rules clearly state that the court should permit the defendant to read the PSI. This insures that the facts about the defendant are accurate and reliable. Several types of information are exempt, but the court must provide a written summary of the findings to the defendant.

The evaluation and the recommendation are two extremely important components of the PSI. This is supported by the fact that in the majority of cases, the judge follows the recommendation of the probation officer. The three critical areas that must be considered include: the offense, the community, and the defendant.

Recently, there has been a movement to submit privately prepared presentence reports. These reports have generally augmented the court-ordered PSI with special attention given to sentencing alternatives.

Notes

1. For a thorough discussion of the early development of the presentence investigation report see "The Presentence Report: An Empirical Study of Its Use in the Federal Criminal Process," *Georgetown Law Journal* 58 (1970): 12–27.
2. These functions are adapted from the Administrative Office of the U.S. Courts,

The Presentence Investigation Report, Publication No. 105, p. 1 (Washington, D.C.: Government Printing Office, revised September 1978).

3. Several cases in which the disclosure issue has been tested include: *Kent v. United States*, 383 U.S. 541 (1966); *Baker v. United States*, 287 F. 2d 5 (9th Cir., 1961); and *Gardner v. Florida*, 20 Cr.L. 3083 (1977).

4. For example, in Cincinnati, Ohio, a single probation department serves both the Municipal Court and the Court of Common Pleas, yet each court requires a different presentence investigation report. The Court of Common Pleas does not permit probation officer recommendations to be included in the report, but the Municipal Court requires one.

Study Guides

1. What are the five major functions of the presentence investigation report?
2. What are the five core areas of a presentence investigation report? Justify each area.
3. What types of information are exempt from disclosure?
4. What does Carter recommend concerning the length of the presentence reports? Do you agree with his position? Defend your answer.
5. Why is the recommendation so important?
6. What is a privately commissioned presentence report?

Key Terms

alterative plan
confidentiality
disclosure
disposition
investigation

presentence investigation
private presentence investigation
reports
supervision plan

References

CARTER, ROBERT. *Prescriptive Package on Pre-Sentence Investigations*. Unpublished draft, Washington, D.C.: Law Enforcement Assistance Administration, 1976.

―――. *Presentence Report Handbook: Prescriptive Package*. Washington, D.C.: Law Enforcement Assistance Administration, 1978.

CARTER, ROBERT, AND WILKINS, LESLIE T. "Some Factors in Sentencing Policy," *Journal of Criminal Law, Criminology and Police Science* 58 (1967):503–14.

CZAJKOSKI, EUGENE H. "Exposing the Quasi-Judicial Role of the Probation Officer," *Federal Probation* 37 (1973):9–13.

EVANS, SANDRA S., AND SCOTT, JOSEPH E. "Social Scientists as Expert Witnesses: Their Use, Misuse and Sometimes Abuse," *Law and Policy Quarterly* 5 (1983):181–214.

Federal Rules of Criminal Procedure, Rule 32 (Appendix A). In *The Presentence Investigation Report*. Washington, D.C.: Administrative Office of the United States Courts, Publication No. 105, September 1978.

GITCHOFF, THOMAS G. "Expert Testimony at Sentencing," *American Jurisprudence Proof of Facts*, Vol. 21, pp. 1–9. Rochester, N.H.: Lawyers Cooperative Publishers, 1980.

HIGGENS, JOHN. "Confidentiality of Presentence Reports," *Albany Law Review* 28 (1964):31–47.

MILLS, ROBERT B. *Offender Assessment*, pp. 177–79. Cincinnati, Ohio: Anderson Publishing, 1980.

The Presentence Investigation Report. Washington, D.C.: Administrative Office of the United States Courts, Publication No. 105, September 1978.

"The Presentence Report: An Empirical Study of Its Use in the Federal Criminal Process," *Georgetown Law Journal* 58 (1970):12–27.

RODGERS, THOMAS R.; GITCHOFF, THOMAS G.; AND PAUR, IVAR O. "The Privately Commissioned Pre-Sentence Report: A Multidisciplinary Approach," *Criminal Justice Journal* 2 (1979):271–79.

United States Department of Justice, Law Enforcement Assistance Administration, *State and Local Probation and Parole Systems*. Washington, D.C.: Government Printing Office, 1978.

Recommended Readings

Allen, Harry E., et al. *Critical Issues in Adult Probation Summary Report* (Washington, D.C.: U.S. Department of Justice, Law Enforcement Assistance Administration, National Institute of Law Enforcement and Criminal Justice, 1979). This recent study of probation presents an examination of the critical issues surrounding the presentence investigation report. A good summary of the literature is included.

Carter, Robert M. "The Presentence Report and the Decision-Making Process." In *Probation, Parole and Community Corrections*, edited by R. Carter and L. Wilkins, pp. 201–11 (New York: John Wiley & Sons, 1976). This article describes a decision-making game that is useful in understanding the presentence process.

Mills, Robert B. *Offender Assessment* (Cincinnati, Ohio: Anderson Publishing, 1980). This is a comprehensive casebook on offender assessment and the investigative process. Sections of interest include specific areas of the presentence report and actual case practice.

Rothman, David J. *Conscience and Convenience: The Asylum and Its Alternatives in Progressive America* (Boston: Little, Brown, 1980). Chapter 3, "Watching Over the Offender," provides a critical assessment of the early use of probation and the development of the presentence investigation.

5

Granting Probation

Free administration decision making based on individual characteristics of the offender has given way to the offender's relative success at plea bargaining. . . . Nowadays it is likely that the prosecutor has communicated the plea bargaining agreement to the probation officer, and the latter's recommendation takes into consideration the prosecutor's agreement with the offender.

—Herbert Callison

As noted in Chapter 3, a recent national study defined probation as:

> . . . a sentence which establishes the defendant's legal status under which his freedom in the community is continued or only briefly interrupted, subjected to supervision by a "probation organization" and subject to conditions imposed by the court. The sentencing court retains the authority to modify the conditions of the sentence or resentence the offender if he [or she] violates the conditions.[1]

Currently, probation is a privilege, not a right.[2] It is an "act of grace" extended by the sentencing judge who presided over the trial (although a few states permit the jury that determined guilt to award or recommend probation). Of all the principal groups of offenders in America—probationers, jail inmates, prison inmates, and parolees—the largest group is the probationers. The United States Department of Justice (1984) found that 63 percent of all convicted offenders were on probation, 11 percent were on parole, 18 percent were in prison, and 9 percent were in jail.[3] On the basis of 100,000 people in the population, the population rate was almost 897 on probation, 147 on parole, 245 in prison, and 120 in jail. Numerically, there were 1,500,000 probationers supervised by at least 20,000 caseload supervision staff, with a national average caseload of almost seventy-five offenders per officer.[4] What is the process by which so large a proportion of offenders are placed on probation?

Enabling Legislation

As the reader will recall from Chapter 3, both state and federal jurisdictions enacted statutes that permit the granting of probation, as well as define certain categories of offenses for which probation may not be granted. These acts could include all crimes of violence, crimes requiring a life sentence, armed robbery, rape or other sex offenses, use of a firearm in the commission of a felony, crimes against the government, or status as a second-time or multiply convicted offender.

Yet, despite the existence of legislatively defined exclusion, granting probation is a highly individualized process that usually focuses on the criminal rather than the crime. The general objectives of probation (Federal Judicial Center) are:

1. Reintegrate amenable offenders
2. Protect the community from further antisocial behavior
3. Further the goals of justice
4. Provide probation conditions (and services) necessary to change offenders and to achieve the above objectives

While probation granting is individualized, judges and corrections personnel generally recognize the advantages of probation that were identified in Chapter 3: use of community resources to reintegrate offenders who are thus forced to face and hopefully resolve their individual problems while under community supervision; fiscal savings over imprisonment; avoidance of prisonization,[5] which tends to exacerbate the underlying causes of criminal behavior; keeping offenders' families off local and state welfare rolls; a relatively successful process of correcting offender behavior (60 to 90 percent success rates have been reported); and a sentencing option that can permit "selective incapacitation."[6]

Probation, the most frequent disposition for offenders and widely recognized for its advantages, has also received strong endorsement from numerous groups and commissions, including the prestigious National Advisory Commission on Criminal Justice Standards and Goals (1973: 159), the

General Accounting Office (1981), and the American Bar Association (1970: 27). The National Advisory Commission recommended that probation be used more extensively, and the ABA endorsed probation as the presumed sentence of choice for almost all felonies. Finn (1984) has recently argued that universal use of probation would reduce prison populations.

Granting Probation

Sentencing is a complicated process, and sentencing judges frequently find that the disposition of the case (sentence) has already been determined—by the prosecutor, not the judge! This is because, prior to the determination of guilt, the prosecuting attorney and defense counsel have engaged in plea bargaining. During this interaction, any (or even all!) of the following trial elements may have been negotiated:

1. The defendant's pleading guilty to a lesser crime but one that was present in the illegal behavior, for which the penalty is considerably more lenient
2. The frequency of the crime ("number of counts") to which the defendant will plead guilty
3. The number of charges that will be dropped
4. Whether the prosecutor will recommend that the defendant receive probation or be sentenced to incarceration in jail or prison
5. The recommended length of time (months or years) of incarceration
6. If sentences will be consecutive or concurrent[7]

It appears that the judiciary tend to accept and acquiesce to the negotiation outcomes. However, in many cases, judges still decide the sentence, one alternative of which may be probation.

The process of granting probation begins after the offender either pleads guilty (frequently for favorable personal considerations) or is adjudicated guilty following a trial.[8] For those offenders whose crime falls within the list of probation-eligible offenses, or in those states where mandated by law, a presentence investigation will be ordered (described in Chapter 4). It will be recalled that a presentence investigation report, designed to assist the court in determining the most appropriate sentence, is a document resulting from an investigation of an offender that was undertaken by a probation agency (or other designated authority or, sometimes, private agency) at the request of the criminal court.

Based on observations of the defendant at trial—including demeanor, body language, evidence of remorse, and behavior—as well as the recommendation in presentence reports and the prosecutor's recommendation for sentence, jurists attempt to determine the appropriate sentence for a

particular individual. Judges are aware that individualized justice demands that the sentence fit not only the crime but also the criminal.

The role of the presentence report recommendation is a major factor,
for the extent of concurrence between the probation officer's recommendations and the judge's sentencing decision is quite strong. Liebermann,
Schaffer, and Martin (1971) found that, when probation was recommended, judges followed that recommendation in 83 percent of the cases;
Carter (1966) found an even stronger agreement: 96 percent of the cases.
Liebermann et al. (1971) also found that, when the recommendation was
for imprisonment, the judge agreed in 87 percent of the cases.[9]

Role of Defense Counsel

Judges, after ordering a presentence investigation, will schedule a sentencing hearing, which is a court session designed to deliberate, consider, and
determine offender's sentence. The prosecutor will submit a sentencing
memorandum, with recommendation. Defense counsel also has an important, even crucial role here. At this point, defense counsel can:

1. Contest the accuracy of the presentence investigation facts
2. Give notice beforehand as to which parts will be contested
3. Present relevant facts not included in the presentence report
4. Present evidence and arguments on behalf of the client
5. Subpoena witnesses (sometimes even the victim)
6. Call and cross-examine the presentence investigator
7. Authorize a private presentence investigation report (discussed
   below)
8. Prepare a sentencing memorandum
9. Present sentencing alternatives

In order to refute the court's presentence report, defense counsel
would need access to the report. In sixteen states and the federal system,
mandatory disclosure of the report is required by statute. A wide variety of
other policies exists in the remaining thirty-four jurisdictions, ranging from
denial of request to permitting access upon request. The most frequent
court response appears to be access, with certain sensitive or source-
identifying information deleted or summarized.

As mentioned in Chapter 4, the private presentence investigation report (allowable in many states, California[10] and Ohio being just two of
them) is a tactic currently used by a few defense counsels, and entails hiring a creditable practitioner to prepare a presentence report similar in
scope to that which the court-designated officer would prepare. Frequently more detailed than the latter's report, the privately prepared PSI
often identifies the offender's strengths and needs, proposes a comprehen-

sive treatment program using existing public or private social agencies, and details a comprehensive plan for addressing each need, which would lead to the offender's reintegration into the community while on probation. The benefits and effects of private presentence reports have not yet been researched.[11]

Other Sentencing Factors

While the judge may have observed the defendant at trial and have the presentence investigation report available for assistance in sentencing, there are other factors that can influence the decision to grant or deny probation. The roles of these factors are not yet conclusively researched, but they include the size of the state's prison population and the scarcity of prison cells[12]; local probation caseload size; local unemployment rates; the quality of probation officers and services; attitudes of probation officers[13]; availability of alternative dispositions (such as fines, halfway houses, or drug treatment programs); personal and philosophical characteristics of sentencing judges (Hogarth); judicial environment and practices in the court district; and any plea bargain that the defendant might have struck with the prosecutor (Callison, 1983: 106–107). Such factors may play subtle roles in granting or denying probation.

Conditions of Probation

When probation is granted, the court may impose certain reasonable conditions on the offender, which the probation officer is expected to monitor in the supervision process. These must not be capricious, and may be both general (required of all probationers) or specific (required of an individual probationer). General conditions include obeying laws, submitting to searches, not associating with known criminals, reporting regularly to the supervising officer, notifying the officer of any change in job or residence, not being in possession of a firearm, refraining from excessive use of alcohol, and not leaving the court's jurisdiction for long periods of time without prior authorization.

Specific conditions are generally tailored to the needs of the offender or philosophy of the court. For reintegration or other such purposes, the court may impose conditions of medical or psychiatric treatment; residence in a halfway house or residential center; active involvement in Alcoholics Anonymous; participation in a methadone maintenance program (if the probationer has a heroin dependence); restitution or victim compensation; no use of psychotropic drugs (such as cocaine or marijuana); observing a reasonable curfew; no hitchhiking; staying out of bars and poolrooms (particularly if the probationer is a prostitute); group counseling; vocational training; or other court-ordered requirements. Such required conditions are specifically designed to assist the probationer in the successful completion of probation.

Two recent but related trends in the conditions the court may impose are restitution and community work orders. Restitution requires the offender to make payment (perhaps monetary) to a victim to offset the damages done in the commission of the crime. If the offender cannot afford to repay at least a part of the loss suffered by the victim, it is possible to restore the victim's losses through personal services. Probation with restitution thus has the potential for being a reparative sentence and Galaway (1983) argues that it should be the penalty of choice for property offenders. Restitution can lessen the loss of the victim, maximize reconciliation of the offender and community, and marshal community support for the offender, perhaps through enlisting a community sponsor to monitor and encourage the offender's compliance.

Community work orders as conditions of probation appear to be increasingly used in conjunction with probation, particulary if there are no direct victim losses or the nature of the crime demands more than supervised release. Examples of community work orders would include requiring a dentist convicted of driving while intoxicated to provide free dental services to a number of indigents, or ordering a physician to provide numerous hours of free medical treatment to jail inmates, perhaps on Saturday mornings. Juveniles may frequently be ordered to work for community improvements through litter removal, cutting grass, painting the homes of the elderly or public buildings, or driving shut-ins to market or to visit friends and relatives. Both restitution and community work orders can serve multiple goals: offender punishment, community reintegration, and reconciliation.

Alternative Probation Procedures

In addition to the most frequent procedures described above, there are six other variations of granting probation that need to be discussed before we consider the legal process of revoking probation of those who cannot or will not abide by court-imposed conditions of liberty in the community: prosecutorial probation, court probation without adjudication, shock probation, intermittent incarceration, split sentences, and modification of sentence.

While probation most frequently is imposed by a trial judge after a guilty plea or trial, it may also replace the trial completely, in which case it is called "probation without adjudication." In practice, the process embraces two separate programs, one operated by the prosecutor (a form of deferred prosecution) and the other by the judge in those limited number of jurisdictions in which the state legislation permits a bifurcated process (determining guilt, followed by adjudication as a felon). Both result in probation but are vastly different.

Deferred Prosecution Probation

Part of the broad power accorded a prosecutor in the United States is the ability to offer the accused deferred prosecution. In those programs in which the prosecutor grants deferred prosecution, the accused will generally be asked to sign a contract accepting moral (but usually not legal) responsibility for the crime and agreeing to make victim restitution, to undergo specific treatment programs (Alcoholics Anonymous, methadone maintenance, psychotherapy, etc.), to report periodically to a designated official (usually a probation officer), and to refrain from other criminal acts during the contract period. If these conditions are satisfied, the prosecutor dismisses (*nolle pros*) the charge. *If* the accused does not actively participate and cooperate in the program the prosecutor can, at any time during the contract period, carry the case forward to trial. Deferred prosecution can, although it is infrequent, lead to a unique probation organization within the office of the prosecutor.

Probation by Withholding Adjudication

This process refers to a judge's optional authority that is available in those states (such as Florida) where statutes permit a bifurcated process: first determine guilt and then declare the defendant a convicted felon. By refraining from the declaration of guilty felon, the judge can suspend the legal process and place the defendant on probation for a specific time period, sometimes without supervision being required (a "summary" or nonreporting probation). Thus the judge gives the offender a chance to demonstrate his or her ability and willingness to adjust and reform. The offenders know that they can still be returned to court for adjudication of guilt and sentencing, and frequently imprisonment.

The advantages of this option fit squarely in the general philosophy of probation. Not only is treatment in the community emphasized, but the collateral benefits are considerable:

> [The judge] places him on probation without requiring him to register with local law enforcement agencies as a previously convicted felon; without serving notice on prospective employers of a previous conviction; without preventing the offender from holding public office, voting, or serving on a jury; without impeding the offender from obtaining a license that requires "reputable character"; without making it more difficult than others to obtain firearms; in short, without public or even private degradation.[14]

Shock Probation

In 1965, Ohio became the first of currently fourteen states that enacted an early release procedure generally known as "shock probation." The assumptions and features underlying this innovative program were described by the then director of the Ohio Adult Parole Authority. It was

1. A way for the courts to impress offenders with the seriousness of their actions without a long prison sentence
2. A way for the courts to release offenders found by the institutions to be more amenable to community-based treatment than was realized by the courts at time of sentence
3. A way for the courts to arrive at a just compromise between punishment and leniency in appropriate cases
4. A way for the courts to provide community-based treatment for rehabilitable offenders while still observing their responsibilities for imposing deterrent sentences where public policy demands it
5. [A way to afford] the briefly incarcerated offender a protection against absorption into the "hard rock" inmate culture.[15]

Vito and Allen (1981) note that shock probation is a program of judicial reconsideration of the original sentence. Convicted defendants, originally sentenced to prison for varying numbers of years may, through their own motion or that of their legal counsel or even through direct motion by the court, be recalled to court and have the remainder of their sentences suspended and be placed on probation. When granted release to the community on probation, these offenders are supervised by probation officers under the same rules and regulations that apply to other probationers, including the possibility of probation revocation. Both the eligibility requirements and sentence length are fixed by statute, although the sentencing judge may shorten the period of supervision in the community.

The effectiveness of shock probation has been evaluated by a number of researchers, the most sophisticated of which was by Vito (1978). Effectiveness—as measured by a variety of failure indicators—ranges from a success rate of 78 percent to 91 percent. Farmer (1981) reported that, of the 13,012 offenders released under shock probation in Ohio from 1966 until 1979, only 1,389 (10.6 percent) were reinstitutionalized.

Shock probation has also been acclaimed (Reid, 1976) as a program that permits the offender a reduction in the time he or she would have spent in prison; a chance to be quickly reintegrated into the community; a mechanism by which to maintain family and community ties; an opportunity to avoid prisonization; a speedy judicial review of sentence; and an early release mechanism that both reduces prison populations and the costs of imprisonment (Vito, 1978).

Critics have argued that shock probation combines philosophically incompatible objectives: punishment and leniency. Other criticisms (Reid, 1976) are that the defendant is further stigmatized by the incarceration component of shock probation, and that the existence of a shock probation sentence may encourage the judiciary to rely less on probation than previously. But the most damaging criticism is by Vito and Allen:

> . . . the fact of incarceration is having some unknown and unmeasurable effect upon [the more unfavorable] performance of shock probationers. . . . It could be that the negative effects of incarceration are affecting the performance of shock probationers.[16]

The overall effects and effectiveness of shock probation remain unknown. Until more research is conducted, perhaps the best tentative conclusion is that the program is no worse than probation and incarceration, is less costly than imprisonment, and may be just as effective in preventing recidivism as is probation.

Combining Probation and Incarceration

There are a number of alternatives to placing an offender on probation, other than shock probation, that include a period of incarceration. The U.S. Department of Justice (1983) notes:

> Although the courts continue to use [probation] as a less severe and less expensive alternative to incarceration, most courts are also given discretion to link probation to a term of incarceration—an option selected with increasing frequency. Combinations of probation and incarceration include:
>
> *split sentences*: where the court specifies a period of incarceration to be followed by a period of probation [see Parisi, 1981]
>
> *modification of sentence*: where the original sentencing court may reconsider an offender's prison sentence within a limited time and change it to probation
>
> *intermittent incarceration*: where an offender on probation may spend weekends or nights in jail.[17]

How frequently sentencing judges use these options is not yet known (see also Parisi, 1980).

Probation Revocation

Once placed on probation, offenders are supervised and assisted by probation officers who are increasingly using existing community agencies and services to provide individualized treatment based on the offender's needs.

Assuming the offender meets the court-imposed conditions, makes satisfactory progress in resolving underlying problems, and does not engage in further illegal activities, probation agencies may request the court to close the case. This would terminate supervision of the offender and probation. Probation may also be terminated by the completion of the period of maximum sentence, or by the offender having received "maximum benefit from treatment."

In supervising a probationer, officers should enforce the conditions and rules of probation pragmatically, considering the client's particular and individual needs, legality of decisions they must make while supervising clients, the clarity of expectations by the probationer of assistance from the supervising officer (and expectations of the probationer), and the potential effects of enforcing rules on a client's future behavior and adjustment (Koontz, 1980).

Probationers vary in their ability to comply with imposed conditions, some of which may be unrealistic, particularly those that require extensive victim restitution or employment during an economic period of high unemployment. Some probationers are also indifferent or even hostile, unwilling or psychologically unable to cooperate with their probation supervisor or the court. Others commit technical violations of court orders that are not per se new crimes but are seen as harbingers of future illegal activity. In these circumstances, probation officers must deal with technical probation violations.

Probation officers, charged with managing such cases, may determine that technical violators need a stern warning or that court-imposed conditions should be tightened (or relaxed, depending on individual circumstances). These determinations may lead to an offender's reappearance before the court for a warning or redefinition of conditions. Judges and probation officers, ideally, collaborate in such cases to protect the community or increase the probability of successful reintegration. Offenders are frequently returned to probation, and supervision and treatment continue.

If the warning and new conditions are not sufficient, or the offender repetitively violates conditions of probation, or is arrested for an alleged new crime, a probation revocation hearing may be necessary. If the probationer is not already in jail for the alleged new crime, a warrant may be issued for his or her arrest.

A probation revocation hearing is a serious process, posing potential "grievous loss of liberty" for the offender. Both probation officers and judges vary considerably as to what would constitute grounds for revoking probation and resentencing to imprisonment. Punitive probation officers (see Chapter 7) may contend that technical violations are sufficient for revoking probation; judges may believe that the commission of a new crime would be the only reason for revocation.

The due process rights of probationers at a revocation hearing were generally ignored until 1967, when the United States Supreme Court issued an opinion regarding state probationers' rights to counsel at such hearings (*Mempa v. Rhay*). This case provided right to counsel if probation were revoked under a deferred sentencing statute, but this decision did not specify that a court hearing was required. That issue was resolved in *Gagnon v. Scarpelli* (1972) a landmark case in due process procedures in probation (see Chapter 3).

Summary

This chapter has described the court options and procedures for placing offenders on probation, as well as some issues in supervising offenders. It should be obvious that probation requires a judge to weigh "individualization" of treatment as opposed to "justice" or "just deserts." Underlying this perplexing problem is the belief in individualized treatment. Unfortunately, at this time we lack sufficient technical knowledge of treatment to successfully implement the philosophy of individualized, reintegrative treatment for *all* offenders. This issue is more fully explored in Chapter 9, which deals with caseload supervision and strategies.

Notes

1. Harry E. Allen, Eric Carlson, and Evalyn Parks, *Critical Issues in Probation: Summary Report* (Washington, D.C.: U.S. Department of Justice, 1979), pp. 12–13.
2. *Gagnon v. Scarpelli*, 411 U.S. 778, 93 S. Ct. (1972).
3. Bureau of Justice Statistics, *Probation and Parole 1983* (Washington, D.C.: U.S. Department of Justice, 1984).
4. The figures for January 1, 1984, were 1,502,247 adults on probation, up 11 percent from 1982. The rate of imprisonment at January 1, 1984, had reached 245/100,000 population, up 50 percent from 1982.
5. Prisonization refers to the socialization process by which the inmate learns the prison culture, a cluster of folkways and mores that indoctrinates the new inmate into the inmate world. Prisonization is believed to interfere with the ability of the inmate to function as a law-abiding citizen following release.
6. Selective incapacitation refers to a policy of identifying high-risk offenders for incarceration on the premise that, while imprisoned, such offenders would be incapable of committing further criminal acts, and may be deterred from illegal behavior when released. See Andrew von Hirsch, "The Ethics of Selective Incapacitation," *Crime and Delinquency* 30 (1984):175–94.

7. If a concurrent sentence, the offender would start serving time for *all* crimes for which convicted on the day of arrival in prison. If a consecutive sentence, the offender *must* generally serve the minimum sentence for the first crime before beginning to serve time for the second offense. Offenders vastly prefer the concurrent to the consecutive sentence compromise, since they would thus be eligible for release from prison much earlier!

8. There is considerable evidence that forcing the prosecutor (and thus the court) into a trial, rather than pleading guilty for considerations, will invite a much longer sentence. One study found that ordinary drug dealers who demand a trial receive prison sentences that average 36 months longer than those who plead guilty. For big drug dealers, the average prison sentence lengths are more than 126 months longer. See Ruth Peterson, and John Hagan, "Changing Conceptions of Race: Toward an Account of Anomalous Findings of Sentencing Research," *American Sociological Review* 49 (1984):56–70.

9. For an excellent discussion of this issue, see Allen et al., *supra* note 1.

10. The legal framework for California, for example, can be found in Chapters 1204 and 1170(b) of the California Penal Code, and Chapter 18 U.S.C. 3577.

11. Fred Cohen, "How and Why to Use Experts in Sentencing: A Comment," *Criminal Law Bulletin* 15 (1979):151–56.

12. Unfortunately, when prison overcrowding occurs and there is a scarcity of prison beds, judges may find themselves in the uncomfortable position of placing high-risk offenders on probation. This could result in higher recidivism and crime rates, and a decline in the public's support for probation as a sentencing outcome. See, for example, Bruce Cory, and Stephen Gettinger, *Time to Build? The Realities of Prison Construction* (New York: Edna McConnell Clark Foundation, 1984).

13. The attitudes and decisions of probation officers are significant in determining what sentencing disposition to recommend to the judge. See J. Katz, "The Attitudes and Decisions of Probation Officers," *Criminal Justice and Behavior* 9 (1983):455–75.

14. Harry E. Allen, Paul Friday, Julian Roebuck, and Edward Sagarin, *Crime and Punishment* (New York: Free Press, 1981), pp. 361–62.

15. Cited in Harry E. Allen, and Clifford E. Simonsen, *Corrections in America* (New York: Macmillan, 1981), p. 161.

16. Gennaro F. Vito, and Harry E. Allen, "Shock Probation in Ohio: A Comparison of Outcomes," *International Journal of Offender Therapy and Comparative Criminology* 25 (1981):74.

17. Bureau of Justice Statistics, *supra* note 3, p. 3.

Study Guides

1. What are the general objectives of probation?
2. What are the advantages of probation?
3. How effective is probation?

4. How is probation granted?
5. What types of information are generally found in a presentence report?
6. What is the extent of concurrence between the presentence investigation report recommendation and the judge's sentencing disposition?
7. What can a defense counsel do to increase the chances of his or her client being placed on probation?
8. Differentiate between general and specific conditions of probation.
9. What are the advantages of probation without adjudication?
10. What are the advantages and criticisms of shock probation?
11. How can probation be revoked?

Key Terms

individualized sentencing
Mempa v. Rhay and *Gagnon v. Scarpelli*
presentence investigation
prisonization
private presentence investigation
probation

probation revocation
probation without adjudication
prosecutorial probation
sentencing hearing
shock probation
technical probation violation

References

ALLEN, HARRY E.; CARLSON, ERIC W.; AND PARKS, EVALYN. *Critical Issues in Probation: Summary Report*. Washington, D.C.: U.S. Department of Justice, 1979.

ALLEN, HARRY E.; FRIDAY, PAUL; ROEBUCK, JULIAN; AND SAGARIN, EDWARD. *Crime and Punishment*. New York: Free Press, 1981.

ALLEN, HARRY E., AND SIMONSEN, CLIFFORD E. *Corrections in America*. New York: Macmillan, 1981.

American Bar Association Project on Standards for Criminal Justice. *Standards Relating to Probation*. Approved Draft, 1970.

Bureau of Justice Statistics. *Bulletin: Probation and Parole, 1982*. Rockville, Md.: National Crime Justice Reference Service, 1983.

CALLISON, HERBERT G. *Introduction to Community Based Corrections*. New York: McGraw-Hill, 1983.

CARTER, ROBERT M. "It Is Respectfully Recommended . . ." *Federal Probation* 30 (1966):38–40.

_____. *Presentence Report Handbook*. Washington, D.C.: Law Enforcement Assistance Administration, 1978.

CLEMMER, DONALD. *The Prison Community*. New York: Holt, Rinehart and Winston, 1958.

FARMER, GEORGE. "Letter to the Editor," *International Journal of Offender Therapy and Comparative Criminology* 25 (1981):75–76.

FINN, PETER. "Prison Crowding: The Response of Probation and Parole," *Crime and Delinquency* 30 (1984):141–53.

Gagnon v. Scarpelli, 411 U.S. 778 (1972).

GALAWAY, BURT. "Probation as a Reparative Sentence," *Federal Probation* 46 (1983):9–18.

HOGARTH, JOHN. *Sentencing as a Human Process.* London: Heinemann Educational, 1972.

KATZ, J. "The Attitudes and Decisions of Probation Officers," *Criminal Justice and Behavior* 9 (1983):455–75.

KOONTZ, JOHN. "Pragmatic Conditions of Probation," *Corrections Today* 42 (1980):14–44.

LIEBERMANN, E.; SCHAFFER, R.; AND MARTIN, C. *The Bronx Sentencing Project: An Experiment in the Use of Short-Form Presentence Report for Adult Misdemeanants.* New York: Vera Institute of Justice, 1971.

Mempa v. Rhay, 389 U.S. 128 (1967).

National Advisory Commission on Criminal Justice Standards and Goals. *Corrections.* Washington, D.C.: Government Printing Office, 1973.

National Council on Crime and Delinquency. *Probation in the United States: 1979.* San Francisco: National Council on Crime and Delinquency, 1981.

PARISI, NICOLETTE. "Combining Incarceration and Probation," *Federal Probation* 46 (1980):3–10.

_____. "A Taste of the Bars," *Journal of Criminal Law and Criminology* 72 (1981):1109–23.

President's Commission on Law Enforcement and Administration of Justice. *Corrections.* Washington, D.C.: Government Printing Office, 1967.

REID, SUE TITUS. *Crime and Criminology.* Hinsdale, Ill.: Dryden Press, 1976.

VITO, GENNARO F. *Shock Probation in Ohio: A Comparison of Attributes and Outcomes.* Unpublished doctoral dissertation, Ohio State University, 1978.

VITO, GENNARO F., AND ALLEN, HARRY E. "Shock Probation in Ohio: A Comparison of Outcomes," *International Journal of Offender Therapy and Comparative Criminology* 25 (1981):70–75.

VON HIRSCH, ANDREW. "The Ethics of Selective Incapacitation," *Crime and Delinquency* 30 (1984):175–94.

6

Granting Parole

Most inmates do not serve their entire prison sentence, but are released from correctional institutions in a variety of ways, among them pardon and conditional release—more commonly called parole. At present, approximately 75 percent of those released from prison are released to parole supervision. Contemporary parole may be defined as the release of offenders from correctional institutions after they have served a portion of their sentence, under conditions that facilitate reintegration to society, while placing the ex-offender under the continued custody of the state and with the possibility of reincarceration in the event of misbehavior.[1]

As was noted in the previous chapter, parole was originally implemented as a method of releasing reformed inmates at the ideal time. The primary focus of parole is the rehabilitation and eventual reintegration of the offender to society. But it also serves as a decompression period that helps the offender make the adjustment between the institution and the outside world. As such, parole is an integral component of the indeterminate sentence.

The indeterminate sentence serves as both the philosophical and operational foundation of parole. Sanctions are determined by the legislature, in establishing minimum and maximum terms; by the sentencing judge, in determining the specific sentencing range; and by correctional and parole officials, in determining how long individuals will be incarcerated. Judges have little impact upon the actual length of time the inmate will serve once the sentence is pronounced.

Overview of the Parole Process

The parole process begins in the courtroom when the judge sentences an individual to a prison term by stating the minimum and maximum length of time the individual is to serve. At the expiration of a certain portion of that sentence, less credit granted for good behavior and performance of duties, an individual becomes *eligible* for parole. The amount of the sentence that must be served and the amount of credit that can be given for good behavior and performance of duties vary from state to state. In Nebraska, an individual sentenced to a three- to five-year term can become eligible for parole at the end of two years and five months if they have behaved "properly" within the institution.[2] This does not mean that a release will actually occur; it only means that the individual is eligible to be released. There are a number of states that have mandatory parole release statutes which state that at the expiration of a certain portion of the sentence, inmates must be released onto parole, unless the inmate chooses not to be released. A number of inmates refuse to be released onto parole because they do not want to be subject to a parole officer's supervision and consequently they choose to serve their entire prison sentence ("max out").

Regardless of whether these individuals wish to max out or receive parole, information concerning their personal characteristics and backgrounds are compiled by institutional officers. Treatment progress is continually evaluated, and at some point in time, the staff begins working with offender's friends, family, and employers to develop a release plan.

This information, along with the presentence and institutional progress reports, is periodically brought to the attention of the releasing authority, usually a parole board. Some states review inmates' progress on a yearly basis, even though they are not eligible for release. In accordance with the eligibility guidelines and an interview with the offender, the parole board decides whether to release the offender on parole. If the decision is to deny release, a future rehearing date is usually set. If a release is to be effected, the parole board then determines when and where the release is to be made. A contract, usually including very specific conditions of parole, is also established. Once a release has been achieved, inmates (now called parolees) come under the supervision of parole officers.

Current Operations

Parole is a complex procedure and has many functions and processes that differ from one jurisdiction to another. Traditionally, parole includes four basic functions:

1. Selecting and placing prisoners on parole
2. Aiding, supervising, assisting, and controlling parolees in the community
3. Returning parolees to prison if the conditions of parole are not met
4. Discharging parolees when supervision is no longer necessary or when sentence is completed

Parole, unlike probation, is an administrative process located within the executive branch of every state, as well as the federal government. This may soon change, however, for nine states (California, Colorado, Connecticut, Illinois, Indiana, Maine, Minnesota, New Mexico, and North Carolina) have virtually eliminated the discretionary releasing power of these parole boards. Two of these states (Maine and Connecticut) have abolished both their parole boards and parole supervision. Only those persons sentenced under the old law are being placed on parole. Fifteen other jurisdictions (Alaska, California Youth Authority, District of Columbia, the federal system, Florida, Georgia, Maryland, Missouri, New Jersey, New York, Oklahoma, Oregon, Pennsylvania, Utah, and Washington) have developed various systemwide parole guidelines that have restricted the discretionary powers of the parole boards. The operation of parole, obviously, is not at all uniform.[3]

State parole systems vary widely in terms of their organizational makeup and administrative procedures. Most parole boards are independent state agencies that only administer parole. Depending on the state, there are anywhere from three to twelve members on a parole board. Only twenty-four states have any statutory requirements for specific qualifications for parole board members, and even those are usually stated in such broad terms as "possessing good character" or "judicious temperament" (Carlson, 1979). The governor is directly responsible for parole board appointments in forty-five states; Wisconsin and Ohio appoint parole board members from a civil service list. In 1967, the President's Commission on Law Enforcement and Administration of Justice recommended that parole board members be appointed solely on the basis of competence.

The *National Strategy* volume of the National Advisory Commission (1973) stated that each parole jurisdiction that had not already done so should, by 1975, establish parole decision-making bodies for adult and juvenile offenders that are independent of correctional institutions. These boards may be administratively part of an overall statewide correction services agency, but they should be autonomous in their decision-making authority and separate from field services. The board responsible for the parole of adult offenders should have jurisdiction over both felons and misdemeanants (1973: 413).

Parole Selection Process

In most jurisdictions, individual cases are assigned to individual members of the parole board. They review each case and make initial recommendations. These recommendations are usually accepted, although occasionally the board as a whole may seek to obtain more details. While there are some jurisdictions that make the final release decision solely on the basis of written reports, most states conduct some type of a formal hearing. The hearing may be with one member of the parole board, the assembled board as a whole (*en banc*), or handled by a hearing examiner with no members of the board present. Occasionally, prison staff are also interviewed. Some states send the board members and/or hearing examiners to the institutions to conduct the hearings, while others bring those to be interviewed to the board/examiners.

Parole selection guidelines differ widely from state to state. The U.S. Supreme Court has consistently held parole to be a privilege and, consequently, held that a full complement of due process rights do not need to be afforded at parole-granting hearings (*Greenholtz v. Inmates of the Nebraska Penal and Correction Complex*, 99 S. Ct. 2100 [1979]. As a result, the states have been given the opportunity to establish whatever inmate privileges they feel are appropriate at parole-granting hearings.

Inmates are permitted the use of counsel in twenty-one states and are allowed to present witnesses in nineteen. The rationale for the parole decision must be formally articulated in eleven parole jurisdictions. Most states have established regulations as to the amount of time an inmate is required to serve prior to parole eligibility. In sixteen states, eligibility is obtained upon completion of the minimum sentence. In ten states, as well as the federal system, eligibility is achieved upon completion of one-third of the maximum sentence. Other states use the number of prior felony convictions and length of prior sentences to calculate eligibility rules. Even in the states that use the same eligibility guidelines, there is such a wide variation in the length of the minimum and maximum prison terms handed down for the same offense that, in reality, there are literally as many variations in eligibility as there are parole jurisdictions. In addition to time factors, some states restrict the use of parole for those convicted of various serious personal offenses, such as first degree murder, kidnapping, aggravated rape, etc.[4]

If an inmate does not meet parole standards, the sentence is continued, and a date set for the next parole review. If parole is approved, the individual is prepared for release to the parole field service authority. Just how long an inmate must wait to hear the verdict varies greatly. The inmate receives word immediately in many jurisdictions. In others, and in those jurisdictions where no hearings are held, inmates are notified by the prison staff or by mail. Receipt by the inmate of formal written notification varies from immediately in several states to as long as three to four weeks in New Jersey.

The parole-granting hearing is a very significant event for inmates. Regardless of the outcome, the result will greatly affect their lives. They realize that a single inappropriate word or action could jeopardize their freedom for years to come. Yet despite the significance of the decision, Mitford (1971) found that the California Youth Authority averaged less than seventeen minutes per case. Some feel that, in other states, the amount of time is probably less; Scott (1974) found the median in Indiana to be eight seconds. The national average is probably between twelve and fifteen minutes per case. This means that parole boards are hearing approximately fifteen to twenty cases per day. The *Corrections* volume of the National Advisory Commission (1973) recommended that no more than twenty cases be heard in a single day.

It is difficult to determine exactly how long a parole board deliberates because they operate in relative secrecy. Hearings are closed, and decision-making criteria are not really known to outsiders. Indeed, a major problem in the parole process is a reluctance on the part of most parole boards to clearly articulate standards and guidelines for release. As Porter (1958: 227) has stated, there is nothing more cruel, inhumane, and frustrating than serving a prison term without knowledge of what will be measured and what rules determine release readiness. This discretionary use (and occasional abuse) of power has come under close scrutiny and criticism by both academicians and politicians, and some have called for abolition of both parole and the indeterminate sentence.

Shock Parole

On January 1, 1974, a new criminal code became law in the state of Ohio. Part of this new code was designed to provide for the early release of inmates by placing them on parole after six months of incarceration. This type of release is called shock parole and is limited for use with first offenders—the basic penological theory behind its use is that of deterrence. Hopefully, the first offender will be "shocked" by the harsh realities of prison life and inspired to avoid criminal behavior upon release. At the same time, it attempts to perform a rehabilitative function by avoiding the possible negative effects of incarceration by releasing the first offender as soon as possible. These offenders can be released on parole, after serving six months in prison, provided that (Vaughan, 1980: 225):

1. The offense for which the prisoner was sentenced was an offense other than murder or aggravated murder.

2. The prisoner has not previously been convicted of any felony for which, pursuant to sentence, he was confined for 30 days or more in a penal or reformatory institution in this state or in the United States.

3. The prisoner is not a dangerous offender (psychopathic) as defined in the Revised Code.

4. The prisoner does not need further confinement in a penal or reformatory institution for his correction or rehabilitation.

5. The history, character, condition, and attitudes of the prisoner indicate that he is likely to respond affirmatively to early release on parole and is unlikely to commit another offense.

The discretionary authority to release an inmate on shock parole rests entirely with the parole board. Hearings on shock cases are held in the same manner as regular parole hearings.

Early research on the program (Vaughan et al., 1976: 275–79) examined the factors related to the parole board's decision to release an inmate on shock parole. It was discovered that, among 1,980 shock candidates from 1974, one was most likely to be granted shock parole if one: (1) were female, (2) were nonblack, (3) were younger, (4) were better educated, (5) were incarcerated for embezzlement, (6) received a lower maximum sentence, or (7) had less prior criminal involvement as indicated by total time previously served in jails and prisons. However, it is not possible to reach any definite conclusion about the motives of the parole board on the basis of this evidence. It is possible that these factors are related to a single important variable, such as severity of present offense, and should not be interpreted in an attempt to find the ultimate causes of shock parole decision making.

The research also compared the on-parole performance of shock and regular parolees in an effort to examine the effectiveness of the program. Vaughan et al. (1976: 279–82) did a four-month follow-up investigation on the performance of fifty-six shock and sixty regular parolees released in July 1974 and used arrest and parole violation as indicators of recidivism. They discovered that 14 percent of the shock cases and 22 percent of the regular parolees had been arrested. It was also reported that 2 percent of the shock cases and 6 percent of the regular parolees violated their conditions of release. Due to the small size of the sample and the preliminary nature of the study, the authors caution that "no final conclusions can be drawn at this time concerning the relative adjustment of shock parolees compared to 'regular' parolees."

Despite such tentative findings and negative public attitudes, an early release mechanism like shock parole can provide certain benefits if it is properly administered. In these times of nationwide overcrowding in correctional institutions, shock parole can send a definite message to the non-dangerous offender and help decrease the staggering financial cost of incarceration. It can also cause a number of problems since it gives the parole board another measure of discretionary power over the inmate. It is clear that shock parole is an innovation that bears further analysis and investigation.

Factors Influencing Parole Decisions

In theory, parole decisions should be based upon the factors outlined in state statutes. In practice, however, it appears that parole boards are influenced by a wide variety of criteria, not all of which are articulated by law. Furthermore, some states do not have *any* legal guidelines.

In his study of 325 males and 34 females facing a parole decision in a Midwest state in 1968, Scott (1974) examined the factors that influenced the parole decision. He determined that the seriousness of the crime, a high number of prison disciplinary reports, age (older inmates), a low level of education, a marital status of single, and (surprisingly) a good institutional record were factors that *lengthened* an inmate's sentence. Prior record and race were determined to have no effect upon the parole decision.

However, in his study of 243 inmates in an eastern facility, Carroll (1976) found that race did play a significant role in this determination. A number of factors that were not related to the parole decision for white prisoners were important for blacks. Blacks who participated in treatment programs or were older were more likely to be released. The supposition is that these blacks were perceived as nonmilitant and therefore less likely to cause problems upon release.

For the purposes of this analysis, we will explore the release criteria that influence parole boards, as suggested by Dawson (1966):

1. Factors for granting parole based upon the probability of recidivism
2. Factors for granting parole other than probability of recidivism
3. Factors for denying parole other than probability of recidivism

Factors for Granting Parole Based on the Probability of Recidivism

Perhaps the most basic aspect of the decision-making process is estimating the probability that an individual will violate the law if and when released on parole. This is known as the recidivism factor. Parole boards, as quasi-political entities, are extremely sensitive to the public criticism that may arise when parolees violate parole, especially if they commit a serious offense. Just how parole boards determine the probability of recidivism is unclear. As early as 1928, Burgess (1928) advocated the need to develop methodologically sound prediction tables for potential parolees that were based upon socioeconomic data. Since this observation, many such scales and tables have been developed (Babst, Inciardi, Jarman, 1970; Bromley and Gathercole, 1969; Gottfredson, Babst, Ballard, 1958; Glaser, 1962; Wilkins and MacNaughton-Smith, 1964). For more than fifty years, the value of prediction devices has been recognized as a means of standardizing parole release and more accurately assessing recidivism probability; yet they are seldom used, for a variety of reasons.

A substantial resistance to the use of prediction tables stems from a firm belief in the uniqueness of each case. Prediction devices do, in fact, predict group behavior, but they cannot specifically predict what will happen to an individual. Tied in closely with this notion of individuality is the fact that prediction devices are unable to quantify such subjective, intangible criteria as mental attitude and success drive.[5]

Another set of factors that limit the use of prediction instruments are the legal, traditional, and political environments of the community. Indeed, the restrictions imposed by certain laws and traditions can render a prediction device virtually useless. For example, overtly differentiating release on the basis of race, even if quantitatively substantiated, would clearly violate the Civil Rights Act. Even when prediction devices incorporate legal criteria, parole boards must carefully weigh their subjective assessment of current community perspectives relevant to the case decisions under consideration. In other words, parole boards must be sensitive to public attitudes. The recent decision in California to rescind parole for Sirhan Sirhan, convicted murderer of Senator Robert Kennedy, illustrates the impact of possible public outcry over the release of a "dangerous" offender.

Just what information is used to reach a probability figure is not fully known. It is possible, however, to examine criteria that seem to recur with some frequency. Perhaps the factor of greatest concern in reaching a probability of recidivism figure is the psychological adjustment or change in inmates' attitudes. There is a traditional assumption in corrections that offenses are committed as a result of personal problems, and unless a change in attitude occurs while under correctional treatment and control, the probability of recidivism will be high. Parole boards also consider whether inmates participate in institutional programs, their prior experience outside the institution under supervision, their criminal record, how well they adjusted to institutional life and regimentation, and a host of rather nebulous aggravating and/or mitigating circumstances that may or may not be related to each of the above factors—or to recidivism by the parole candidate. However, many jurisdictions now use parole decision-making guidelines.

Factors for Granting Parole Other Than Probability of Recidivism

There are occasions when inmates are granted parole despite the parole board's belief that they possess a relatively high probability of recidivism. In instances when offenders are believed not likely to commit a crime of a *serious* nature, the parole board may vote to grant parole. This factor is often accompanied by a determination that the inmate will gain little additional benefit from further institutionalization. For example, although an inmate may be an alcoholic with a long record of public intoxication arrests, the parole board may grant a release because it feels that the individual is relatively harmless, and that continued institutionalization will very likely have little further impact upon the alcoholism problem.

Occasionally, situations arise when inmates have but only a short period of time to serve before the completion of their sentences. When such circumstances arise, parole boards frequently parole these individuals, despite what may be a high perceived probability of recidivism, in order to provide even a brief period of supervisory control and, more importantly, to assist the parolee in the environmental decompression and social reintegration process. Some 26 percent of 1981 parolees were released on mandatory parole, required under postrelease supervision and determinate sentencing laws (Scott, 1982: 6). This perspective is built upon the basic principle that those released from an institution under the care of a parole authority perform better than those who are granted an unconditional, unsupervised release. These are the mandatory supervision parolees.

An additional criteria that may swing a parole board, despite an apparent high recidivism probability, is the length of time served. If an inmate has failed to respond to institutional treatment but has served a relatively long sentence, the parole board may grant parole under the conviction that these individuals have paid their dues, and that perhaps they will succeed on parole to avoid being sent back. Occasionally, the maturation process will play an important role. When lengthy sentences are mandated for young persons, the parole board may affect an early release, noting the general process of maturation that will enable these individuals to adopt more acceptable patterns of behavior once released.

Factors for Denying Parole Other than Probability of Recidivism

There are circumstances when individuals may not be granted a release despite a relatively low recidivism probability. For example, when inmates have demonstrated occasional outbursts of violent and assaultive behavior, parole boards tend to be somewhat reluctant to grant a release. As previously noted, parole boards are extremely sensitive to public criticism, and while the probability of violent attack may be very small, the seriousness of the incident would likely attract considerable media attention. Consequently, release in such a situation will often be denied. Community attitudes and values often play major roles in overriding the recidivism probability factors. For example, murderers have traditionally been good parole risks in terms of the likelihood of parole success. However, whether and how quickly they should be paroled is often a function of community attitudes. If a community attitude is unfavorable, parole is likely to be denied, for the release of such an inmate might expose the parole board to bitter public criticism, and most parole boards prefer to keep an inmate in prison rather than incur the public's anger.

There are also occasions when parole is used as a tool to support and maintain institutional discipline. Individuals may possess very high potential for success on parole, but continually violate institutional rules and regulations. In these situations, parole will frequently be denied. Occasionally, an inmate with a drug abuse problem may be counseled by the parole board to enroll in an existing drug-dependency program, sending a clear message to the inmate population that such rehabilitation programs are appropriate and functional for release. In this way, parole can be viewed as an incentive for good behavior and a sanction against inappropriate conduct. There are even situations when parole may be denied so as to benefit the inmate. Circumstances occasionally arise when inmates are making rapid progress in academic pursuits, or may be receiving and responding to necessary medical and/or psychological treatment. The parole board may temporarily postpone such a case for a few months to give these individuals the opportunity to complete their high school work, for example, or recover from surgery performed to correct facial abnormalities or some other physical deformities.

Finally, there are situations when the parole board may feel that individuals are good risks but ineligible for release because they have not served the minimum terms as fixed by the sentencing judge. Some have expressed a concern over the fact that the courts occasionally err in handing down sanctions more severe than are necessary. Correctional officials, after more careful observation and evaluation than the courts could originally consider, may clearly document greater progress than the court expected. Nevertheless, as previously noted, state parole statutes may mandate a minimum time to be served (calculated as a percentage of the minimum or maximum sentence) that even the parole board cannot ignore.

There are some similarities in the present federal system. Parole eligibility for all federal inmates is determined within the first 120 days of incarceration in a federal institution. During that time, each case is considered and a future or presumptive parole release date is established (Stone-Meierhoefer and Hoffman, 1982). It should be emphasized that inmates are not released within 120 days but, rather, parole eligibility is considered and inmates are able to have their release date established. There are some skeptics who feel that 120 days is not sufficient time to make an accurate assessment. On the other hand, it removes the uncertainty factor from the release decision.

Some state jurisdictions are adopting an early-decision model called the Mutual Agreement Program (MAP). In a MAP contract system, shortly after the offender enters the institution, correctional officials, parole officials, and individual offenders meet to develop a program plan that clearly details the areas in which the offender has to improve, and the extent of the improvement needed, in order to be granted parole and, once paroled, to be released from supervision. The MAP plan also involves the establishment of an exact date of release *if* the contract is met. This serves to eliminate the uncertainty factor so prominent in traditional parole and, furthermore, provides offenders with the opportunity to participate in the development of a treatment plan tailored to their own specific needs.

Parole Board Release Decisions

All persons who are eligible for parole are not automatically granted a release. Occasionally, parole boards will not release individuals who could be safely released. This is partially, a desire by parole boards to minimize the number of persons who are classified as good risks and released, but who the board feel are in reality bad risks and expected to fail on parole. Failed parole is a problem the boards seek to minimize (Wiggins, 1984).

At present, however, criminologists have not been able to predict well. In fact, prediction accuracy has a rather dismal track record (Smykla, 1984; Monahan, 1981). As a result, there is now a general tendency to overpredict dangerousness, and this results in more persons being classified as bad risks, fewer persons being granted parole, and an increase in prison populations (Monahan, 1981). Although such tendencies have come under intense criticism, overprediction of dangerousness continues (Morris, 1974; Smykla, 1984). This is probably due to the perception that overprediction is viewed as having smaller short-term costs. In the short-run, it may be cheaper to incarcerate large numbers of offenders than to permit a few dangerous persons to roam the streets and commit crimes. Such an approach is quite costly in the long-run, however, as more and more persons are housed and cared for within the prison system. Furthermore, there are indications that after the extended prison sentences are served, the former inmates will commit more serious crimes more frequently than they would have prior to their incarceration.

While the courts have ruled that parole cannot be denied on the basis of race, religion, or national origin,[6] they have really not become involved in parole board policies and practices. This is due in large part to the fact that the Supreme Court has consistently held parole to be a privilege rather than a right (*Greenholz*, 1979). Consequently, there is no constitutional mandate that there even be any formal parole release guidelines, no right to obtain access to institutional files, and no right to counsel at the hearing. Indeed, there is no constitutional requirement that there even be a formal hearing. The state is under no constitutional obligation to articulate the reason for denial of parole and there is no right of appeal.

While parole is not protected by the U.S. Constitution, most states have adopted laws and/or administrative policies that do outline parole procedures. Some even allow inmates access to their files and permit the presence of legal counsel. At present, the U.S. Parole Commission and twenty-three states offer inmates the opportunity to internally appeal parole release hearing decisions (O'Leary and Hanrahan, 1977: 42–47). Up to this point, however, the courts have continued to refuse to become involved in any type of review of a negative parole board decision. Many feel that the time will soon come when the courts will mandate basic rules of procedures for parole hearings, and perhaps even become actively involved in actual appellate reviews. If the latter were to occur, the parole decision, at this point an administration matter, could become a judicial matter. In other words, indeterminate sentences, which are now a joint venture between the judiciary and the executive branch, could become the sole possession of the judiciary.

Conditions of Parole

Parole is in essence a contract between the state and the offender. If the offender is able to abide by the terms of the contract, freedom is maintained. If a violation of these conditions occurs, or if a parolee is charged with a new crime, the parole board may revoke parole and return the offender to prison. The offender must abide by the contract, and stay under parole supervision for the period of time outlined by the parole board. While every state has its own policies and procedures, parole usually lasts more than two but less than seven years. Some states have in fact become rather liberal and permit discharge from parole after a very short time, as long as the offender has diligently adhered to the prerelease contract. While the exact content of the contracts varies from state to state, and from individual to individual, the following federal guidelines cover the majority of the conditions that are usually adopted:

1. You shall go directly to the district showing on this CERTIFICATE OF PAROLE (unless released to the custody of other authorities). Within three days after your arrival you shall report to your parole advisor if you have one, and to the United States Probation Officer whose name appears on this certificate. If in any emergency you are unable to get in

touch with your parole advisor, or your probation officer or his office, you shall communicate with the United States Board of Parole, Department of Justice, Washington, D.C. 20537.

2. If you are released to the custody of other authorities, and after your release from physical custody of such authorities, you are unable to report to the United States Probation Officer to whom you are assigned within three days, you shall report instead to the nearest United States Probation Officer.

3. You shall not leave the limits of this CERTIFICATE OF PAROLE without written permission from the probation officer.

4. You shall notify your probation officer immediately of any change in your place of residence.

5. You shall make a complete and truthful written report (on a form provided for that purpose) to your probation officer between the first and third day of each month, and on the final day of parole. You shall also report to your probation officer at other times as he directs.

6. You shall not violate any law. Nor shall you associate with persons engaged in criminal activity. You shall get in touch immediately with your probation officer or his office if you are arrested or questioned by a law-enforcement officer.

7. You shall not enter into any agreement to act as an "informer" or special agent for any law-enforcement agency.

8. You shall work regularly, unless excused by your probation officer, and support your legal dependents, if any, to the best of your ability. You shall report immediately to your probation officer any change in employment.

9. You shall not drink alcoholic beverages to excess. You shall not purchase, possess, use, or administer marijuana or narcotic or other habit forming or dangerous drugs, unless prescribed or advised by a physician. You shall not frequent places where such drugs are illegally sold, dispensed, used, or given away.

10. You shall not associate with persons who have a criminal record unless you have the permission of your probation officer.

11. You shall not have firearms (or other dangerous weapons) in your possession without the written permission of your probation officer, following prior approval of the United States Board of Parole.

12. You shall, if ordered by the Board pursuant to Section 4203, Title 18, U.S.C., as amended October 1970, reside in and/or participate in a treatment program of a Community Treatment Center operated by the Bureau of Prisons, for a period not to exceed 120 days.

Parole conditions were once much more restrictive than they are today. Within the past three or four decades there has been a very clear and conscious effort to reduce both the number and the restrictive nature of parole conditions. The courts have ruled that parole conditions, to be valid, must be constitutional, reasonable, clear, and contribute to the rehabilitation and/or protection of society.[7] As del Carmen (1984) points out, these are rather nebulous terms that frankly continue to leave parole boards rather broad discretion in imposing conditions of parole.

Parole Revocation

In 1972, the U.S. Supreme Court established procedures for parole revocation with the case of *Morrissey v. Brewer* (1972). In this case, the Supreme Court said that once parole is granted, it is no longer just a privilege but a right. Consequently, the Court ruled that parolees should be granted certain due process rights in any parole revocation proceeding. While the Court did not grant a full array of due process rights in *Morrissey*, it did advance the mandate of fundamental fairness. The Court required the following minimum due process rights in the event of a parole revocation proceeding.

1. Parolee given advanced written notification of the inquiry, its purpose, and alleged violation
2. A disclosure to the parolee of the evidence against him or her
3. The opportunity to be heard in person and present witnesses and documentary evidence
4. The right to confront and cross-examine adverse witnesses
5. A neutral and detached hearing body
6. A written statement by the hearing body as to the evidence relied upon and reasons for revoking parole

The case of *Morrissey* also established a dual state procedure, including a preliminary inquiry at the time of the alleged parole violations as well as a formal revocation hearing. Left unanswered, however, was the right to counsel, and whether or not the Exclusionary Rule should apply to revocation cases. One year later, in the case of *Gagnon v. Scarpelli* (411 U.S. 778 [1972]) the Court held that parolees do have a limited right to counsel in revocation proceedings and the hearing body must determine, on a case-by-case basis, whether counsel should be afforded. While it need not be granted in all cases, ". . . Counsel should be provided where, after being informed of his right, the . . . parolee requests counsel, based on a timely and colorable claim that he had not committed the alleged violation or, if the violation is a matter of public record or uncontested, there are substantial reasons in justification or mitigation that make revocation inappropriate."

The Exclusionary Rule issue remains unanswered. While illegally seized evidence cannot be used in a criminal trial, many states do permit such evidence to be used in parole revocation cases. To date, the courts have generally upheld this practice.[8]

Problems with Parole Board Discretionary Power

During the 1970s, dramatic shifts occured in the field of corrections. Dissatisfied with high recidivism rates, many states opted to amend the traditional indeterminate sentencing model and adopt some of the aspects of a determinate or fixed sentencing model (see Table 6–1). The use of the indeterminate sentence in the United States represented a grand experiment in controlling if not eliminating criminal behavior. Indeterminate sentencing, in which the judge sets limits within legislatively determined minimum and maximum sentences (e.g., one to seven years for burglary), would focus upon the individual criminal and his or her needs, rather than establishing a fixed penalty for certain *types* of crime. It sought to maximize the possibility of criminal rehabilitation through the use of various educational, vocational, and psychological treatment programs in the institution, and the use of a parole board that would release the inmate on parole at the optimum moment when change had occurred.

Table 6–1
Sentencing Modes by State

State	Type of Sentencing	Mandatory Sentencing	Mandatory Offenses
Alabama	Determinate	Yes	Repeat felony
Alaska	Determinate, presumptive	Yes	Murder, kidnapping, firearms, repeat felony
Arizona	Determinate, presumptive	Yes	Firearms, prior felony convictions
Arkansas	Determinate	Yes	Robbery, deadly weapons
California	Determinate, presumptive	No	
Colorado	Determinate, presumptive	No	
Connecticut	Determinate	Yes	Sex assault with firearm, burglary, repeat felony, assault on elderly
Delaware	Determinate	Yes	Murder, kidnapping, prison assault, robbery, narcotics, deadly weapons, habitual criminal, obscenity, others
Florida	Indeterminate	Yes	Drugs
Georgia	Determinate	Yes	Armed robbery, burglary, drugs
Hawaii	Indeterminate	No	

Table 6–1 (*Continued*)

State	Type of Sentencing	Mandatory Sentencing	Mandatory Offenses
Idaho	Determinate	Yes	Firearms, repeat extortion, kidnap or rape with bodily injury
Illinois	Determinate	Yes	Major offenses, specified felonies and offenses, repeaters, weapons
Indiana	Determinate, presumptive	Yes	Repeat felony, violent crime, deadly weapons
Iowa	Indeterminate	Yes	Forcible felonies, firearms, habitual offenders, drugs
Kansas	Indeterminate	Yes	Sex offense, firearms
Kentucky	Indeterminate	No	
Louisiana	Indeterminate	Yes	Drugs, violent crime
Maine	Determinate	No	
Maryland	Determinate, guidelines	Yes	Repeat violent offenders, handgun
Massachusetts	Indeterminate	Yes	Firearms, auto theft, drug trafficking
Michigan	Indeterminate	Yes	Murder, armed robbery, treason, firearms
Minnesota	Guidelines	No	
Mississippi	Determinate	Yes	Armed robbery, repeat felony
Missouri	Determinate	Yes	Dangerous weapons, repeat felony
Montana	Indeterminate	Yes	Firearms
Nebraska	Indeterminate	No	
Nevada	Determinate	Yes	2nd degree murder, 1st degree kidnapping, sexual assault, firearms, repeat felony
New Hampshire	Indeterminate	Yes	Firearms
New Jersey	Determinate, presumptive	Yes	Sexual assault, firearms
New Mexico	Determinate, presumptive	Yes	Firearms
New York	Indeterminate	Yes	Specified violent and nonviolent felonies
North Carolina	Determinate, presumptive	Yes	Armed robbery, 1st degree burglary, repeat felony with firearm

Table 6-1 (*Continued*)

STATE	TYPE OF SENTENCING	MANDATORY SENTENCING	MANDATORY OFFENSES
North Dakota	Determinate	Yes	Firearms
Ohio	Indeterminate	Yes	Rape, drug trafficking
Oklahoma	Determinate	No	Repeat felony
Oregon	Indeterminate, guidelines	Yes	Drugs
Pennsylvania*	Indeterminate, guidelines	Yes	Selected felonies with firearms, within 7 years of prior convictions, in or near public transportation
Rhode Island	Indeterminate	No	
South Carolina	Determinate	Yes	Armed robbery, drugs, bomb threat
South Dakota	Indeterminate	No	
Tennessee	Determinate, indeterminate	Yes	Specified felonies, firearms, repeat felony
Texas	Determinate	Yes	Repeat felony, violent offenses
Utah	Indeterminate	No	
Vermont	Indeterminate	Yes	Drugs, violent crime
Virginia	Indeterminate	No	
Washington	Indeterminate	Yes	Firearms, rape, repeat felony
West Virginia	Indeterminate	Yes	Firearms in felony
Wisconsin	Indeterminate	No	
Wyoming	Indeterminate	No	

*Pennsylvania updated as of December 1982.

SOURCES: Richard S. Morelli, Craig Edelman, and Roy Willoughby, "A Survey of Mandatory Sentencing in the U.S." (Pennsylvania Commission on Crime and Delinquency, September 1981); Criminal Courts Technical Assistance Project, "Judicial and Executive Discretion in the Sentencing Process: Analysis of Felony State Code Provisions" (Washington, D.C.: American University, January 1982); Michael Kanvensohn, "A National Survey of Parole-Related Legislation" (San Francisco: Uniform Parole Reports, December 1979).

Through this "medical model of corrections," it was argued that such parole board decision making would offer several benefits:

1. It would provide an incentive for rehabilitation by linking it to release from prison.
2. This incentive would also apply as a mechanism to control the prison population, ensuring inmate discipline and safety.
3. Another latent function of parole would be to provide a mechanism to control the size of the prison population.

4. Similarly, the parole board would share the responsibility for societal protection with the judiciary through its control over prison release procedures. The board could also serve as a check and balance to judicial discretion by reducing sentencing disparities (such that inmates who committed the same crime would serve approximately the same amount of actual time in prison).

However, a number of factors combined to question the efficacy and fairness of the medical model. Penologists, such as Martinson (1974) and MacNamara (1977), reviewing the outcome of research reports on correctional rehabilitation programs, concluded that the medical model failed to cure criminals, reduce recidivism, or protect the public. Others (Morris, 1974) argued that the medical model harmed the inmates because program participation was coerced. Inmates correctly believed that their release on parole was tied to, and dependent upon, such participation. From the inmates' point of view, the decisions of the board were arbitrary, unpredictable, and not subject to external review by any other governmental body (Irwin, 1977). In fact, a number of studies (see Goodstein, 1980) have indicated that inmate frustration over failure to obtain release on parole is a factor that contributes to prison violence.

By the same token, others have argued that reckless decision making by parole officials has contributed to violence within communities. While most parole boards are granted absolute immunity from damages or injury caused by inmates they release onto parole,[9] there are a growing number of exceptions. In one particular case, the supreme court in Arizona levied a civil liability against members of the Arizona Board of Parole for their grossly negligent decision to release an inmate onto parole who subsequently killed one man and seriously harmed another while robbing a bar.[10] The keys in these parole board liability cases appear to be the concepts of recklessness and gross negligence, concepts subject to interpretation from one court to another and from one part of the country to another. Consequently, this issue will not be easily resolved.

Parole Board Decision-Making Guidelines: The U.S. Parole Commission

Concerns over some of these issues have led a number of jurisdictions, including the Federal Parole System, to adopt parole release guidelines. The U.S. Parole Commission developed its system of parole decision-making guidelines in 1974. It has been stated that these guidelines were developed in response to Senate 1437, legislation that would create a sentencing commission (Krajick, 1979; McCall, 1978). The major complaint against parole board decision making has been, and remains, the great amount of unchecked discretionary power. The parole decision-making guidelines propose to structure this discretionary power to promote equity and fairness,[11] and also to reduce sentencing disparity. The task was to make the decisions of the parole board less arbitrary and more explicit.

A central portion of these guidelines is based upon the salient factor scoring scale (Hoffman and Adelberg, 1980). Figure 6–1 is a copy of the scale [12] currently used by the U.S. Board of Parole examiners. The scale consists of six items. With each case, the examiner assigns a score to each item. The sum of the six items ranges from 0 to 10; the higher the score, the better the prospects for success on parole. This predictive score is then collapsed into eight categories. This task completed, the examiner then consults the guidelines as detailed in Figure 6–2, which indicates the amount of prison time an offender should serve with a certain record and who has been convicted of an offense of a given severity. In sum, the examiner uses the information from Figure 6–2 to rank the severity of the present offense and the parole prognosis (salient factor score) of the individual offender. Note that for offenders who commit serious crimes, no limits are established for time to be served. In this fashion, the guidelines system attempts to structure the discretionary power of the parole board while at the same time maintaining equity and fairness (Hoffman, 1983).

However, board examiners are permitted to deviate from the guidelines. As Hoffman and Adelberg (1980: 45) point out, the use of a salient factor score with a guidelines system does not mean the elimination of clinical judgment. The examiners can shorten or lengthen the amount of time specified by the guidelines when, in their judgment, the case at hand appears to merit such consideration. However, when such a step is taken, the examiner is required to state the specific factors present that led to such a judgment. Again, the emphasis is upon the articulation of those factors that influence parole board decision making.

Sigler (1978: 329) describes the due process mechanisms in this process. The inmate receives the board's decision within fifteen days of the hearing, and if the decision is negative, he receives the reasons for the decision in writing. The recommendation of the examiner is reviewed by the chief hearing examiner or regional director; the action may be modified or referred to the National Appellate Board. The decision of the appeals board is then forwarded to the inmate.

If the inmate disagrees with the negative decision or the parole date, these decisions may be appealed to the regional director. This individual may advance a set-off date up to six months, change the salient factor score or offense severity rating, and adjust the release date accordingly. The power to grant parole where it has been denied or vice versa, or to advance a set-off date by more than six months, requires the signature of another regional director. If this signature is not obtained, the original recommendation must stand.

Figure 6-1   Salient Factor Score (SFS/81)

A.   PRIOR CONVICTIONS/ADJUDICATIONS (ADULT OR JUVENILE)
     None .... = 3
     One .... = 2
     Two or three = 1
     Four or more = 0

B.   PRIOR COMMITMENTS OF MORE THAN 30 DAYS (ADULT OR
     JUVENILE) ....
     None .... = 2
     One or two ..... = 1
     Three or more .. = 0

C.   AGE AT CURRENT OFFENSE/PRIOR COMMITMENTS .../..............
     Age at commencement of the current offense:
        26 years of age or more .. = 2*
        20-25 years of age .... = 1*
        19 years of age or less .. = 0
        *EXCEPTION: If five or more prior commitments of
        more than thirty days (adult or juvenile), place
        an x here ____ and score this item .... = 0

D.   RECENT COMMITMENT-FREE PERIOD (THREE YEARS) ....
     No prior commitment of more than thirty days (adult or
     juvenile), or released to the community from last such
     commitment at least three years prior to the commence-
     ment of the current offense .... = 1
     Otherwise .... = 0

E.   PROBATION/PAROLE/CONFINEMENT/ESCAPE STATUS VIOLATOR THIS
     TIME ....
     Neither on probation, parole, confinement, or escape
     status at the time of the current offense; nor committed
     as a probation, parole, confinement, or escape status
     violator this time .... = 1
     Otherwise .... = 0

F.   HEROIN/OPIATE DEPENDENCE ....
     No history of heroin or opiate dependence = 1
     Otherwise .... = 0

TOTAL SCORE ....

   In the final stage, a dissatisfied inmate may either accept the decision
or appeal the regional director's decision by going to court. Finally, the inmate can appeal any board decision in the courts.
   Despite the remedies, this guidelines system has its critics (Krajick,
1978: 41-42). First of all, there is the problem that has plagued all attempts at the prediction of criminal behavior—"false positives": those inmates whose success is predicted but who would fail upon release. The
Commission reports that 63 percent of the inmates with a poor risk score (0
to 3) will be successful, yet they will be held longer because of factors in
their backgrounds that are beyond their control. In fact, the Commission

Figure 6-2   Guidelines for Decision Making

[Guidelines for Decision Making, Customary Total Time
to Be Served Before Release (Including Jail Time)]

Offense Characteristics: Severity of Offense Behavior	Offender Characteristics: Parole Prognosis (Salient Factor Score 1981)			
	Very Good (10-8)	Good (7-6)	Fair (5-4)	Poor (3-0)
Category One (formerly "low severity")	Adult Range = 6 months	6-9 months	9-12 months	12-16 months
	(Youth Range) (= 6) months	(6-9) months	(9-12) months	(12-16) months
Category Two (formerly "low moderate severity")	Adult Range = 8 months	8-12 months	12-16 months	16-22 months
	(Youth Range) (= 8) months	(8-12) months	(12-16) months	(16-20) months
Category Three (formerly "moderate severity")	Adult Range 10-14 months	14-18 months	18-24 months	24-32 months
	(Youth Range) (8-12) months	(12-16) months	(16-20) months	(20-26) months
Category Four (formerly "high severity")	Adult Range 14-20 months	20-26 months	26-34 months	34-44 months
	(Youth Range) (12-16) months	(16-20) months	(20-26) months	(26-32) months
Category Five (formerly "very high severity")	Adult Range 24-36 months	36-48 months	48-60 months	60-72 months
	(Youth Range) (20-26) months	(26-32) months	(32-40) months	(40-48) months

Figure 6-2 *(continued)*

Offense Characteristics: Severity of Offense Behavior	Offender Characteristics: Parole Prognosis (Salient Factor Score 1981)			
	Very Good (10–8)	Good (7–6)	Fair (5–4)	Poor (3–0)
Category Six (formerly "greatest I severity")	Adult Range 40–52 months	52–64 months	64–78 months	78–100 months
	(Youth Range) (30–40) months	(40–50) months	(50–60) months	(60–76) months
Category Seven (formerly included in "greatest II severity")	Adult Range 52–80 months	64–92 months	78–110 months	100–148 months
	(Youth Range) (40–64) months	(50–74) months	(60–68) months	(76–110) months
Category Eight* (formerly included in "greatest II severity")	Adult Range 100 months	120 months	150 months	180 months
	(Youth Range) (80) months	(100) months	(120) months	(150) months

*Note: For Category Eight, no upper limits are specified due to the extreme variability of the cases within this category. For decisions exceeding the lower limit of the applicable guideline category by more than 48 months, the pertinent aggravating case factors considered are to be specified in the reasons given (e.g., that a homicide was premeditated or commited during the course of another felony, or that extreme cruelty or brutality was demonstrated).

removed two factors (marital status and education) from the salient factor scale because they felt them to be class or status biased. Along with the false positives issue, prisoners are very much aware of the fact that the scale does not take prison behavior into account. The Commission's policy is to expect good institutional behavior, not to reward it. One inmate, serving four years for hijacking a truck, remarked (Krajick, 1978: 43):

> When I came here, they said, "When you get out is up to you." But it's not up to me. It's up to those mechanical charts that they look everything up on. . . . I've dedicated every minute I've been here to getting out. . . . Worked and gone to school, and stayed out of trouble, till there wasn't anything else I could do. But they don't care. . . . All I'm saying is, don't look at those charts; look at my change, look at my record, look at *me*.

Apparently, maintaining incentives for rehabilitation under the guidelines system is a problem.

However, research indicates that these guidelines appear to have some effect in reducing sentencing disparity among inmates. Gottfredson (1979) collected data on sentence length and time served (presumptive release date) for 4,471 adult cases appearing before the Parole Commission between October 1977 and May 1978. He then grouped the offenders with similar offense severity ratings and similar prior records as ranked by the Commission and the salient factor score categories. Statistical analysis revealed that for every category of equally situated offenders, the variations in decision made by the Commission, as opposed to the sentence imposed by the judge, were markedly smaller. Although Gottfredson cautions that the results are not necessarily attributable to the use of the guidelines themselves,[13] the Parole Commission decisions are less disparate than the judicial decisions. The use of parole board decision-making guidelines attempts to deal with the traditional problems of the parole process. They do not represent a panacea, but they are an alternative to either the typical method, outright abolition, or the use of determinate sentencing.

Abolition of Parole

While some criminologists and practitioners have been content to alter various aspects and procedures of the parole process, others have called for its complete abolition. The states of Maine and Connecticut, as previously discussed, have, for all intents and purposes, abolished parole; the state of New York, if it adheres to the recommendations made by the Citizens Inquiry on Parole and Criminal Justice, may be next.

In their monograph on the abolition of parole, von Hirsch and Hanrahan (1980) also made a number of suggestions concerning the use of parole, particularly violations of due process rights in the parole process, revocation proceedings, and conditions of release. The authors suggest that a parolee who is accused of committing a new crime, and could be returned to prison on a charge of parole violation, does not have full protection of the law. A revocation proceeding requires a lower standard of proof than a court proceeding or the alleged new offense. For this reason, von Hirsch and Hanrahan (1980: 117) recommend the abolition of the separate system of adjudication for parolees. Any parolee who is believed to have committed a new crime should, instead, be criminally charged and prosecuted.[14]

The authors offer two other *caveats* regarding parole supervision. One is the question of cost-effectiveness: How costly is parole supervision to the taxpayer? To determine this aspect as well as ascertaining the effectiveness of parole supervision in reducing recidivism,[15] von Hirsch and Hanrahan call for "sunset" legislation for parole. Under this concept, a state would continue parole services for a fixed period (i.e., five years) and would submit the question of parole effectiveness to testing. At the end of this period, the results would be evaluated and future planning with regard to parole would rest upon these findings. Finally, the authors assert that services should be offered to any ex-offender who might need them, but they should be voluntary, with no penalties for refusal. Again, these suggestions call for a rather different style of parole supervision or, in the case of the "desert model," outright abolition of parole.

The abolition of parole, however, presents a number of significant problems. Von Hirsch and Albanese (1979) outlined a number of the difficulties associated with the elimination of parole release: One of the proposed substitutions for parole is the use of sentencing guidelines for judges. (Guidelines of this type have been adopted by Minnesota, Utah, and Pennsylvania and on a selected and/or experimental basis in six other states [Maryland, Massachusetts, Rhode Island, Vermont, Washington, and Wisconsin].)[16] But the major question then becomes who will administer these guidelines—a sentencing commission (composed of judges or a special board established by the legislature) or will the parole board retain its power over the length of confinement?

Von Hirsch and Albanese state that one of the problems associated with a sentencing commission is that this body, unlike the parole board, would not have the authority to enforce its own rules. Enforcement would depend upon review by the overburdened higher court judges. In addition, the Commission would have to deal with establishing sentence lengths— real time in prison—set by the judges' sentences. The problem with this is that the Commission may appear to be lenient. Such sentiment by the public and the legislature has led to the demise of sentencing guidelines in several states (Eskridge, 1985). The public debate, as von Hirsch and Albanese predicted, has focused on (among other topics) the supposed leniency of the guidelines rather than on such concepts as fairness and workability. These authors caution that it may be better to utilize parole board decision-making guidelines rather than establish a sentencing commission.

Whatever the change, one should be aware of the argument by Sigler (1978: 335): "I say that as long as we use imprisonment in this country, we will have to have someone, somewhere, with the authority to release people from imprisonment. Call it parole, call it what you will. It's one of those jobs that has to be done."

Summary

There is considerable contemporary discussion relative to the value of parole. Indeed, there are those who oppose the indeterminate sentencing mode in general[17] and wish to see parole abolished in particular. Concerns over these issues, and the perceived ineffectiveness of the present parole system, have led twenty-four jurisdictions to either abolish parole altogether or dramatically adjust the entire parole process (see Table 6–2). Allen and Seiter (1983) note that, of all community programs, parole faces perhaps the greatest challenge. There are new indications, however, that pragmatism in the form of simple economics may renew an interest in parole. As our jail and prison populations swell above capacity, criminal justice planners and politicians will be forced to either construct new facilities or develop alternative models. Parole emerges as a relatively inexpensive alternative model and, perhaps more importantly, one that is already in place. There is a need, though, to improve the parole process so as to overcome the deficiencies detailed above.

Even if this apparent renewed interest in parole phases out and parole as we know it is abolished in a stampede toward the determinate sentencing model, the need to assist inmates in their transition from the institution to the free community will remain. The problems facing released inmates are usually temporal or material: obtaining employment, suitable housing, financial aid, etc. Parole officers, indeed the entire parole system, should perhaps shift from the present supervisory role to that of a brokerage-clearinghouse role, with the responsibility of assisting ex-inmates to meet temporal needs.[18] Services should be requested and received voluntarily, with no sanction for refusal. In sum, it may be well for parole to become a release process in which voluntary services are provided to help ex-offenders readjust to the community. Whether one prefers this perspec-

Table 6–2
Jurisdictions That Have Adjusted Traditional Parole Processes

ADJUSTMENT	STATES
Parole boards no longer have discretionary release power	California, Colorado, Connecticut, Illinois, Indiana, Maine, Minnesota, New Mexico, North Carolina
Guidelines for paroling decisions are written into statutes	Federal system, Florida, New York
Guidelines for pending decisions are systemwide policy but not written into statutes	Alaska, California Youth Authority, District of Columbia, Georgia, Maryland, Missouri, New Jersey, Oklahoma, Oregon, Pennsylvania, Utah, Washington
Guidelines for paroling decisions are selectively applied	California (CDC), Minnesota
Eliminated parole office supervision and parolees	Connecticut, Maine

SOURCE: Adopted from Bureau of Justice Statistics, *Setting Prison Terms* (Washington, D.C.: August 1983), and Bureau of Justice Statistics, *Probation and Parole 1982* (Washington, D.C.: September 1983).

tive or not, it will in all likelihood surface as the future role of parole in the U.S.

Notes

1. This is an extrapolation of the definition developed in the *Attorney General's Survey of Release Procedures* (Washington, D.C.: Government Printing Office, 1939), p. 4.
2. The offender's mandatory release date in Nebraska is calculated as follows:
   For all odd numbered maximum terms MR = (MAX − 1)/2 + 11 months
   For all even numbered maximum terms MR = MAX/2 + 5 months
3. Such intrastate variations may also be true within states. For example, Sutton recently observed that the decision to place an individual in prison or not, and the length of the sentence per se, may be more a function of the county where the sentence was handed down than the nature of the offense. See Paul L. Sutton, *Criminal Sentencing in Nebraska: The Feasibility of Empirically Based Guidelines* (Williamsburg, Va.: National Center for State Courts, 1981).
4. For a description of the Canadian experience with violent offenders on parole, see Jim Hackler and Laurel Gould, "Parole and the Violent Offender," *Canadian Journal of Criminology* 23 (1981):407–20.
5. Pritchard conducted an analysis of offender characteristics related to recidivism. He discovered in 177 independent samples of probationers and parolees that the most common factor related to recidivism was the stability of employment. Of course, finding employment for parolees is beyond the scope of parole boards. David A. Pritchard, "Stable Predictors of Recidivism: A Summary," *Criminology* 17 (1979):15–21.
6. See *Block v. Potter*, 631 F. 2d 233 (3d Cir. 1980); *Candelaria v. Griffin*, 641 F. 2d 868 (10th Cir. 1980); *Farris v. U.S. Board of Parole*, 384 F. 2d 948 (7th Cir. 1973).
7. See *U.S. v. Consuelo-Gonzales*, 521 F. 2d 259 (9th Cir. 1975); *Porth v. Templar*, 453 F. 2d 330 (19th Cir. 1971).
8. See *State v. Malone*, 403 So. 2d 1234 (Supp. Ct. of La., September 8, 1981); *United States ex rel. Santos v. New York State Board of Parole*, 441 F. 2d 1216 (2nd Cir., 1971), cert. denied, 404 U.S. 1025 (1972); *Catta v. Fitzharris*, 521 F. 2d 246 (9th Cir., 1975), cert. denied, 423 U.S. 827 (1975); *People v. Anderson*, 536 P. 2d 302 (Colo. Sup. Ct., 1975).
9. See *Keeton v. Procunier*, 468 F. 2d 810 (9th Cir., 1972); *Bennett v. People*, 406 F. 2d 36 (9th Cir., 1969).
10. *Grimm v. Arizona Board of Pardons and Parole*, 115 Ariz. 260 (1977).
11. As defined by Gottfredson, Hoffman, Sigler, and Wilkins (1980: 7), equity and fairness means that "*similar* persons are dealt with in *similar* ways in *similar* situations. Fairness thus implies the idea of similarity and of comparison."
12. This scale was constructed through the use of a random sample of federal prisoners (N = 2,497) released in 1970. A two-year follow-up period was used for each case and all three major types of release were utilized (parole, mandatory

release, and expiration of sentence). An additional sample of 2,149 offenders released during 1971–72 was used to validate the factors on the scale (Hoffman and Adelberg, 1980: 44). In addition, this scale was revalidated (Hoffman and Beck, 1980) using a sample of federal prisoners released in 1976 (N = 1,260).

13. Galvin and Polk (1981) have proposed an agenda for research on parole guidelines, calling for a coherent program of research to accompany the implementation of guidelines.

14. The principle of commensurate deserts states that the severity of the punishment must be commensurate with the severity of the offense. For a full discussion of the concept and a sentencing structure based upon it, see von Hirsch (1974).

15. In a recent study, Martinson and Wilks (1977) examined the arrest, conviction, and reincarceration rates of a "batch" of parolees taken from a survey of criminal justice research reports. The authors examined these three rates within forty-three batches and compared the rates of the parolees against those of offenders who were released directly from imprisonment without parole supervision (i.e., max out). They discovered that, in the overwhelming majority of comparisons, the mean recidivism rate for the parolees was substantially lower than that for the max out group. On this basis, the authors concluded that "The evidence seems to indicate that the abolition of parole supervision would result in substantial increases in arrest, conviction, and return to prison."

16. For a more detailed discussion of sentencing guidelines see Alfred Blumstein, Jacqueline Cohen, Susan Martin, Michael Tonry, eds., *Research on Sentencing: The Search for Reform* (Washington, D.C.: U.S. Department of Justice, 1983).

17. For an excellent review of this discussion see Robert Martinson, Ted Palmer, and Stuart Adams, *Rehabilitation, Recidivism, and Research* (Hackensack, N.J.: National Council on Crime and Delinquency, 1976).

18. Parolees generally view parole officers most favorably when they assist in meeting immediate, concrete needs. Parolees are least appreciative of the "control functions" and parole supervision.

Study Guides

1. Define parole. How does it differ from probation?
2. Describe the parole release process.
3. Distinguish between parole eligibility and granting parole.
4. What are the roles of the parole board?
5. What are the rights of parolees?
6. What are the purposes of parole?
7. Since parole boards are quasi-political entities, what external factors tend to influence their decisions to parole?
8. From the inmate's perspective, how can parole be seen as inequitable?

9. How can parole decision-making procedures be used to benefit the inmate?
10. What is the purpose of shock parole? Do you think that it can be effective as a method for dealing with offenders?
11. What is wrong with traditional parole board discretionary power? How can parole board decision-making guidelines solve these problems?
12. Hoffman has stated (Krajick, 1978: 43) that the parole board decision-making guidelines are "more complex than they appear on the surface. They look just like a tidily packaged chart, but it takes long training and daily experience to use them." In spite of this, consult Figure 6–1 and Figure 6–2 and, acting as a parole board member, reach a decision regarding the following case: Joseph S. is a convicted heroin pusher with a record of three prior convictions. He has served a previous sentence of three years in a maximum security institution. He committed his current offense while on parole. He is an addict himself and has no record of employment. In spite of this, his institutional record is impeccable. He is married and has a young daughter. What is Joe's salient factor score? How much time should he serve for his present offense before he is released on parole?
13. Should parole supervision be abolished? Why or why not?
14. Do you see any problems with the federal parole board decision-making guidelines? How do you feel about the possibility of "false positives"?

Key Terms

continuance

determinate sentencing

eligibility versus release

Gagnon v. Scarpelli

Greenholtz v. Inmates of Nebraska Penal and Correctional Complex

indeterminate sentence

mandatory supervision releases

Morrissey v. Brewer

Mutual Agreement Program (MAP)

parole board

parole contract

parole d'honneur

parole

parolee

parole release plan

recidivism factor

revocation

salient factor scores

shock parole

References

ABADINSKY, HOWARD. *Probation and Parole*. Englewood Cliffs, N.J.: Prentice-Hall, 1977.

ALLEN, HARRY E., AND SEITER, RICHARD. *Community Based Corrections*. New York: Holt, Rinehart and Winston, 1983.

American Correctional Association. *Manual of Correctional Standards*. Rockville, Md., 1971.

BABST, D. V.; INCIARDI, J. A.; AND JAMAN, D. R. *The Uses of Configural Analysis in Parole Prediction Research.* New York: Narcotics Control Commission, 1970.

BALLARD, K. B., AND GOTTFREDSON, D. M. *Predictive Attribute Analysis and Prediction of Parole Performance.* Vacaville, Calif.: Institute for the Study of Crime and Delinquency, December 1963.

BROMLEY, E., AND GATHERCOLE, C. E. "Boolean Prediction Analysis: A New Method of Prediction Index Construction," *British Journal of Criminology* 17 (1969):287–92.

BURGESS, E. W. "Factors Determining Success or Failure on Parole." In *The Workings of the Indeterminate Sentence Law and the Parole System in Illinois,* edited by Bruce Harmo, E. W. Burgess, and C. L. Landeson. Springfield: Illinois State Board of Parole, 1928.

CARLSON, ERIC, AND PARKS, EVALYN. *Contemporary United States Parole Board Practices.* Tuscon: University of Arizona, 1979.

CARNEY, LOUIS. *Probation and Parole: Legal and Social Dimensions.* New York: McGraw-Hill, 1977.

CARROLL, LEO. "Racial Bias in the Decision to Grant Parole," *Law and Society Review* 11 (1976):93–107.

Citizens' Inquiry on Parole and Criminal Justice, Inc. "Parole in Crisis: A Report on New York Parole." In *Corrections in the Community,* edited by G. Killinger and P. F. Cromwell, pp. 297–314. St. Paul, Minn.: West, 1978.

DAWSON, ROBERT O. "The Decision to Grant or Deny Prole: A study of Parole Criteria in Law and Practice," *Washington University Law Quarterly,* June 1966, pp. 248–85.

ESKRIDGE, CHRIS W. "Sentencing Guidelines: To Be or Not to Be?" *The Champion* 9 (1985): 17–24.

EVJEN, VICTOR H. "Current Thinking on Parole Prediction Tables," *Crime and Delinquency* 8 (1962):210–26.

Gagnon v. Scarpelli, 411 U.S. 788 (1972).

GALVIN, JAMES L., AND POLK, KENNETH. "Parole Guidelines: Suggested Research Questions" *Crime and Delinquency* 27 (1981):213–24.

General Accounting Office. *Federal Parole Practices.* Washington, D.C.: GAO, 1982.

GLASER, DANIEL. "Prediction Tables as Accounting Devices for Judges and Parole Boards" *Crime and Delinquency* 8 (1962):239–58.

GOODSTEIN, LYNNE. "Psychological Effects of the Predictability of Prison Release: Implications for the Sentencing Debate," *Criminology* 18 (1980): 363–84.

GOTTFREDSON, D. M., BABST, D. V.; AND BALLARD, K. B. "Comparison of Multiple Regression and Configural Analysis Techniques for Developing Base Expectancy Tables," *Journal of Research in Crime and Delinquency* 5 (1958):72–80.

GOTTFREDSON, DON B.; HOFFMAN, PETER B.; SIGLER, MAURICE H., AND WILKINS, LESLIE. "Making Parole Policy Explicit." In *Criminal Justice Research,* edited by S. M. Talarico, pp. 2–20. Cincinnati, Ohio: Anderson 1980.

GOTTFREDSON, MICHAEL R. "Parole Guidelines and the Reduction of Sentencing Disparity: A Preliminary Study," *Journal of Research in Crime and Delinquency* 16 (1979):218–31.

Greenholtz v. Inmates of the Nebraska Penal and Correction Complex, 442 U.S. 1 (1979).

HAYNER, NORMAN S. "Why Do Parole Boards Lag in the Use of Prediction Scores?" *Pacific Sociological Review* 1 (Fall 1958):70–79.

HOFFMAN, PETER B. "Screening for Risk: A Revised Salient Factor Score (SFS/81)," *Journal of Criminal Justice* 11 (1983):539–47.

HOFFMAN, PETER B., AND ADELBERG, SHELDON. "The Salient Factor Score: A Nontechnical Overview," *Federal Probation* 45 (1980):185–88.

HOFFMAN, PETER B., AND BECK, JAMES L. "Revalidating the Salient Factor Score: A Research Note," *Journal of Criminal Justice* 8 (1980):185–88.

IRWIN, JOHN. "Adaptation to Being Corrected: Corrections from the Convict's Perspective." In *The Sociology of Corrections*, edited by R. G. Leger and J. R. Stratton, pp. 276–300. New York: John Wiley and Sons, 1977.

JOHNSTON, NORMAN, AND SAVITZ, LEONARD, EDS. *Justice and Corrections*. New York: John Wiley and Sons, 1978.

KRAJICK, KEVIN. "Parole—Discretion Is Out, Guidelines Are In," *Corrections Magazine* 4 (December 1978): 39–49.

LAGOY, STEPHEN P.; HUSSEY, FREDERICK A.; AND KRAMER, JOHN H. "A Comparative Assessment of Determinate Sentencing in the Four Pioneer States," *Crime and Delinquency* 24 (1978):385–400.

MACNAMARA, DONAL E. J. "The Medical Model in Corrections: *Requiescat in Pax*," *Criminology* 14 (1977):435–38.

MANHEIM, HERMANN, AND WILKINS, LESLIE T. *Prediction Methods in Relation to Borstal Training*. London: Her Majesty's Stationary Office, 1955.

MARTINSON, ROBERT. "What Works? Questions and Answers About Prison Reform," *Public Interest* 25 (Spring 1974):22–25.

MARTINSON, ROBERT, AND WILKS, JUDITH. "Save Parole Supervision," *Federal Probation* 41 (1977):23–26.

MCCALL, CECIL C. "The Future of Parole—In Rebuttal of S. 1437" *Federal Probation* 42 (1978):3–10.

MITFORD, JESSICA. "Kind and Unusual Punishment in California," *Atlantic Monthly* 227 (March 1971):79–87.

MONAHAN, JOHN. *Predicting Violent Behavior: An Assessment of Clinical Techniques*. Beverly Hills, Calif.: Sage Publications, 1981.

MORRIS, NORVAL. *The Future of Imprisonment*. Chicago: University of Chicago Press, 1974.

Morrissey v. Brewer, 408 U.S. 471 (1972).

National Advisory Commission on Criminal Justice Standards and Goals. *A National Strategy to Reduce Crime*. Washington, D.C.: Government Printing Office, 1973.

National Advisory Committee on Criminal Justice Standards and Goals. *Corrections*. Washington, DC.: U.S. Department of Justice, 1973.

National Council on Crime and Delinquency, Uniform Parole Reports. *Parole in the United States: 1979*, pp. 1–48. Washington, D.C.: Government Printing Office, December 1980.

O'LEARY, V., AND NUFFIELD, J. *The Organization of Parole Systems in the United States*, pp. 1–67. Hackensack, N.J.: National Council of Crime and Delinquency, 1972.

O'LEARY, VINCENT, AND HANRAHAN, KATHLEEN. *Parole Systems in the United States: A Detailed Description of Their Structure and Procedure*, 3rd edition. Hackensack, N.J.: National Council on Crime and Delinquency, 1977.

PORTER, EVERETTE M. "Criteria for Parole Selection." In *Proceedings of the American Correctional Association*, pp. 109–12. New York: American Correctional Association, 1958.

PRASSEL, FRANK. *Introduction to American Criminal Justice*. New York: Harper and Row, 1975.

President's Commission on Law Enforcement and Criminal Justice. *Task Force Report: Corrections*. Washington, D.C.: Government Printing Office, 1967.

The Pretrial Reporter, Vol. 5, No. 2 (April 1981): 3.

PRITCHARD, DAVID A. "Stable Predictors of Recidivism: A Summary." *Criminology* 17 (1979):15–21.

SCOTT, GILBERT. "Probation and Parole Numbers Increasing BJS Study Shows," *Criminal Justice Newsletter* 13 (August 30, 1982):5–6.

SCOTT, JOSEPH. "The Use of Discretion in Determining the Severity of Punishment for Incarcerated Offenders," *Journal of Criminal Law and Criminology* 65 (1974):214–224.

SCOTT, JOSEPH E.; DINITZ, SIMON, AND SHICHOR, DAVID. "Pioneering Innovations in Corrections: Shock Probation and Shock Parole," *Offender Rehabilitation* 3 (1978):113–22.

SIGLER, MAURICE. "Abolish Parole?" In *Corrections in the Community*, edited by G. Killinger and P. R. Cromwell, pp. 325–35. St. Paul, Minn.: West, 1978.

SMYKLA, JOHN O. *Community-Based Corrections: Principles and Practices*. New York: Macmillan, 1981.

———. "Prediction in Probation and Parole: Its Consequences and Implications." Paper presented at the Annual Meeting of the Academy of Criminal Justice Sciences, Chicago, Illinois, 1984.

STANLEY, DAVID T. *Prisoners Among Us: The Problem of Parole*, pp. 34–46. Washington, D.C.: The Brookings Institute, 1976.

STONE-MEIERHOEFER, BARBARA, AND HOFFMAN, PETER B. "The Effects of Presumptive Parole Dates on Institutional Behavior: A Preliminary Assessment," *Journal of Criminal Justice* 10 (1982):283–97.

———. "Presumptive Parole Dates: The Federal Approach," *Federal Probation* 46 (1982):41–50.

STUDT, ELLIOT. "The Reentry of the Offender into the Community." In *Community-Based Corrections: Theory, Practice and Research*, edited by Paul G. Boesen and Stanley E. Grupp. Santa Cruz, Calif.: Davis Publishing Co., 1976.

SUTTON, PAUL L. *Criminal Sentencing in Nebraska: The Feasibility of Empirically Based Guidelines*. Williamsburg, Va.: National Center for State Courts, 1981.

TRAVIS, LAWRENCE F., III, AND LATESSA, EDWARD J. "A Summary of Parole Rules—Thirteen Years Later, Revisited Thirteen Years Later." Paper presented at the Annual Meeting of the Academy of Criminal Justice Sciences, Louisville, Kentucky, March 26, 1982.

TRESTER, HAROLD B. *Supervision of the Offender*. Englewood Cliffs, N.J.: Prentice-Hall, 1981.

TUCKER, JULIE. "Federal News Clips" *On the Line* 5. College Park, Md.: American Correctional Association, September 1982.

VAUGHAN, DIANE. "Shock Probation and Shock Parole: The Impact of Changing Correctional Ideology." In *Corrections: Problems and Prospects*, edited by D. M. Peterson and C. W. Thomas, pp. 216–37. Englewood Cliffs, N.J.: Prentice-Hall, 1980.

VAUGHAN, DIANE; SCOTT, JOSEPH E.; BONDE, ROBERT H.; AND KRAMER, RONALD C. "Shock Parole: A Preliminary Evaluation," *International Journal of Criminology and Penology* 4 (1976):271–84.

VON HIRSCH, ANDREW, AND ALBANESE, JAY S. "Problems with Abolishing Parole Release: The New York Case," *Criminal Law Bulletin* 15 (1979):416–35.

VON HIRSCH, ANDREW, AND HANRAHAN, KATHLEEN J. "Abolish Parole?" In *Corrections: An Issues Approach*, edited by M. D. Schwartz, T. R. Clear, and L. F. Travis, pp. 109–29. Cincinnati, Ohio: Anderson, 1980.

WIGGINS, MICHAEL E. "False Positives/False Negatives: A Utility Cost Analysis of Parole Decision Making." Paper presented at the Annual Meeting of the Academy of Criminal Justice Sciences, Chicago, Illinois, 1984.

WILKINS, L. E., AND MACNAUGHTON-SMITH, P. "New Prediction and Classification Methods in Criminology," *The Journal of Research in Crime and Delinquency* 1 (1964):19–32.

Recommended Readings

Carroll, Leo. "Racial Bias in the Decision to Grant Parole," *Law and Society Review* 11 (1976):93–107. This study focuses upon racial differences and factors related to the parole decision in an eastern state.

Dawson, Robert O. "The Decision to Grant or Deny Parole: A Study of Parole Criteria in Law and Practice," *Washington University Law Quarterly*, June 1900, pp. 248–85. This piece reviews the actual criteria used by parole boards to reach decisions in Kansas, Michigan, and Wisconsin.

Stanley, David T. *Prisoners Among Us: The Problem of Parole* (Washington, D.C.: The Brookings Institute, 1976), pp. 34–46. This piece describes what actually happens in parole board hearings themselves, how decisions are made, and how inmates are notified of those decisions.

Vaughan, Diane; Scott, Joseph E.; Bonde, Robert H.; and Kramer, Ronald C. "Shock Parole: A Preliminary Evaluation," *International Journal of Criminology and Penology* 4 (1976):271–84. The results of this study may be inconclusive, but they also represent the only published data available on shock parole.

7

Roles of Probation and Parole Officers

. . . a parole officer can be seen going off to his/her appointed rounds with Freud in one hand and a .38 Smith and Wesson in the other hand. It is by no means clear that Freud is as helpful as the .38 in most areas where parole officers venture. . . . Is Freud backup to the .38? Or is the .38 carried to support Freud?

—David Fogel

As Fogel (McCleary, 1978: 10–11) succinctly indicates, the role of the probation or parole officer (PO)[1] has traditionally been viewed as a dichotomy. The supervision role involves both maintaining *surveillance* (societal protection) over as well as *helping* or treating the offender (counseling, rehabilitation, reintegration). The PO is often left to his or her own devices with regard to which role would be most appropriate. This dilemma is likely to remain with us at least through this decade even though calls from several quarters of the criminal justice system point toward coming changes in the role of the PO. This chapter describes and outlines the boundaries of this role conflict as it has developed over time, the problems associated with it, and some of the proposed changes in the area.

Responsibilities of Probation and Parole Agencies

To begin, it is necessary to examine what duties and responsibilities are held in common by probation and parole agencies. O'Leary (1974) has argued that parole resembles probation in several ways. With both, information is gathered and presented to a decision-making authority (either a judge or a parole board). This authority has the power to release (parole) or suspend the sentence (probation) of the offender. In turn, the liberty that the offender enjoys is subject to certain conditions which are imposed by the decision-making authority. If these conditions are not obeyed, the offender may be sentenced, or returned, to prison.

On the other hand, parole differs from probation in distinct ways. The offender on parole has served a portion of his or her sentence in a correctional facility. The decision to release the offender from prison is an administrative one, made by the parole board. The decision to grant probation lies entirely with the court. As Wallace (1974: 950) has written, "Probation is more than a process; it connotes an organization, basically a service agency, designed to assist the court and to perform particular functions in the administration of criminal justice."

Despite these differences, probation and parole agencies share one particular and significant function: They provide supervision of offenders in the community. The basic question remains: What is the purpose of supervision? To Wallace, the function of supervision, drawn from the social work field, is based upon the casework model. Supervision is the basis of a treatment program. The PO uses all the information available about the offender to make a diagnosis of that person's needs and to design a treatment plan. One example of a treatment plan for probationers, emphasizing the need for reintegration, was suggested by the President's Task Force on Corrections (1967: 30):

> . . . developing the offender's effective participation in the major social institutions of the school, business and the church . . . which offer access to a successful career.

Yet, providing treatment is only one aspect of supervision. In addition, the PO is expected to maintain surveillance of those offenders who make up the caseload.

A classic definition of surveillance was provided by the National Conference on Parole (Studt, 1978: 65):

> Surveillance is that activity of the parole officer which utilizes watchfulness, checking, and verification of certain behavior of a parolee without contributing to a helping relationship with him.

Although these statements indicate that the treatment and surveillance roles of the PO are almost diametrically opposed, several authors have indicated that they coexist as a part of the agency's mission. Some authors—such as Glaser (1969), McCleary (1978), and Studt (1978)—have noted that the PO has two missions: to rehabilitate the offenders who are amenable to treatment, while simultaneously protecting society from those who prove to be dangerous.

In his study of parole officers at work, McCleary (1978: 112) discovered that POs typically reviewed their caseload to identify the presence of "dangerous men." This term stereotypically refers to the offender who does not demonstrate willingness to accept the PO as a therapist. The dangerous man does not respond in a rational manner to the threats or promises made by the PO. It is this responsibility that leads the PO to label him or her dangerous and, as such, a prime candidate for surveillance.

Despite this evidence, other scholars have suggested that POs perceive their roles in different ways because of their particular view of the job as well as the appropriate role that they perceive they should follow. From this perspective, it is the PO's perception of the purpose of supervision that determines which of the two goals is most appropriate in a given client's case.

Role Typologies

In one of the first studies of types of officers, Ohlin and his associates (1956: 211–25) developed the following typology of PO styles:

> 1. The *punitive* officer, who perceives himself as the guardian of middle-class morality; he attempts to coerce the offender into conforming by means of threats and punishment, and emphasizes control, the protection of the community against the offender, and the systematic suspicion of those under supervision.
>
> 2. The *protective* officer, who vacillates literally between protecting the offender and protecting the community. His tools are direct assistance, lecturing, and, alternately, praise and blame. He is perceived as ambivalent in his emotional involvement with the offender and others in the community as he shifts back and forth in taking sides with one against the other.
>
> 3. The *welfare* officer, who has as his ultimate goal the improved welfare of the client, achieved by aiding him in his individual adjustment within limits imposed by the client's capacity. Such an officer believes that the only genuine guarantee of community protection lies in the client's personal adjustment, since external conformity will only be temporary and, in the long run, may make a successful adjustment more difficult. Emotional neutrality permeates his relationships. The diagnostic categories and treatment skills which he employs stem from an objective and theoretically based assessment of the client's needs and capacities.

Glaser (1969: 293) later extended this typology to include, as a fourth category, the *passive* officer, who sees his job as a sinecure requiring only minimum effort. For example, Erickson (1977: 37) has satirically offered the following gambit to officers who wish to "fake it" and have an "ideal, trouble-free caseload":

> "I'm just so busy—never seem to have enough time." A truly professional execution of this ploy does require some preparation. Make sure that your desktop is always inundated with a potpourri of case files, messages, memos, unopened mail, and professional literature. . . . Have your secretary hold all your calls for a few days and schedule several appointments for the same time. When, after a lengthy wait, the probationer is finally ushered into your presence, impress him (or her) with the volume of your business. . . . Always write while conversing with the subject, and continue to make and receive telephone calls. Interrupt your dialogue with him to attend to other important matters, such as obtaining the daily grocery list from your wife or arranging to have your car waxed. Apologize repeatedly and profusely for these necessary interruptions and appear to be distracted, weary, and slightly insane. Having experienced the full treatment, it is unlikely that the probationer will subsequently try to discuss with you any matters of overwhelming concern. He could even feel sorrier for you than he does for himself. You should henceforth be able to deal with him on an impersonal basis, if indeed he tries to report anymore at all.

The complete typology is presented in tabular form in Figure 7–1. The key distinction in this figure is the manner in which the PO personally views the purpose of the job of supervision. Personal preference and motivations of the PO will often determine the style of supervision that is followed.

A similar typology was developed by Klockars (1972: 550–52), based on the working philosophy of the PO. The first style that he presented is that of the "law enforcer." Such officers are primarily motivated by: (1)

Figure 7–1   Typology of PO Supervision Styles

Emphasis on Control

		High	Low
Emphasis on Assistance	High	Protective Officer	Welfare Officer
	Low	Punitive Officer	Passive Officer

SOURCE: Frank C. Jordan and Joseph M. Sasfy, *National Impact Program Evaluation: A Review of Selected Issues and Research Findings Related to Probation and Parole*, p. 29. Washington, D.C.: Mitre Corporation, 1974.

the court order and obtaining offender compliance with it, (2) the authority and decision-making power of the PO, (3) officer responsibility for public safety, and (4) police work—the PO as police officer of the agency.

The second category is that of the "time server." This individual feels that the job has certain requirements to be fulfilled until retirement—"I don't make the rules; I just work here." The third type is the "therapeutic agent," a PO who accepts the role of administrator of a form of treatment (usually casework oriented) to help the offender. Finally, the "synthetic officer" attempts to blend treatment and law enforcement components by "combining the paternal, authoritarian, and judgmental with the therapeutic." The synthetic officer attempts to solve what Miles (1965a) terms the "probation officer's dilemma" by balancing the administration of criminal justice (offender is wrong but responsible for own behavior) with treatment (casework, offender is sick) goals. In sum, Klockar's typology rounds out the original scheme developed by Ohlin by providing an example through which the PO can integrate the best of each possible role.

Czajkoski (1973) expanded on the law enforcement role of the officer's job by outlining the quasi-judicial role of the probation officer. He develops his thesis on five lines of functional analysis. The first line examines the *plea bargain*. Since the decision to grant probation is largely determined by plea bargaining, Czajkoski cites Blumberg's (1974) argument that the probation officer serves to "cool the mark" in the confidence game of plea bargaining by assuring the defendant of how wise it was to plead guilty. In this fashion, the PO certifies the plea bargaining process—a task that can significantly undermine the helping/counseling role of the PO.

The second line of quasi-judicial functioning by the PO occurs at the *intake* level. For example, at the juvenile level, the PO is often asked which cases are appropriate for judicial processing. Like the prosecutor, this function permits the probation officer to have some control over the intake of the court.

The third quasi-judicial function of the probation officer concerns setting the *conditions* of probation, a power the judge often gives the probation officer. This often leads to discretionary abuses, since indefinite conditions (often moralistic or vague in terms of offender's *behavior*) can become a vehicle for maintaining the moral status quo as interpreted by the probation officer. In addition, probation conditions can become substitutions for, or even usurp, certain formal judicial processes. For example, the monetary obligations of the probationer (such as supporting dependents) can be enforced by the probation officer, rather than by a court that is specifically designed to handle such matters (see Schneider et al., 1982).

The fourth quasi-judicial role is concerned with probation *violation* procedures. Czajkoski contends that such procedures are highly discretionary, especially in view of the vague and all-encompassing nature of the probation conditions, which are usually not enforced until the officer has reason to believe that the probationer is engaged in criminal activity.

The final quasi-judicial role of the probation officer concerns the ability to administer *punishment*. Since the officer may restrict the liberty of his or her charge in several ways, this is tantamount to punishment. In this fashion, Czajkoski highlights some of the actions officers take that relate to his or her function as a quasi-judicial official, and illustrates more ways in which the PO uses discretionary power in judicial-like ways.

Tomaino (1975) also attempts to reveal some of the hidden functions of probation officers. Figure 7–2 summarizes the Tomaino typology. Once again, concern for control is contrasted with concern for rehabilitation. To Tomaino, the key probation officer role is the "Have It Make Sense" face. This role attempts to integrate the often-conflicting concerns of societal protection and offender rehabilitation. Accordingly, Tomaino recommends that the officer stress goals, not offender personality traits, to ". . . organize legitimate choices through a collaborative relationship which induces the client to act in accord with presocial expectations." Perhaps, as Linden (1975) suggests, the probation officer can create a learning situation for the offender and induce a desire for change.

A different but related role for the probation officer is also presented by Arcaya (1973), who stresses the counseling aspect of probation. Arcaya recommends that the officer adopt a "dwelling presence" in which he or she openly accepts the ambiguity of feelings and responsibilities attached to probation work and uses it to develop an awareness of the officer's own humanity within the client. To accomplish this objective, the officer should blend "active listening" (putting aside all preconceptions and thus permitting the probationer to define himself) and "responsive talking" (a dialogue with the probationer to conceptualize and situate the offender's world in the knowledge that the client can serve as his or her own best advisor). In this fashion, the officer can develop a style of emphathetic understanding that goes beyond any original preconceptions of the offender's background, crime, or even social status.

Unlike the previous authors, Smith and Berlin (1974) consider the role of probationer as an involuntary client. They feel the probationer qualifies as an involuntary client because of the "degree of injury to self resulting from disregarding the conditions established by the agency." In view of this occurrence, Smith and Berlin suggest that the probation officer adopt the role of "community resource agent" to bring the offender into contact with the agency and community resources designed to satisfy those needs.

In sum, these authors indicate that the PO has a range of choices concerning the style of supervision to be followed and the ultimate goal of the entire probation/parole process. There is a strong emphasis here upon blending the need for control with the need for counseling. The PO must choose which style to adopt based upon the individual client (severity of the offense, amenability to treatment) and the nature of the situation. POs clearly have the discretionary power to either enforce the law (i.e., condi-

Figure 7-2   The Five Faces of Probation Supervision

Concern for Rehabilitation (vertical axis, 1–9)
Concern for Control (horizontal axis, 1–9)

The 1/9 Face
Help-Him-Understand

Probationers will want to keep the rules once they get insight about themselves. The PO should be supportive, warm and nonjudgmental in his relations with them.

The 9/9 Face
Have-It-Make-Sense

Probationers will keep the rules when it is credible to do so because this meets their needs better. The PO should be open but firm, and focus on the content of his relations with probationers.

The 5/5 Face
Let-Him-Identify

Probationers will keep the rules if they like their PO and identify with him and his values. The PO must work out solid compromises in his relations with the probationers.

The 1/1 Face
It's-Up-To-Him

Probationers should know exactly what they have to do, what happens if they don't do it, and it is up to them to perform.

The 9/1 Face
Make-Him-Do-It

Probationers will keep the rules only if you take a hard line, exert very close supervision, and stay completely objective in your relations with them.

Source: Louis Tomaino, "The Five Faces of Probation," *Federal Probation* 39 (1975):43.

tions of supervision) or offer help and treatment. No doubt, the world view of the PO also plays a crucial role in this decision.

Self-Images of the PO

How do probation and parole officers see themselves and their work? The following studies focused upon agents to secure their views concerning what the appropriate goals of supervision should be and, within the criminal justice system, where such agents primarily identify with their allegiance.

In an early study, Miles (1965b) surveyed all 116 probation and parole officers on duty in Wisconsin on a single day. In addition, forty-eight officers were interviewed and accompanied into the field by the researchers. On the basis of these data, Miles discovered that a majority of these officers basically identified with the field of corrections (61.5 percent). The clear majority of individuals identified themselves as probation officers when dealing with judges (81 percent), social agencies (69 percent), and potential client employers (79 percent). These officers emphasized their identification with correctional work and did not wish to have this primary link absorbed by another area (for example, social work).

The survey also uncovered what is considered to be the basic dilemma of probation in terms of its primary goal: offender rehabilitation versus societal protection. Apparently, experience plays the key role in the officer's resolution of this problem. The experienced officer cited societal protection as the primary responsibility, while seeking to maximize the client's potentialities in a nontherapeutic manner. On the other hand, the inexperienced officer is more concerned with the therapeutic function. It appears that this dilemma may be resolved with the passage of time, by the novice officers either resigning their positions in frustration, or adjusting their conceptions to meet those of the more experienced majority. Miles concluded that, until legislatures of the various states provide precise definitions of the functions of probation and parole officers, the dilemma of what is the fundamental goal will not be resolved.

In a similar study, Sigler and Benzanson (1970) conducted a survey of a random sample of New Jersey probation officers in an attempt to learn about their role perceptions. The authors randomly selected 130 of the 522 probation officers serving the New Jersey's twenty-one counties and achieved a response rate of 55.4 percent. As Table 7–1 illustrates, in every situation, the probation officer asserted his or her desire to be identified with the field of probation. The clear implication from this survey is that probation officers believe that probation is a separate profession and should not be confused or identified with other criminal justice agencies or functions.

Table 7–1
Preferences for Identification Among Probation Officers

Situation	Percentage Citing "Probation Officer"
1. Preference for identification by judges	79
2. Self-identification	66
3. To employers of probationers	76
4. Description of their professional activities to community leaders (correctional work)	35
5. To friends	62
6. To police (representative of the probation department)	85

Source: Adapted from Jay A. Sigler and Thomas E. Benzanson, "Role Perceptions Among New Jersey Probation Officers," *Rutgers Camden Law Journal* 2 (1970):256–60.

In a similar study, von Laningham, Taber, and Dimants (1966) sent questionnaires to 417 adult probation officers in selected probation services across various regions, levels of urbanization, and levels of education, and received a response rate of 85.1 percent. The subjects were asked to rate the appropriateness of fifty-two tasks performed by probation officers. As a result, seven categories were ranked by the respondents according to their perceived degree of conformity to the proper role of the PO (von Laningham et al., 1966: 101–104.

1. *Referral Function.* Probation officer refers his or her client to other community resources for help or assistance.

2. *Advice and Guidance.* Providing fairly direct advice or guidance for day-to-day living.

3. *Court Consultant.* A well-established role in which the probation officer interprets for the court the social and personal factors of the client for decision-making purposes.

4. *Psychotherapy.* Utilizes the techniques based largely upon psychological orientation and is concerned with deep-seated emotional problems. Only agreed upon for use with the "unduly suspicious," "reckless risk-taking," or alcoholic probationer.

5. *Law Enforcement.* Detecting and apprehending violators. Only considered appropriate for two examples—checking to see if an alcoholic probationer is attending AA or if a probationer has made court appearances without your knowledge.

6. *Environmental Manipulation.* Attempt to directly influence the persons and organizations important in the probationer's adjustment. In this case, only one example was considered appropriate—speaking to a loan company on a probationer's behalf.

7. *Conduct Establishment and Enforcement.* The use of the officer's authority to attempt to coerce the probationer into behaving in accordance with the prevailing moral system of the community as perceived by the officer.

These ratings give some indication of the functions of the probation officer considered most proper by practitioners in the field. The ranking order evident in this study, particularly the importance placed on the referral and guidance functions, is significant, and may reflect the large number of college-educated probation officers in this sample.

Similarly, Dembo (1972) tested three dimensions of parole officer orientation by surveying ninety-four New York State parole officers with between four and five years of on-the-job experience. The three dimensions were (1972: 194–96):

1. *Conception of the Parolee.* The divergent ways that officers see their clients . . . viewing the parolee as essentially *anti-social* . . . or as an *individual* in a positive sense.

2. *View of Parole Purpose.* The distinction between police and social work approaches to deviant behavior

3. *Belief in Method of Law Enforcement.* The use of parole rules to deter crime and literal enforcement of their intent imply a punitive orientation toward the parolee.

The results revealed the presence of two distinct groups of parole officers with regard to their belief in the efficacy of reintegration. The parole officers who had high reintegration scores were liberal, either preferred to supervise difficult cases or had no preferences as to type of client, and did not prefer the use of control on clients. On the other hand, officers who had low reintegration scores tended to be conservative; preferred to handle low-risk cases; were dissatisfied with the political factors of the job, the long hours, and the constant crisis situations encountered in their work; and possessed high control attitudes. Dembo's study indicates, once again, that the role assumed by the PO and the underlying view of the proper function of supervision are related to the personal attitudes and beliefs of the officers themselves.

To test their view of the officer-client relationship, Studt (1978) interviewed 11 agents and 125 parolees in order to examine the interaction between the purpose of supervision as viewed by the client, as well as the officer. She focused on three dimensions of the client's experience: (1) the kinds of help provided by the agent, (2) the usefulness of supervision to the parolee, and (3) the kinds of events that cause "trouble" and may terminate parole for the parolee.

On the first measure, type of help provided, Studt (1978: 169) discovered that the more practical and specific the agent's action (i.e., helping the parolee find a job), the more likely this action would be remembered by the client as helpful. Conversely, the more the officer directs his efforts toward what the client considers a "personal affair" (i.e., "managing their social life"), the more probable the client will remember this action as help given but the less likely he or she will remember it as help received. It would seem that these parolees favor a less intrusive form of supervision based on the treatment rather than the surveillance model.

With regard to the usefulness of the parole period, Studt (1978: 173) discovered that parolees were not hesitant to admit that the experience had been useful in several ways. Specifically, the parolees felt that the agents were most useful when they needed someone "higher up to go to bat for them" and to "kick around pros and cons when making decisions." The officers' responses on this point were also supportive of the treatment model. They felt that they were most useful when they "kept him working steadily" or when the parolee "needed help with personal problems."

As one would expect, the officer and client perceptions of the disadvantages of parole differed sharply. Parolees clearly felt that the personal problems for which they needed help were a direct result of the fact that they were on parole. On the other hand, officers were apt to state that the parolee was better off than persons with similar problems because the agent was there to help, or that client complaints were excuses and rationalizations for their own inadequacies.

Studt also encountered vast differences between the officer and client perceptions of what constitutes "trouble" on parole. The officers were likely to make a causal connection between living conventionally (i.e., middle-class life-style) and the ability to avoid crime.[2] Parolees tended to think of "success" on parole as simply "not committing crime." It is clear that the parolees were voicing their objections to the *technical* conditions of parole, the violation of which could result in a prison term, and which typically are aimed at the urban, lower-class life-style.

In sum, Studt found that parolees view their officers as helpful when they contribute to their survival in the community, but they do not accept either the officer's responsibility for supervising their personal life-styles or the relevance of what they felt were overly intrusive conditions of parole.

Overall, the studies examined reveal that POs are aware of the surveillance/treatment dichotomy that exists with regard to style of supervision. A number of factors (age, education, years of job experience) are related to or influence the PO's style and method of supervision. Yet, in general, there is a distinct lack of consensus over which style of supervision should dominate.

Policy Implications and Management Concerns

For these reasons, the POs, their respective agencies, and their clients must deal with the consequences of role confusion. The split between treatment and surveillance has attracted a great deal of attention as changes in sentencing statutes (toward determinate or fixed sentences) and the general shift to the political right in the criminal justice system affect the roles and purposes of the PO.

The absence of a distinct and defined purpose has definite consequences for an organization. A typology of bureaucratic organizations developed by Blau and Scott (1962) serves to illustrate the difficulties that could result in role confusion. The basics of this typology are presented in Table 7–2. The key to this typology is the "prime beneficiary" of the organization. Put simply, the prime beneficiary is the person who benefits most from the operations of the agency. The key question is: Where do probation and parole agencies fit in? Clearly, the choice is between the Service and Commonwealth organizations. This choice again illustrates the persistent dichotomy between providing treatment (service to clients) and surveillance (protection of the public). For this reason, probation/parole agencies are classic examples of agencies that have "dual beneficiaries." This split becomes a source of conflict and concern to the organization that must decide which should be the primary and which should be the second-

Table 7-2
Blau and Scott Typology: Who Benefits?

Type of Organization	Prime Beneficiary	Basic Problem
Mutual benefit	Rank and file members	Internal democratic control
Business concern	Owners and managers	Efficiency of operations
Service	Clients	Professional service to client
Commonwealth	Public at large	External democratic control

Source: Adapted from Peter Blau and W. Richard Scott, *Formal Organizations: A Comparative Approach*, pp. 40–57. San Francisco: Chandler, 1962.

ary choice. Should these agencies serve the public, or should they attempt to provide for and protect the interests of their clients?

Several authors have addressed the consequences of this dilemma with regard to parole and probation. Blumberg (1974: 154–58) has written that probation officers suffer from "civil service malaise" due to their lack of genuine professional status in the court organization. He also argues that probation officers have no "service ideal" because their primary allegiance is to the organization rather than their clients. Studt (1978: 189–90) concludes that the community will not provide the agency with the resources necessary to reintegrate offenders; that the agency's technology will emphasize surveillance to alert the community to dangerous persons; and that the officers will focus on the nature of the life-style of their clientele. In addition, this problem will lead clients to be selective about the kinds of help they might seek from the agency and to view the agency's offer of help as hypocritical.

Can this dilemma be resolved? Several potential solutions have been offered from various quarters. Fogel and Thompson ("Swing," 1981: 34) have suggested that Fogel's "justice model" (1975) might be applied to probation:

> The probation officer is neither a cop nor a counselor; he/she is an officer of the court. As such, he/she is responsible for monitoring compliance with the demands of justice . . . [and] ensuring that the essence of probation is carried out.

They recommend that the officer should adopt a "compliance orientation," strictly carrying out the sanctions imposed by the court. A contract should be developed among the court, the probation officer, and the client "so that all parties know exactly what to expect and have some recourse if the rights and obligations specified in the sentence fail to be carried out."

Not all persons associated with probation, however, agree with this contention. The California Probation, Parole and Correctional Association ("Swing," 1981: 34) has stated:

> Decisions constantly must be made between the relative risk of law violation at the present time and the probable long-term gain if a probationer is to be allowed the opportunity to develop an improved life-style. The role of the probation officer is complicated by his dual orientation . . . yet he must resist being stereotyped as a member of either camp if he is to be effective in planting the seeds of change.

Here the treatment-surveillance dichotomy is viewed as a strength, rather than a weakness.

In California, where the determinate sentence has been in force since 1977, Gettinger (1981: 34–35) reports that a "new model" of parole supervision has been developed. This model is characterized by:

1. The use of Risk Assessment Scale to assign parolees to different types of supervision. A needs score is also assigned.
2. Different types of supervision. Any parolee with a score of 7.5 or above is considered a "control" case. A parolee with a score of 5 to 7.5 is also a control case, unless his or her needs are above 7.5, in which case it will be handled as a service case.
3. Minimum supervision. Any case that scores below 3.75 on both risks and needs is put into a separate caseload with few reports required and services provided only upon request.
4. Specializaton of parole agents by style of supervision. "Control" agents are forbidden to handle problems outside of their specialities.
5. Specific direction by supervisors. They tell a parole agent exactly what actions to take on each case and how many hours per month they are to devote to it.

This method of supervision constitutes an attempt to balance the conflicting needs of treatment and surveillance. It also represents an effort to maintain some aspect of parole supervision under a determinate sentencing structure with an emphasis upon control and maintaining societal protection.[3]

Again, some authors have disagreed with this new development. A foremost opponent is Conrad (1979: 21), who has written:

> We can hardly justify parole services on the basis of the surveillance model. What the parole officer can do, if it should be done at all, can better be done by the police. The pushing of doorbells, the recording of "contacts," and the requirement of monthly reports all add up to expensive pseudoservices. At best, they constitute a costly but useless frenzy of activity. But more often than not, I suspect, they harass and humiliate the parolee without gaining even the illusion of control.

Summary

It is probable that the treatment-surveillance dichotomy will remain with us forever. Recent developments suggest that surveillance is likely to become the primary emphasis—especially for clients who constitute a demonstrable risk to society. Here, conclusions made recently by Marshall and Vito (1982: 37) are particularly relevant:

> . . .It is the manifest duty of the probation officer to keep the court aware of the conduct of the probationer. Here, the official charge to the officer and the directive to the client is most clear: Maintain or abide by the conditions of probation or face the consequences (i.e., violation and incarceration). The argument can be made that the protection of society was always paramount; the helping or treatment role was always secondary.

In short, the conflict between counseling and surveillance is simply part of the job of the PO and a duality that makes their positions in the criminal justice system vital, unique, and necessary.

Notes

1. Throughout this chapter, when the abbreviation PO is utilized, it is meant to designate both probation and parole officers. Their views with regard to their role as well as the dilemmas that they face are so intimately related that this abbreviation will not misrepresent the opinions, findings, and conclusions of the various authors.

2. Blumberg (1974: 159) also spoke to this tendency of the PO. Blumberg feels that supervision provides an "unanticipated job bonus"—experiencing the life of the client vicariously, which is often "a stark, heady contrast to the conventional and pedestrian style of life of the minor civil servant."

3. In their study of 49 career criminals convicted of armed robbery, Petersilia, Greenwood, and Lavin (1977: 49–51) discovered that these offenders were not prevented from engaging in criminal activity through the strict monitoring by their parole officers. This response could be considered as evidence that an increase in the level of surveillance by parole officers, even with "high risk" cases, may not achieve the desired effect.

Study Guides

1. How should the treatment-surveillance dichotomy be handled? Should the PO emphasize one method of supervision over the other?

2. Which of the role typologies would you follow if you were a PO? Give the reasons for your selection.

3. How are the duties and responsibilities of probation and parole agencies alike? Different?
4. What would be the characteristics of a "good" PO? Of the "worst" PO?
5. What are the quasi-judicial roles of the PO?
6. Contrast liberal, reintegrative POs with their conservative, low-reintegrative counterparts.

Key Terms

civil service malaise	passive officer
client surveillance	prime beneficiary
compliance orientation	protective officer
dangerous men	punitive officer
five faces of probation	synthetic officer
new model	welfare officer

References

ARCAYA, JOSE. "The Multiple Realities Inherent in Probation Counseling," *Federal Probation* 37 (1973):58–63.

BLAU, PETER, and SCOTT, RICHARD W. *Formal Organizations: A Comparative Approach.* San Francisco: Chandler, 1962.

BLUMBERG, ABRAHAM S. *Criminal Justice.* New York: New Viewpoints, 1974.

CONRAD, JOHN. "Who Needs a Door Bell Pusher?," *The Prison Journal* 59 (1979):17–26.

CZAJKOSKI, EUGENE H. "Exposing the Quasi-Judicial Role of the Probation Officer," *Federal Probation* 37 (1973):9–13.

DEMBO, RICHARD. "Orientation and Activities of the Parole Officer," *Criminology* 10 (1972):193–215.

ERICKSON, CHARLES L. "Faking It: Principles of Expediency as Applied to Probation," *Federal Probation* 41 (1977):36–39.

FARE, K. F., and DWOSKIN, S. I. "Managing Probation Programs in an Era of Diminishing Resources," *Corrections Today* 44 (1982):68–70.

FOGEL, DAVID. *We Are the Living Proof . . .* Cincinnati, Ohio: W. H. Anderson, 1975.

GETTINGER, STEPHEN. "Separating the Cop from the Counselor," *Corrections Magazine* 7 (June 1981):34–41.

GLASER, DANIEL. *The Effectiveness of a Prison and Parole System.* Indianapolis, Ind.: Bobbs-Merrill, 1969.

HALL, PAUL, and SMITH, ROBERT. "Development of the Probation Counseling Relationship Scale," *Journal of Offender Rehabilitation* 2 (1981):20–32.

HARDEMAN, DALE G. "The Function of the Probation Officer," *Federal Probation* 24 (1960):3–8.

JORDAN, FRANK C., and SASFY, JOSEPH H. *National Impact Program Evaluation: A Review of Selected Issues and Research Findings Related to Probation and Parole.* Washington, D.C.: Mitre Corporation, 1974.

KLOCKARS, CARL B. "A Theory of Probation Supervision," *Journal of Criminal Law, Criminology and Police Science* 63 (1972):550–57.

LINDEN, JACK. "The Future of Probation: A Field Officer's View," *Federal Probation* 39 (1975):22–28.

MARSHALL, FRANKLIN H., and VITO, GENNARO F. "Not Without the Tools: The Task of Probation in the Eighties," *Federal Probation* 46 (1982):37–40.

McCLEARY, RICHARD. *Dangerous Men: The Sociology of Parole.* Beverly Hills, Calif.: Sage Publications, 1978.

MILES, ARTHUR P. "The Reality of the Probation Officer's Dilemma," *Federal Probation* 29 (1965a):18–22.

_____. "Wisconsin Studies the Function of Probation and Parole," *American Journal of Corrections* 27 (1965b):21–32.

OHLIN, LLOYD E.; PIVEN, HERMAN; and PAPPENFORT, D. M. "Major Dilemmas of the Social Worker in Probation and Parole," *National Probation and Parole Association Journal* 2 (1956):21–25.

O'LEARY, VINCENT. "Parole Administration." In *Handbook of Criminology* edited by Daniel Glaser, pp. 909–48. New York: Rand McNally, 1974.

PETERSILIA, JOAN; GREENWOOD, PETER; and LAVIN, MARVIN. *Criminal Careers of Habitual Felons.* Santa Monica, Calif.: Rand Corporation, 1977.

President's Commission on Law Enforcement and Administration of Justice. *Task Force Report: Corrections.* Washington, D.C.: Government Printing Office, 1967.

SCHNEIDER, P. R.; GRIFFITH, W. R.; and SCHNEIDER, A. L. "Juvenile Restitution as a Sole Sanction or Condition of Probation: An Empirical Analysis," *Journal of Research in Crime and Delinquency* 19 (1982):47–65.

SIGLER, JAY A., and BENZANSON, THOMAS E. "Role Perceptions Among New Jersey Probation Officers," *Rutgers Camden Law Journal* 2 (1970):256–60.

SMITH, ALEXANDER B., and BERLIN, LOUIS. "Self Determination in Welfare and Corrections: Is There a Limit," *Federal Probation* 38 (1974):3–6.

STUDT, ELLIOT. *Surveillance and Service in Parole.* U.S. Department of Justice: National Institute of Corrections, 1978.

"A Swing to the Right?," *Corrections Magazine* 7 (March 1981):34.

TOMAINO, LOUIS. "The Five Faces of Probation," *Federal Probation* 39 (1975): 41–46.

VON LANINGHAM, DALE E.; TAUBER, MERLIN; and DIMANTS, RUTA. "How Adult Probation Officers View Their Responsibility," *Crime and Delinquency* 12 (1966):97–104.

WALLACE, JOHN A. "Probation Administration." In *Handbook of Criminology*, edited by Daniel Glaser, pp. 949–69. New York: Rand McNally, 1974.

Recommended Readings

Conrad, John. "Who Needs a Door Bell Pusher?" *The Prison Journal* 59 (1979):17–26. Building upon his experience as a PO, a noted scholar gives his strong opinions on the proper role of supervision.

McCleary, Richard. *Dangerous Men: The Sociology of Parole* (Beverly Hills, Calif.: Sage Publications, 1978). Based upon participant observation, this is an in-depth examination of a parole agency and the supervision styles of its officers.

Studt, Elliot. *Surveillance and Service in Parole* (U.S. Department of Justice: National Institute of Corrections, 1978). Intensive interviewing was utilized in this study, which reveals the roles of the parole officer and parolee and how they interact in the supervision process.

8

The Education and Training of Probation and Parole Officers

During the past fifteen years, several national commissions and studies have recommended formal education as a means of significantly improving the delivery of justice in this country (President's Commission, 1967; American Bar Association, 1970; National Advisory Commission, 1973a; National Manpower Survey, 1978; Sherman et al., 1978). Graduate level education and frequent in-service training for probation and parole officers have also been advocated for many years. The emerging philosophy now requires undergraduate degree education as a prerequisite for quality probation and parole service, and continuous in-service training as a means of maintaining and improving both service and skills (President's Commission, 1967; Loughery, 1975; National Advisory Commission, 1973b; Senna, 1976).

The Issues

Since 1959, the National Probation and Parole Association has recommended that all probation and parole officers should hold at least a bachelor's degree supplemented by at least one year of graduate study or full-time field experience. This recommendation reflects the assumption that

144

an educated officer is more competent and mature and thus in a better position to efficiently perform the varied functions of probation and parole. However, it was not until the 1967 President's Commission on Law Enforcement and Administration of Justice Task Force Report, which led to the Law Enforcement Education Program, that federal funds were made available for higher education of justice system personnel, including a college education for probation and parole officers. In 1970, the American Bar Association (1970: 92) reaffirmed the National Probation and Parole Association's minimum standards, and suggested that probation and parole officers should hold a master's degree. The American Bar Association also noted that, while few departments have achieved this standard, many have nonetheless encouraged their personnel to become increasingly involved in pursuing higher education.

There are a number of arguments for requiring probation and parole officers to have a formal, post–high school education. Comanor (1968: 44) has suggested that the philosophy of professional education as a *necessary* preparation for entry into such a position has several practical advantages for field supervision agencies: They are:

1. Responsibility for basic preparation for the field is assumed by the student, in an educational institution. This represents a large-scale investment of time, money, and educational skill that will not be required of the employing organization;
2. The graduate degree is a positive indicator of the suitability of the new employee for the position, reducing loss of organizational efficiency through errors of recruitment and slowness in assuming a full workload;
3. It reduces the scope of training for which the organization and field must take responsibility, permitting focus on advanced work and innovation, instead of directing efforts to elementary knowledge;
4. A common base of knowledge is assured, enhancing internal communication and cooperation, and facilitating interaction and influence with other fields and organizations;
5. The professional perspective—i.e., the profession's social accountability and the learning of contemporary concepts at the graduate level—protects against organization introversions and intellectual isolation.

Unfortunately, Comanor did not provide empirical data to support these points, nor did he make an attempt to ascertain the exact nature and extent of the education that would lead to the greatest benefit for the probation or parole systems. The literature in the field is replete with sometimes contradictory educational curriculum proposals or models. Each model seems to have raised a series of personnel and operational issues as various departments have sought to adhere to one or another form of the proposed standards for preservice educational and in-service training and education programs.

A lengthy debate has surfaced in the past years as to the differences, roles, and functions of education versus training, not only in the general field of criminal justice, but particularly in probation and parole. Criminal justice education has evolved to the point where it now possesses a dual role: description and policy. Lower-level undergraduate courses focus on the structures and processes of the justice system, while upper-level courses generally adopt a public policy and "cause and consequence" perspective and stress a critical view of justice system operations, problems, and potential solutions. Inherent in this dual role is education's responsibility to critique and challenge in order to facilitate change, all the while knowing that there are few (if any) definitive answers but, rather, many potential solutions, each of which has costs and benefits. Formal education, in sum, seeks to create an attitude of inquiry and to develop abilities necessary to facilitate that inquiry.

Training, on the other hand, involves a one-way transfer of knowledge, usually in the form of specific skills, facts, and procedures to be learned by the trainees. Furthermore, training in a criminal justice context usually implies a practical or a "nuts and bolts" curriculum, such as workshops in the appropriate use of force, emerging rights of offenders, arrest techniques, interrogation procedures, preparing a presentence report, crisis intervention techniques, and the use of firearms. While educational curricula seek to ask and answer questions, training programs attempt to solve immediate problems.

While both education and training are needed, the National Advisory Commission (1973a: 170) clearly states that care must be taken to separate the academic nature of the college criminal justice curriculum from training content. However, as Sherman et al. (1978) later noted, there is an unavoidable overlap between training courses and educational programs, with no clear boundary between the two.

This issue has emerged as a major point of contention in the criminal justice discipline. Many weaker programs in academic institutions have developed training-oriented criminal justice curricula and, for at least the past decade, have tried to pass these off as legitimate educational programs. Many educators feel that with the demise of the Law Enforcement Education Program (LEEP) and the resulting reduction of the number of in-service students, the training-oriented college programs that catered to agency training needs will be forced to close or adapt their curricula to the educational approach.

Closely tied to this issue of education versus training has been a constant movement to professionalize probation and parole. They very term "professionalism" has become a major goal of contemporary corrections.

Professionalism suggests a personal, internal commitment to an inherent code of ethics and accompanying self-discipline. Professionalism also demands high levels of knowledge and skills obtained only through rigorous, formal education and training. Entry into a profession is controlled by guidelines established by the profession, and control is maintained over professionals by professional colleagues. Both the probation and parole services are legitimately striving to be viewed as a profession, for many see the achievement of professionalism as the ultimate solution to most problems in the probation and parole systems.

Yet, as many have stressed, professionalism might be a mixed blessing. Niederhoffer and Blumberg (1976: 16–17) have identified several problems with the professionalization of justice system agents. Professionalism may create a struggle for power that can polarize an agency into two camps: the professionals and the conservatives. By its stress on formal education, professionalism threatens many officers who do not want to go back to school for a variety of reasons, such as: the coursework is perceived not to be job-related and is taught by an instructor who has not "been on the street"; it competes with family demands and leisure time; or it involves unproductive, "Mickey Mouse" busy work. Professionalism also requires changes in policy, techniques, and social relations that can lead to potential intradepartmental turmoil and a general lowering of agency morale if such changes are not monitored and properly managed.

Professionalism intensifies the demand for self-control and autonomy, which some argue runs counter to the democratic ideal of public agencies as a commonweal. The fact that professionalism demands consistent, efficient, and accountable performance can result in a tendency to falsify reports and cover up inadequate performance in an attempt to maintain a high level of prestige and solid performance ratings.

Current Practices

Regardless of the resistance and potential hazards, probation and parole administrators generally are determined to professionalize. The issues have not been whether or not there is a need for preservice education and in-service development, but rather what program would provide the greatest benefit to the officer, the agency, the client, and the system in general. Information obtained by Latessa and Allen (1982), in their recent review of parole in the nation, illustrates this fact. From the data in Table 8–1, it can be seen that more than 80 percent of the jurisdictions in this country require at least a bachelor's degree for initial employment. In addition, many require specific areas of college study, as well as various levels of training and experience. While there is some consensus as to the level of education needed (bachelor's degree), the exact content of undergraduate study is still a matter of some debate. Generally speaking, however, aspiring probation and parole personnel would better prepare themselves for agency entry by enrolling in various sociology, social work, psychology, and criminal justice courses. Myren (1975) points out that care must be taken in academic programs to prepare generalists who would have the skills to manage the system, establish policy, and perform most of the client-related tasks. Increasingly, this seems to be the prevailing philosophy among probation and parole administrators, and many academic programs are responding by developing a broad interdisciplinary curriculum. There is also a growing interest among educators in many fields and disciplines to guarantee all students a common core of learning (Scully, 1977; Fish, 1978). On the other hand, there are those who would rather the academic programs produce specialists with narrow but sophisticated knowledge and skills. While there are some academic institutions that seek to fulfill this latter need, many argue that the development of specialists is a training function, and one better fulfilled by the agency (Academy of Criminal Justice Sciences, 1976).

Evaluation Preservice Educational Standards

The premise that a college graduate is a more capable and competent officer seems to have been generally accepted by criminal justice planners, administrators, and educators, although some are not totally convinced of this position (Eskridge, 1977). In order to assess the impact of preservice education, there must first be agreement on the roles for and functions of probation and parole officers (see Chapter 7). There currently is no consensus on these issues, nor can one reasonably expect such agreement, given the present decentralized system of justice, where "proper function" varies from jurisdiction to jurisdiction and from situation to situation. Before arriving at a decision as to the appropriate role of education, there must also be a determination of the objectives of the correctional system. Education must have a goal, and as long as there are different opinions on such goals (vocational, professional, or humanistic), agreement will be lacking. It has been argued that the establishment of educational standards seem premature when corrections has yet to come to a consensus regarding its own objectives (Schnur, 1959: 28).

Edwards (1973) has stated that a primary task of designing an effective program is to clearly bring into focus what the program is to achieve (reintegration, rehabilitation, community safety). This focus has not been determined in either the area of probation or parole, let alone corrections as a whole. If it were assumed that a dominant function could be defined for probation and parole, several logical steps must be followed to deter-

Table 8–1
Entry Level Requirements for Parole Officers

Jurisdiction	Preservice Education Requirements	Other Requirements
Alabama	Bachelor's degree in social psychology, criminal justice, or related area	Six weeks of law enforcement training prior to achieving permanent status
Alaska	Bachelor's degree; not specific	None
Arizona	High school degree	None
Arkansas	Bachelor's degree in criminology, sociology, or related area	None
California	Some college; not specific	Experience in custody, treatment, and supervision; human services
Colorado	Bachelor's degree in behavioral science	Ability to work with clients, public, agency; written and oral communication skills
Connecticut	Bachelor's degree	College and experience
Delaware	Bachelor's degree in behavioral sciences or related area	None
Florida	Bachelor's degree; not specific	Pass examination
Georgia	Bachelor's degree; not specific	Passing score on competitive examination
Hawaii	Bachelor's degree; not specific	None
Idaho	Some college; social science or criminal justice	Experience in related field
Illinois	Bachelor's degree in law enforcement or human services	Pass civil service examination
Indiana	Some college; fifteen hours in social work, psychology, sociology, crminology, guidance, or criminal justice	Four years full-time paid experience (college training may be substituted for three years of experience)
Iowa	Some college; not specific	Merit examination, two years of experience in casework
Kansas	Some college; humanities	None
Kentucky	Bachelor's degree; not specific	None
Louisiana	Bachelor's degree; not specific	None
Maine	Bachelor's degree; not specific, but social science preferred	None

149

Table 8-1 (Continued)

JURISDICTION	PRESERVICE EDUCATION REQUIREMENTS	OTHER REQUIREMENTS
Maryland	Bachelor's degree; not specific	None
Massachusetts	Bachelor's degree; not specific	No criminal record
Michigan	Bachelor's degree in criminal justice, social work, psychology, sociology	Interview, personal investigation
Minnesota	Bachelor's degree in behavioral science or related area	None
Mississippi	Master's degree in criminal justice, behavioral sciences	Three years of experience in job-related field
Missouri	Bachelor's degree in social work, psychology, behavioral science	Nine hours of college work in criminology or corrections or internship
Montana	Bachelor's degree in behavioral science	None
Nebraska	Not specific, but prefer criminal justice, behavioral science	Valid driver's license
Nevada	Bachelor's degree in behavioral science, social science	One year of experience to reach full journeyman level
New Hampshire	Bachelor's degree in sociology, criminology, behavioral sciences	Prior experience in probation, parole, or social welfare work
New Jersey	Not specific	Valid New Jersey driver's license
New Mexico	Bachelor's degree in corrections, social work, penology, or related field	None
New York	Not specific	Three years of experience in social work setting (may substitute graduate school)
North Carolina	Not specific, but prefer sociology, criminal justice, or corrections	None
North Dakota	Not specific	State civil service
Ohio	Bachelor's degree in behavioral science, counseling, and interview skills	Valid driver's license
Oklahoma	Bachelor's degree in counseling, sociology, psychology, law enforcement, education	None

150

State	Education	Experience
Oregon	Bachelor's degree in behavioral science	Two years of experience with clients in a related or social service or rehabilitation setting; one year must be in correctional setting
Pennsylvania	Not specific	Valid driver's license
Rhode Island	High school degree	Physical examination
South Carolina	Bachelor's degree in sociology, psychology, social science, criminal justice	Experience; parole officer II, one year plus degree; parole officer III, two years plus degree; parole officer IV, three years plus degree
South Dakota	Bachelor's degree in criminal justice or other social science	None
Tennessee	Bachelor's degree in behavioral science	Must be twenty-five years old
Texas	Not specific	Two years of full-time paid experience in people-oriented area
Utah	Not specific	None
Vermont	Not specific	Eighteen months of experience in pertinent field
Virginia	Bachelor's degree in behavioral science	Two years of related experience or equivalent qualification
Washington	Bachelor's degree in social services	One year of experience in social work, police or related area
West Virginia	Bachelor's degree in sociology, psychology, penology, criminal justice, related area	None
Wisconsin	Not available	None
Wyoming	Bachelor's degree in criminal justice, social sciences, counseling	Two years of experience to reach full agent status
District of Columbia	Behavioral science	Two years of experience in related field
Federal	Master's degree; not specific	Two years of experience

Source: Edward J. Latessa and Harry E. Allen, "Management Issues in Parole" (San Jose, Calif.: San Jose State University Foundation, 1982).

mine what comprises a competent performance of that function (competency-based analysis). First, competency must be categorized into basic elements (skills); then some determination must be made as to the significance of each element in contributing to overall probation and parole competency. Once these steps have been achieved and an accurate indicator of competency developed, it would eventually be possible to empirically measure the impact of education upon competency.

Preservice education is defined as a college education received prior to employment as a probation or parole officer. A few researchers (Cohn, 1970; Miles, 1965; and Newman, 1970) have addressed this subject by examining the various probation and parole work elements they perceive as fundamental, and evaluating the impact of education upon those elements. Up to this time, however, there seems to have been no empirical attempts to evaluate and categorize competency into basic elements and to quantitatively ascertain the significance of each element upon probation and parole officer competency. This need has been widely recognized (Sternbach, 1975; Taylor and McEachern, 1966; the California Youth Authority, 1972; and the State of Oklahoma Probation Department, 1973). Without such competency-based analyses, the worth and impact of education upon probation and parole officers' performance will be an open question.

While a competency-based analysis of probation and parole work elements as described above seems unattainable at this time, a cost-benefit review would be helpful. Cost-benefit analyses would help determine the nature, frequency, and quantity of educational investments that would bring the optimum rate of return (in this case optimum competency) at a minimum cost. To undertake this type of study requires clear-cut behavioral objectives and officer functions, as well as a consensus as to what comprises a competent performance in each function. Such determinations are obviously difficult, as has been suggested previously. While extensive difficulties may be present in any attempt to measure output and efficiency of probation and parole agencies, Ostrom (1973) has pointed out that such efforts must be undertaken, for without serious attempts to evaluate the consequences of reform, changes may produce more harm than good. These tasks will be undertaken in the near future.

In addition, there have been only a few attempts to handle these other issues. Cohn (1970) conducted a study involving some 270 probation officers and administrators. He found that the higher the level of education (regardless of the formal area of study), the more lenient the probation administrator tended to be, and conversely, the lower the educational achievement, the more punitive the administrator tended to be. He further reported finding no significant difference between a preservice education major and case judgment. However, he did observe a tendency for undergraduate social work majors to be slightly more punitive in their judgments than undergraduates with other majors. As noted earlier, this has been an issue of great debate in the past few years.

While there are many who concur with Cohn, that the formal concentration of study does not make much difference on attitude or performance, there are those who argue strongly to the contrary, stressing the need for probation and parole officers to immerse themselves in a narrow, specialist-oriented curricula. The current trend, however, seems to be toward the development of generalists. Newman (1970: 90), for example, advocated a liberal arts/general educational preparation, but one with an emphasis on correctional topics. While he suggested that pre-entry education should develop general skills and bring an aura of maturity and professionalism to the officer, he concluded that education (or the lack of it) does not assure a stable and emotionally mature individual. Schnur (1959: 28) basically agrees with Newman that education is not a substitute for personal maturity, and in calling for a moratorium on the establishment of educational standards for probation officers, he argued that what is important is not how the applicants secured their knowledge and ability, but whether they have what it takes to be a good officer. A fifteen-year study by Heath (1977) independently concurs with Newman's observations, suggesting that good grades and other usual measures of academic success do not necessarily correlate with personal maturity and competency in later life. Of course, education contributes to both these qualities.

In part, as a way of overcoming this problem, Myren (1975) suggested that individuals blend their higher education with productive employment in the system. He stated that correctional careerists should be granted systematic educational leaves with pay, or some continuous mixture of part-time education and part-time employment—perhaps the model of the future. Such an arrangement could serve to sensitize individuals to the environments and needs of others, resulting in an immediate positive transfer value of the educational experience to the officer. For the preservice student, internships can provide similar benefits.

Problems with Preservice Educational Standards

Many have suggested that there may be a negative relationship between the establishment of educational standards and officer attitudes. Hostility may develop among older officers who lack the formal education to meet the emerging standards. The mid-career change in the rules forces reorientation in a way that breaks up established work patterns for higher-echelon officers, with the younger but more educated officers often being ostracized as standard breakers (similar to a union's charge of "rate breakers"). Noncompliance may result in a form of negative job mobility, with the better educated, younger officers obtaining the most desired assignments and promotions. The result is that the senior officer is virtually coerced into the classroom. But once they are there, what is the probability that they will be professionalized by the experience?

Not much at all says Davis (1983), who, in complete opposition to Myren (1975), concludes that it may be "dysfunctional to mix the academic world and practical worlds of probation." The academic world focuses upon facts, knowledge, and research, while the practical world of probation focuses upon the operations manuals, obedience to orders, processing cases on time, and solving the problems at hand. The academic world of probation has no bearing on the practical world of probation says Davis (1983: 10), who himself is a probation officer and possesses a Ph.D., and attempts to force a marriage leads to frustration that can be rather intense.

The state of Wisconsin attempted to address several of these issues by examining the impact of education on the function of probation and parole as viewed by 116 officers. The results of this study are interesting. Miles's (1965) analysis of the study suggested that preservice education initially had somewhat of a negative association with the probation and parole officers' work attitudes and opinions. Many academic programs fail to reconcile the principles of traditional casework as presented in schools of social work with the elements of surveillance and law enforcement required by the officer's day-to-day tasks. This reflects the basic role conflict in probation and parole field service: helping versus surveillance. College and university programs should assist students in understanding and coping with these conflicts. Miles also noted that officers who enter probation service without a graduate-level education do not experience this trauma to the same degree and, after several years of experience, there is little difference between the philosophy and practice of the more- and less-educated officers. Furthermore, the National Advisory Committee on Criminal Justice Standards and Goals, (1973b) found that many probation officers who had graduate degrees left the agency, in large part because of frustration over the value of preservice education.

In-Service Development Standards

In-service development is defined as training and education received after being hired as a probation or parole officer. Depending on the department, it can take the form of either the traditional education model or the more technical training approach, though it appears that the latter is the most common form. In-service development has generally been divided into two timeframes, each with its own broad objectives: *orientation training*, and *extended personnel development*. Orientation training is provided to acquaint the probation and parole officer with the community, with the probation and parole department as an organization, and with the basic mechanics of probation and parole services. Extended development is provided to increase levels of skills and to meet individual probation and parole officer needs in increasing their long-term job performance efficiency; this may include both training and education-type curriculum modes. Departments vary widely in the nature and extent of the in-service development they require and offer.

The National Manpower Survey (1978) information shown in Table 8–2 reveals the extent of the in-service development opportunity provided by various agencies during 1975. It was found that approximately 80 percent of all probation and parole agencies provided some form of in-service development programming to their personnel. In 22 percent of all agencies, in-service training (extended personnel development) was the only form of training provided; entry level orientation training was provided in approximately 8 percent of the agencies, while about 50 percent reported offering a combination of both entry-level and in-service development.

Table 8–2

Training Provided to Probation and Parole Officers, by Type of Agency

| | | | PERCENT DISTRIBUTION AGENCIES BY TYPE OF TRAINING PROVIDED | | |
TYPE OF AGENCY	NUMBER OF AGENCIES	TOTAL	Entry Level Only	In-Service Only	Both Entry and In-Service
All agencies	1,748	100.0	8.4	22.0	49.8
All probation agencies	774	100.0	7.9	24.5	39.7
All parole agencies	157	100.0	7.0	19.1	59.9
Combined probation and parole agencies	626	100.0	9.2	20.0	59.5
Adult probation	184	100.0	7.6	23.4	32.6
Juvenile probation	335	100.0	8.7	26.9	39.1
Adult and juvenile probation	255	100.0	7.1	22.4	45.5
Adult parole	50	100.0	10.0	8.0	72.0
Juvenile parole	75	100.0	8.0	25.3	45.3
Adult and juvenile parole	32	100.0	3.1	21.9	75.0
Adult probation and parole	319	100.0	9.4	16.0	66.0
Juvenile probation and parole	185	100.0	10.3	22.2	54.6
Adult and juvenile probation and parole	116	100.0	6.9	27.6	49.1
Other agencies	197	100.0	8.1	20.8	50.8

SOURCE: *National Manpower Survey of the Criminal Justice System* (Washington, D.C.: Government Printing Office, 1978).

The average duration of the courses was reported as approximately one week (thirty-eight hours), although, again, the states vary widely. For example, the Oklahoma Department of Corrections requires an initial 120-classroom-hour orientation training session and an additional 120-classroom-hour developmental period to be certified as a probation officer (Oklahoma Department of Corrections, 1973). Massachusetts requires that all incoming probation officers receive formal orientation training within six months of their appointments and a forty-five-hour developmental training session at least once every three years thereafter (NCCD, 1975b). Florida has no requirements, but recommends forty hours of orientation during the first year with an additional sixty hours during the first year (NCCD, 1975a).

Course curricula also differ greatly. Some in-service development programs were designed to provide basic orientation for lower-level personnel. Most in-service courses, however, tend to be more specialized, and place more emphasis upon topics such as counseling techniques, community resource utilization, and alcohol and drug problems, with correspondingly less emphasis on office procedures, investigative techniques, and case report writing.

Latessa and Allen (1982) looked specifically at areas of in-service development offered by agencies. While job-related training was the more common type, it is interesting to note that a growing number of states are apparently adjusting their traditional in-service curriculum to include an educational component. Of special interest is the apparent diminished appeal of the so-called therapeutic or psychological programming—for many years, for example, sensitivity training had been promoted as essential for the development of officers' awareness of their clients' needs (Edwards, 1973). Perhaps this newly found disinterest is reflective of a general trend in the country. By its very nature, probation and parole are people-oriented services, and any attempt to move them out of that framework must be carefully considered.

Latessa and Allen (1982) also looked at the number of jurisdictions receiving federal financial support for training programs. They found that nearly 70 percent of the jurisdictions where data were available reported, at the time of the survey, to be receiving federal assistance. With the demise of the Law Enforcement Assistance Administration, a number of training programs were phased out and others scaled down. Just what the affect will be on probation and parole operations is difficult to assess; the overall affects of in-service training, including retention, are not yet known.

Many states and jurisdictions have begun to fund continuation training from local and state appropriations. The National Correctional Academy, in the Federal Bureau of Prisons, is developing audiovisual and training manual materials for use by state and local agencies. Latessa and Allen

(1982) found only six existing in-house evaluations of training effectiveness, all of which found training to be providing positive results. The concern, of course, is that these were in-house evaluations and perhaps lacked the objectivity that and outside review would provide. Furthermore, positive results were often operationally defined as organizational goals, such as the ability to meet certification standards and speed of promotion, rather than programmatic achievements and operations. More program evaluations should be undertaken shortly.

Evaluation of In-Service Training Programs

To be successful, training programs should not simply be a series of lectures, but should involve the participants in the learning activities. Probation and parole officer feedback as to the nature of the training is also valuable. The training should involve a good deal of repetition. Management must be willing to reinforce the training effort by offering incentives and rewards for participation, and more importantly, for actually performing in the new way. The value of training is, after all, not just the training, but the transference of the skills obtained in the training situation to the work situation.

Training is undertaken on the assumption that this transference takes place, and that trained officers become more capable officers. Evidence to support the latter, however, is not conclusive. The same criticisms of pre-service education apply here. The establishment of standards in the area of in-service development faces many of the methodological hazards previously detailed. In the absence of any definitive data as to the most beneficial in-service development curriculum, a wide range of suggested curricula have been proposed that are often contradictory.

For example, a Philadelphia project noted considerable ambivalence, differences, and clashes of opinion as to appropriate training functions, content, structure, and activity (Sternbach, 1975). The National Council on Crime and Delinquency report (1975a) on the Florida Parole and Probation Commission noted that expectations of the functions of in-service training were different among key people, all of whom were located higher up in the organization than was the training manager. Depending on who was making demands on the training unit, the expectations were different.

These examples again point to the need to determine the elements of competent or desired probation and parole officer performances, and quantitatively ascertaining the nature and extent of the training needed to produce the greatest training benefit at the least cost. Until this is done, it will be difficult to determine the exact impact of in-service development upon any given agency or the system as a whole.

While many jurisdictions recommend or require that probation and parole officers receive a certain amount of orientation and/or developmental training, meeting the standards is another matter. For example, most officers in Florida reported that they were on the job from one to two months and already had a full caseload before receiving any formal orientation training, and by then it was perceived as irrelevant or redundant. In addition, respondents reported a great deal of anxiety, since the training required a two-week absence from the field (NCCD, 1975a).

On the other hand, other programs have found strong officer acceptance of their training operations. The Cleveland State University Training Institute was rated as "good to very good" by 88 percent of the participants (Unkovic and Battisti, 1968). Seventy percent of the probation officers who participated in a 1974 training program in Kentucky felt that the training had improved some aspects of their service delivery techniques. One hundred percent of these probation officers' clients noted the officers had improved their services in some way since the training (Kentucky Mental Health Manpower Commission, 1974). Smith (1982) suggests that in-service training is an excellent tool to be used to prevent job burnout.

A survey of probation personnel in fifty-two probation departments in California found that probation officers preferred workshops and group sessions to any other form of developmental training (California Youth Authority, 1972). The data in Table 8–3 represent the various techniques, skills, and knowledge covered in these workshops, as well as the percent of the staff judged to be knowledgeable in the area as viewed both by probation department administrators and staff. Interestingly, administrators consistently estimate the knowledge level of the staff higher than the staff actually does.

The state of Florida provides training on such topic areas as alcohol rehabilitation, drug and alcohol abuse training, Minnesota Multiphasic Personality Inventory training, computer terminal operations, reality therapy, transactional analysis, and general management training. Unfortunately, the NCCD (1975a) report claimed that this training was conducted by underprepared instructors who presented inadequate materials. Senna (1976: 72) stated that some states have reported termination of their professional staff development programs because of the loss of financial support and general dissatisfaction, but these are a minority. A California Youth Authority (1972) study of some fifty-two probation departments in California found that staff interest in formal training is influenced by the extent to which they believe it will contribute toward promotions. The report also recognized a need for more extensive in-service development, embracing a much larger number of client-serving staff than had been involved thus far. Seventy percent of the staff did not feel that adequate training was being provided.

Other problems with in-service programs have been reported. A North

Table 8-3
In-Service Development Programs for Parole Officers

Jurisdiction	In-Service Program Content	Federal Fiscal Support of In-Service Development Programs
Alabama	Investigation, report writing, probation/parole supervision, law enforcement	Yes
Alaska	Missing data regarding areas of training	Yes
Arizona	Job-related training	
Arkansas	Personnel policy, criminal justice history of corrections, organization rules, procedures, etc.; weapons, report writing, treatment, inside/outside security in prison, first aid, assisting agencies, classification, self-defense, inmate rights, communications	Yes
California	All functions relating to the practice of casework and parole	Yes
Colorado	Crisis intervention, weighted caseload procedure training	Yes
Connecticut	All job-related areas	Yes
Delaware	Criminal justice system, Delaware code, professional roles and attitudes, resources, classification, report writing, caseloads, casework	Data not available
Florida	All areas of corrections, pretrial, youths, investigations	Yes
Georgia	Policies, procedures, firearms, arrest procedures, security procedures	Yes
Hawaii	Investigation, law, counseling, drug abuse, mental health	No
Idaho	Job-related	Yes
Illinois	Counseling, use of community resources, policy and procedures, firearms, rules of search and seizure, restraint	Yes
Indiana	Job-related training	Data not available
Iowa	Job-related skills, human interaction, legal aspects	Data not available
Kansas	Behavioral science, middle management	No
Kentucky	Law enforcement techniques, management, interpersonal skills, communication	No
Louisiana	Job-related areas	Yes

159

Table 8-3 (Continued)

JURISDICTION	IN-SERVICE PROGRAM CONTENT	FEDERAL FISCAL SUPPORT OF IN-SERVICE DEVELOPMENT PROGRAMS
Maine	Counseling, law enforcement labor relations	Yes
Maryland	Job-related	Yes
Massachusetts	Human behavior, firearms, counseling, resource utilization	Yes
Michigan	Orientation, casework, report writing, personnel management, labor relations, investigation, firearms qualification	Yes
Minnesota	Broad range of subjects, interpersonal skills, management, suicide prevention, etc.	Yes
Mississippi	General job-related training	Yes
Missouri	Job-related for parole officers, basic and advanced reality therapy, alcohol/drug counseling, crisis intervention, employment/family management	No
Montana	Interpersonal communication, legislation, rules of search and seizure; grant from the Board of Crime Control	Yes
Nebraska	Supervision, counseling, state service, legal	No
Nevada	Orientation, law, policies, casework, supervision	No
New Hampshire	Job-related	No
New Jersey	Counseling, case management and supervision, penal code, mental health services	No
New Mexico	Job-related corrections training	Yes
New York	Organization, history, casework techniques, firearms, interview techniques, collateral services	No
North Carolina	Entry level/intermediate level/management	Yes
North Dakota	Legal matters, working with people—sociology, psychology, handling of drug/alcohol/special problems	Data not available
Ohio	Parole entrance training; drug abuse, management, counseling, firearms, practical law	No

160

State	Areas	In-service training
Oklahoma	Caseload management, courtroom demeanor, report writing, time management, investigation techniques, referral agencies, 160 hours of basic law enforcement training	Yes
Oregon	Orientaton, security, management and supervision, on-the-job training, workshops	Yes
Pennsylvania	Orientation, counseling and help skills (reality therapy, TA), case management and supervision skills, legal and enforcement skills, management and administrative skills	Yes
Rhode Island	Job-related areas	Data not available
South Carolina	Agency operation, classification, arrest procedures, casework management, court procedures, organization and management	Yes
Suth Dakota	Stress treatment models and resources development	No
Tennessee	Drug abuse, caseload techniques, job-related areas	No
Texas	Job-related areas, counseling techniques, job placement, interviewing, drug/alcohol abuse	Yes
Utah	Peace officer standards and training, community resources, firearms, legal trends and developments in corrections and social work	Yes
Vermont	Full range of job-related areas	No
Virginia	Counseling, interviewing techniques, management techniques, report writing, self-defense	No
Washington	Orientation, parole officer skills, human behavior, written communication (report writing)	No
West Virginia	All areas are on-the-job training; grant for three one-week parole training sessions	Yes
Wisconsin	"All kinds of things"	Data not available
Wyoming	Job orientation	Yes
District of Columbia	All job-related areas, from secretarial skill brush-up to pistol training for parole officers	Yes
Federal	Orientation, advanced skills, management and supervision training; Federal Judicial Center handles management, outside contractor handles crisis intervention	

Source: Edward J. Latessa and Harry E. Allen, "Management Issues in Parole" (San Jose, Calif.: San Jose State University, 1982).

Carolina study found definite resistance to training among probation officers, especially when the training was viewed as a threat to their established roles and work patterns. To combat such difficulties, the study called for wide flexibility in the nature and timing of the coursework, and stressed the need for the development of personal relations between the trainees and the trainers (North Carolina University Training Center on Delinquency and Youth Crime, 1956).

In Horne and Passmore's review of the impact of in-service development at the Rockville (Indiana) Training Center, they found a substantial amount of opposition from the staff, who viewed the training material as irrelevant. Resistance took the form of absenteeism, tardiness, failure to read assignments, and a refusal to try new skills on the job. They also found that officers who seriously attempted to develop their skills through training and education were rewarded with promotions to positions that removed them from direct contact with clients. This is somewhat of a paradox, a typical modified Peter Principle of rewarding those who have fine-tuned their abilities and skills in handling clients with a promotion that removes them from the very clients with whom they were educated and trained to deal. Other states and jurisdictions are aware of this pitfall and take steps to avoid it.

To overcome staff resistance, the Joint Commission on Correctional Manpower and Training (Jelinek, 1967) stressed the need to conduct an officer needs assessment and to develop in-service curriculum around officer-identified needs.[1] Bensinger (1977) found just such a preprogram needs assessment crucial to the success, as measured in the form of participant support, of in-service correctional development programs in Chicago. It was further noted that the interests of agency administration officials must also be considered when developing training materials.

From the evidence obtained to date, it appears that, from the individual officer's perspective, in-service training and education programs are extremely time-consuming. It could detract from available client time and may compete with family and leisure time. Voluntary programs, on the other hand, can create a dilemma for the officer who does not wish to participate but feels pressured by those who do. Many agencies attempt to ease this burden by allowing for education and training sessions on agency time. Latessa and Allen (1982) found that more than 60 percent of the parole agencies currently grant leave-time for college. By the same token, they found salary incentives for educational activity offered in only six states and promotion priority in seven states. Bensinger (1977) suggests that a direct link between training and promotion, salary increments, favorable job assignments, and other relevant factors must be established. Latessa and Allen (1982) report that no incentives for in-service educational activity were offered in nearly 70 percent of the parole agencies.

Sternbach's (1975) review of the Philadelphia project found training to have the greatest impact upon new officers who lack previous relevant education. He found, however, that the value of that initial training and all subsequent in-service development decreased as time on the job increased. Furthermore, he found no connection between in-service development, which in Philadelphia included a series of mandatory university undergraduate- and graduate-level courses, and competency in the human services field. Even if interpersonal skills could be developed in some in-service development setting, or even in a preservice educational environment, the practice of subsequently overwhelming the officer with a large caseload probably negates the value of that training and education. The value of in-service development may be predominantly short-run in impact, and thus its cost may not be worth such a minimal long-run benefit.

The state of Connecticut, however, asserts that the benefits are worth the costs. Connecticut has recognized that, with her new emphasis on hiring younger, relatively highly educated persons as probation officers, there is a likelihood of greater turnover in the adult probation officer ranks. It is felt, however, that this turnover can be reduced by offering explicit training and educational assistance to probation officers, and rewarding those who involve themselves in these pursuits (Connecticut Department of Adult Probation, 1974). Many emphasize that educational and training opportunities must be made available to probation and parole officers, and valid rewards in terms of advancement given for their efforts, not only to increase the quality of the officer, but also to avoid the frustration that could develop among educated officers when and if an undereducated supervisor is placed over them. Latessa and Allen (1982) found that approximately 15 percent of the parole agencies grant promotion priority to those who successfully complete in-service training and education programs. Schnur (1959) had already questioned the practice of seniority advancement as a threat to the entire concept of trained and educated officers. A seniority system, when coupled with a lack of a lateral entry system for the well-educated and trained, can promote negative selection of personnel. The best person for the job should be selected, regardless of years of experience, since experience alone is no guarantee that a particular individual can do a job better than someone with less experience. (Twenty-five years of experience could be one year simply repeated twenty-five times.) By the same token, well-educated and trained officers offer no guarantee that they will do a job better than anyone else. The education and training may have given them tools, but they must know how to use them in the field, and they must be willing to continue to use them properly.

An agency's traditional organization can also confound in-service training activities. Horne and Passmore (1977) experienced a significant amount of disruption in their training program due to work shift changes, emergencies, and other unavoidable interferences. The Philadelphia project report referred to an isolation of the training unit from the department communication network (Sternbach, 1975: 2), while a Florida report stated that area trainers and supervisors experienced some degree of frustration because the central office training unit staff did not encourage their attempts to provide meaningful and innovative staff development (NCCD, 1975).

The best organizational location for the in-service training function is as yet an unresolved issue. Larger states—such as California, New York, and Texas—have long struggled with the problems of how to organize a probation and parole officer development plan that would meet the needs of officers from small, rural departments as well as those from larger, urban departments.[2] Two basic approaches have emerged in the past few years, and both have experienced at least some operational success. The first approach, which seems to be the most popular, advocates a centralized program. Proponents of this concept—such as California, Connecticut, Florida, and Kentucky—opt for a centralized in-service development unit located in the state department of corrections, with mandatory training and education requirements for all officers. In Florida, some problems developed because local training officers felt overburdened with work and reacted negatively to divided supervision (i.e., their chief probation officer and the central office training unit staff). Administrators in other agencies realize that personnel training in this centralized approach must be handled at all levels by personnel whose sole responsibility is training.

Taylor and McEachern (1966) have advocated a national training program developed by the federal government for distribution to the line personnel through training units in the various state departments of correction, an increasingly popular approach. Taylor and McEachern reported that some degree of state and local objections to such a proposal would arise, and pointed out that:

1. It has become increasingly important that a means be found to introduce social and behavioral science research directly into the working operations and training operations of the departments.
2. When the smaller department invests its time and money training its officers, it is often only to lose them a year or so later to larger departments with the advantages of better pay, more facilities, and greater opportunities for advancement; as well as have the resources to become involved in national-level organizations. Consequently, the local association often serves as the primary vehicle to promote information exchange and ongoing training, particularly in the publication of newsletters.

Summary

The fact that probation and parole have not defined substantive goals in the past has and probably will continue to hamper evaluations of the value of preservice education and in-service development in probation and parole work. The need for graduate-level education and frequent in-service staff development programs has been advocated for many years and is becoming a reality. There has come to be a general acceptance of formal education as a prerequisite of quality probation and parole service, and of in-service development as a means of maintaining and improving that service. This need has been identified and encouraged by several national commissions and organizations, as well as by numerous individual writers and researchers. As yet, there is little empirical documentation that education and training can improve overall performance in these environments (Eskridge, 1979).

Despite the lack of empirical support, the need is recognized for preservice education and in-service development projects on agency time, the granting of educational-release time, and for the correlating of program participation with salary increments, favorable job assignments, promotions, and other relevant factors. Program curriculum should reflect predetermined probation and parole officer needs as well as agency administration officials' interest. Aspiring probation and parole professionals should obtain a broad, liberal arts education, augmented with productive employment in the system.

Notes

1. The Joint Commission suggested the adoption of the following program development model: (a) identification of needs, (b) selection of program design, (c) development of curriculum, (d) selection of materials, (e) selection of faculty/ trainers, (f) site selection, (g) relationship of program to other training and trainees, (h) evaluation, and (i) reinforcement and rewards.

2. A study of California probation officers found a very strong positive correlation ($r_s = .94$) between county size and mean level of education among probation officers. That is, the larger the county, the more educated the probation officer population tends to be, and vice versa. See National Probation and Parole Association, *Probation in California* (Sacramento, Calif.: National Probation and Parole Administration, 1957).

Study Guides

1. Differentiate between education and training in both technique and substance. What is the optimum mix for probation and parole officers?
2. What is professionalism? Should probation and parole seek to become a profession? Why or why not?
3. Describe the two types of in-service development programs.

4. Discuss the empirical evidence that has been uncovered relative to the value of educational programming for human services agencies.
5. What are some techniques used to encourage personnel to engage in in-service training?
6. What tactics can correctional administrators use to lessen staff resistance to training?

Key Terms

competency-based education model

education

educational release time

extended development

in-service development standards

in-service training

orientation training

preservice education

preservice standards

professionalism

training

training incentives

training needs assessment

References

Academy of Criminal Justice Sciences. *Accreditation Guidelines for Post-Secondary Criminal Justice Education Programs*. Normal, Ill.: Academy of Criminal Justice Sciences, Illinois State University, 1976.

American Bar Association. *Standards Relating to Probation*. New York: American Bar Association, 1970.

BENSINGER, GAD. "Training for Criminal Justice Personnel: A Case Study," *Federal Probation* 41 (1977):31–35.

BERTINOT, LIBBY, AND TAYLOR, JACK. "A Basic Plan for Statewide Probation Training," *Federal Probation* 38 (1974): 29–31.

California Youth Authority. *Education, Training and Deployment of Staff: A Survey of Probation Departments and the California Youth Authority*. Sacramento, Calif.: California Youth Authority, 1972.

COHN, ALVIN. *Decision-Making in the Administration of Probation Services: A Descriptive Study of the Probation Manager*. Berkeley, Calif.: University of California, 1970.

COMANOR, ALBERT. *Proposals for a Staff Training Program for New Jersey Probation*. New Brunswick, N.J.: Rutgers University, 1968.

Connecticut Department of Adult Probation. *Job Task Analysis and Personnel Organization Study Final Report*. Hartford, Conn.: Department of Adult Probation, 1974.

DAVIS, JAMES R. "Academic and Practical Aspects of Probation: A Comparison," *Federal Probation* 47 (1983):7–10.

EDWARDS, H. FRANKLIN. *Intergroup Workshop for Maricopa County Probation Officers*. Phoenix, Ariz.: Maricopa County Probation Department, 1973.

ESKRIDGE, CHRIS W. "Problems in the Use of Educational Standards: Another Side of the Controversy," *Police Chief* 44 (1977):36–38.

————. "Education and Training of Probation Officers: A Critical Assessment," *Federal Probation* 43 (1979):41–48.

ESKRIDGE, CHRIS, AND ROBERG, ROY. "A New Paradigm for Criminal Justice Education: Some Reflections on a Crime Management Approach," *Journal of Contemporary Criminal Justice* 2 (1981):19–26.

FISH, E. B. "Harvard Tightens Up Curriculum: Ends 'General Education' Program," *New York Times*, May 3, 1978, p. 1.

HEATH, DOUGLAS. "Prescription for Collegiate Survival: Return to Liberally Educate Today's Youth," *Liberal Education*, 1977, pp. 338–350.

HORNE, ARTHUR, AND PASSEMORE, LAURENCE. "In-service Training in a Correctional Setting: Facilitating Change," *Federal Probation* 41 (1977):35–40.

JELINEK, DAVID. "Organizational Assessments for Training." In *Targets for In-Service Training*. Washington, D.C.: Joint Commission on Correctional Manpower and Training, 1967.

Kentucky Mental Health Manpower Commission. *Community Resource Management Training for Kentucky Probation and Parole Officers*. Frankfort, Ky.: Kentucky Mental Health Manpower Commission, 1974.

LATESSA, EDWARD J., AND ALLEN, HARRY E. *Management Issues in Parole*. San Jose, Calif.: San Jose State University Foundation, 1982.

LOUGHERY, DON. "College Education: A Must for Probation Officers?," *Crime and Corrections* 3 (1975):1–7.

MILES, ARTHUR. "The Reality of the Probation Officer's Dilemma," *Federal Probation* 29 (1965):21–25.

MYREN, RICHARD. "Education for Correctional Careers," *Federal Probation* 39 (1975):51–58.

National Advisory Commission on Criminal Justice Standards and Goals. *Criminal Justice System*. Washington, D.C.: Government Printing Office, 1973a.

————. *Corrections*. Washington, D.C.: Government Printing Office, 1973b.

National Council on Crime and Delinquency. *Management Plan Prepared for Florida Parole and Probation Commission*. Austin, Tex.: NCCD, 1975a.

————. *Massachusetts Probation Training Needs*. Austin, Tex.: NCCD, 1975b.

National Manpower Survey of the Criminal Justice System. Washington, D.C.: Government Printing Office, 1978.

National Probation and Parole Association. *Probation in California*. Sacramento, Calif.: National Probation and Parole Association, 1957.

————. "Standards for Selection of Probation and Parole Personnel." In *Practice and Theory of Probation and Parole*, edited by D. Dressler. New York: Columbia University, 1959.

NEWMAN, CHARLES. *Sourcebook on Probation, Parole and Pardons*. Springfield, Ill.: Charles C. Thomas, 1970.

NIEDERHOFFER, ARTHUR, AND BLUMBERG, ABRAHAM. *The Ambivalent Force*. Hinesdale, Ill.: Dryden Press, 1976.

North Carolina University Training Center on Delinquency and Youth Crime. *Probation Training: Context and Method*. Washington, D.C.: U.S. Department of Health, Education and Welfare, Office of Juvenile Delinquency and Youth Development, 1956.

Oklahoma Department of Corrections. *Improved and Expanded Probation and Parole Services: Research Report #5*. Oklahoma City, Okla.: Oklahoma Department of Corrections, 1973.

OSTRUM, ELINOR. "On the Meaning and Measurement of Output and Efficiency in the Provision of Urban Police Services," *Journal of Criminal Justice* 1 (1973):93–111.

President's Commission on Law Enforcement and Administration of Justice. *Task Force Report: Corrections*. Washington, D.C.: Government Printing Office, 1967.

SANCHEZ, MARILYN. "Practical Probation: A Skills Course," *Federal Probation* 41 (1982):77–80.

SCHNUR, ALFRED. "Pre-Service Training," *Journal of Criminal Law, Criminology, and Police Science* 50 (1959):27.

SCULLY, M. G. "Many Colleges Reappraising Their Undergraduate Curricula," *Chronicle of Higher Education* 13 (1977):1.

SENNA, JOSEPH. "The Need for Professional Education in Probation and Parole," *Crime and Delinquency* 22 (1976):67–74.

SHERMAN, LAWRENCE, ET AL. *The Quality of Police Education*. San Francisco: Jossey-Bass, 1978.

SMITH, JAMES O. "Rekindling the Flame: The Use of In-Service Training as Burn-out Training," *Federal Probation* 41 (1982):63–66.

STERNBACH, JACK. *Executive Summary of Evaluation Report: In-Service and Graduate Training Project*. Philadelphia: Philadelphia Probation Department, 1975.

TAYLOR, EDWARD, AND McEACHERN, ALEXANDER. "Needs and Directions in Probation Training," *Federal Probation* 30 (1966):18–24.

TOCH, HANS, AND KLOFAS, JOHN. "Alienation and Desire for Job Enrichment Among Correctional Officers," *Federal Probation* 41 (1982):35–43.

TRESTOR, HAROLD. *Supervision of the Offender*. Englewood Cliffs, N.J.: Prentice Hall, 1981.

UNKOVIC, CHARLES, AND BATTISTI, GLORIA. *Study of Ohio Adult Correctional Personnel and Training Program*. Cleveland, Ohio: Cleveland State University Training Center, 1968.

Recommended Readings

National Manpower Survey of the Criminal Justice System, volumes 1–9 (Washington, D.C.: Government Printing Office, 1978). This exhaustive study offers recommendations for improving the deployment of existing personnel and increasing personnel effectiveness. Criminal justice education and training programs are examined and critiqued.

Sherman, Lawrence, et al. *The Quality of Police Education* (San Francisco: Jossey-Bass, 1978). This volume presents the findings of the National Advisory Commission on Higher Education for Police Officers. While focusing primarily upon police education, the issues raised are relevant and timely to probation and parole education and training.

Myren, Richard. "Education for Correctional Careers," *Federal Probation* 39 (1975):51–58. This article sketches a criminal justice career system of which the corrections education system should be a part. Myren strongly urges the need to develop career generalists and specialists.

9

Service Delivery Strategies

In terms of community safety, the most significant responsibility of a probation or parole agency is supervising offenders. Underlying this duty are the dual objectives of protecting the community and helping the offenders. As Chapter 7 indicated, these objectives are not always compatible.

Depending upon the jurisdiction in which the agency is located, offenders placed on probation and parole may have committed almost any type of criminal offense, and may range from first-time offenders to career criminals. The numbers of offenders placed on probation or released on parole will also vary considerably over time, depending upon the political and fiscal climates in the jurisdiction, existing law in the jurisdiction, size of the prison overpopulation, and the prevailing philosophy toward the use of probation and parole. In addition, there is likely to be variation among probationers and parolees with respect to the type and extent of conditions imposed upon them by the court or parole board. Finally, individuals being supervised will vary considerably in the types of problems they face (family difficulties, educational or employment needs, alcohol or drug abuse). As with the other major responsibilities of a probation or parole agency, supervision necessitates an organizational structure that will enable the agency to protect the community efficiently and effectively, and to provide the necessary support to aid the offender. What strategies are available?

Considering the complexity involved in complying with these duties, it is obvious that the agency will be faced with a number of critical management problems and alternatives from which to choose. Many of these, which will be discussed separately, are, in reality, closely intertwined. They are not "either/or" alternatives. In fact, many strategies can easily be mixed into a variety of combinations.

This chapter addresses the broad area of service delivery and the ways in which probation and parole agencies handle offenders assigned for supervision. The philosophical models of treatment delivery are examined, as well as the planning process of supervision, different levels of caseload size, and new developments in the areas of contracting for services and managing community resources.

Caseload Assignment Models

Offenders are assigned to a probation department by the court, and to a parole department by the parole board.[1] However, the ways in which offenders are individually assigned to available probation and parole officers varies from jurisdiction to jurisdiction.[2] Carter and Wilkins (1976: 391–401) have developed a useful typology of caseload models that includes the major variations in assignment strategies. Underlying their typology is the assumption that the offender population will vary considerably across any characteristic in question.

The first model is called the conventional model and it ignores the differences and similarities among offenders; cases are randomly assigned to available probation or parole officers. Because of the random distribution of the offender population among caseloads, each officer handles a mixture that is generally a miniature reproduction of the entire offender population including, of course, wide variations in personal characteristics. With the conventional caseload model, then, the probation or parole officer must be able to supervise any type of offender who happens to be assigned to his or her caseload, usually a difficult situation.

Closely related to the conventional model is what is called the numbers game model. This type may also ignore differences and similarities across offenders. The object of this model is to numerically balance all caseloads within the department. This balancing may or may not take the personal characteristics of individual offenders into account because the numbers game model can be approached in two ways. First, the number of cases to be supervised can simply be divided by the number of officers available to the department. For example, if a probation department has ten probation officers and eight hundred probationers, every officer will handle a caseload of eighty. Alternatively, the department can select an "ideal size" for each caseload and divide the number of offenders by the ideal size, yielding the number of necessary officers. Under this method, if a department has eight hundred probationers and has selected fifty as its ideal size caseload, then it must provide sixteen probation officers. Variations of the numbers game model may also be used with the other models discussed below.

The third assignment model is called the conventional model with geographic considerations. This one differs from the conventional model in one important respect: The caseload is restricted to residents in one type of geographic area (urban, suburban, or rural). Given the travel time necessary to supervise an entirely rural caseload, the size of a rural caseload is generally smaller than suburban or urban caseloads. Such caseloads, however, are not differentiated on the basis of the personal characteristics of the offenders, except to the extent that the characteristics of urban, suburban, and rural offenders may vary.

The other two assignment techniques recognize the presence of important similarities and differences among offenders. The more elementary of these techniques is called the single-factor specialized caseload model. This groups offenders together on the basis of one single characteristic that they all share—examples include drug or alcohol abuse, mental retardation, age, sex, type of offense, and high potential for violent behavior ("risk"). Despite the existence of a shared characteristic, offenders on each single-factor specialized caseload may vary widely on other characteristics. For example, a caseload restricted to offenders between the ages of eighteen and twenty-one may still include individuals who differ considerably on such variables as type of offense or potential risk to community.

Finally, the most complex assignment model, the vertical model, classifies offenders by two or more factors or characteristics. Often this classification is accomplished by using one of the various prediction devices that estimates the chances of a particular offender's succeeding or failing while under supervision. Prediction devices take a wide variety of individual characteristics into account and stress the similarities among individuals (see Chapter 6 for one example). Once all offenders in the agency are screened according to their probability of success, this classificatory scheme can then be used to create caseloads composed of offenders who have roughly the same chances of success or failure. This model is called vertical because it divides the range of offender characteristics into vertical slices in order to create caseloads.

Caseload size can be varied across both the single-factor and the multifactor classifications. For example, the size of caseloads, when based on the vertical model, are usually varied; it can be decreased in these composed of offenders with a high risk of failure, or increased for those composed of low-risk offenders.

Once the general strategy for managing offenders is established, the officers must deliver needed services to their clients. The remainder of this chapter discusses different strategies employed by probation and parole agencies to deliver those services to offenders under their supervision. Although we discuss these strategies separately, they are not mutually exclusive, and "pure" types are seldom found in actual supervision practices.

Casework Versus Brokerage

The two major orientations or approaches to supervision are casework and brokerage. We will examine each approach, the assumption underlying its use, its advantages and disadvantages, and the major operational concerns. We are discussing "pure" types as though the approaches were mutually exclusive, as if a department would adopt either a casework or a brokerage approach, but could not combine any features of the two. In reality, the two approaches are so mixed that it would be unusual if any two departments exhibited precisely the same approach as extreme positions. Most departments adopt positions somewhere along the continuum.

Casework

The traditional approach to probation and parole supervision has been the casework approach. Casework is not synonymous with social work; rather, it is just one of the three major specialties of social work (the others are community organization and group work).

Many definitions of casework and social casework have been offered. Bowers (1950: 127) has provided this frequently cited definition:

> Social casework is an area in which knowledge of the science of human relations and skills in relationships are used to mobilize capacities in the individual and resources in the community appropriate for better adjustment between the client and all or any part of his total environment.

Meeker (1948: 51–52) has elaborated further:

> The modern emphasis in social casework is upon discovering the positive potential within the individual and helping him exploit his own capabilities, while at the same time revealing external resources in his social and economic environment which will contribute to his ability to assume the mature responsible obligations of a well-adjusted individual.

It is apparent that the basic element in casework is the nature of the relationship between the caseworker and the individual in trouble.

It is obvious from these definitions that casework emphasizes changing the behavior of the offender through the development of a supportive one-to-one relationship. Because of this closeness, this approach views the caseworker as the sole, or at least the primary, agent of treatment for the client.

By following a casework approach, the supervising officer will also follow the basic assumptions of social work. Trecker (1975: 8–9) divides these assumptions into four categories: people, behavior problems, the social worker, and the relationship between society and the offender. One of the assumptions about offenders is that ". . . people can and do change in their behavior when they are given the right help at the right time and in the right amount." With respect to behavior problems, it is assumed that, because people's problems are complex and intertwined with the person's total living situation, treatment of those problems must be individualized. The primary treatment agent is assumed to be the social worker, and his or her other most important tool is the quality of the relationship created with the client. Finally, it is assumed that the client must be motivated to participate in the treatment process; consequently, a key element of the working relationship between the social worker and the client must be the development of the client's desire to change his or her behavior.

A common thread running through these assumptions is the idea that the offender must enter the casework relationship voluntarily, or at least willingly. The relationship involved in correctional supervision, however, does not usually rest on the offender's voluntary participation, but rather on the authority of the probation or parole officer. Under the casework approach, then, it is important to resolve the conflict between the voluntary self-determination of the offender and the authority inherent in the supervising officer's position.

Many authors characterize the authority of the probation or parole officer as an important tool that can be used in the treatment process. Mangrum (1978: 219) refers to the use of "coercive casework" and states, "While it is true that effective casework is not something done *to* or *for* the client, but *with* him, it is also true that sometimes it is a matter of some action which *gets his attention or holds him still* long enough for him to recognize that there *is* motivation from within. . . ." (emphasis added). Studt (1954: 24) notes that it is important for the offender to learn that ". . . authority is power to help as well as power to limit. . . ." Hardman (1959: 249–55) feels that authority, if properly used by the probation officer, can be an extremely powerful tool in social service. He believes that all individuals, including probationers, entertain both positive and negative feelings toward authority, and that a primary responsibility of the caseworker is to help the client understand and accept those conflicting feelings and to learn new ways of controlling and expressing them.

Casework is so extensively used in probation and parole supervision that it is considered the "norm" as a service provision strategy. It basically follows the medical model of corrections in which the supervising officer, through a one-to-one relationship, diagnoses the offender, formulates a treatment strategy, implements that strategy, and, finally, evaluates the offender in light of the treatment.

Following this approach, the probation or parole officer attempts to bring about a mutual interaction with the offender in an effort to promote a psychological and social atmosphere that will enable the offender to be more self-accepting and to interact more acceptably with others. In other words, through the use of this close, helping relationship, the officer attempts to change (positively) the behavior of the offender. Because of the close relationship required by the casework approach, the officer is the primary agent of treatment.

Casework is a way of working with individuals. It is consciously planned to help the offender become better adjusted to the demands of social living. The activities that define the work as "casework" are twofold: (1) the officers are dealing with offenders as individual, and (2) they are consciously controlling what they do so that their activities contribute to the offenders' welfare. Casework is not characterized either by a particular kind of activity on the part of the probation or parole officer, or a particular situation of the offender. For example, while counseling is a large part of casework, it is not the only treatment available. While figuring out what has to be done next, the supervising officer may "cool off" the offender by having him or her jailed on a technical violation. This next step could involve working with the juvenile's teacher, or with the offender's family. Each such activity is a part of casework in the correctional field.

Thus, casework in probation and parole follows the traditional medical model and remains intact in most probation and parole agencies. In reality, however, the supervising officer does not have the time or energy to devote to individual cases. Perhaps the most basic criticisms of the casework approach are that the probation or parole officer tries to be all things to all people, and does not adequately mobilize the community and its support systems. In addition, large caseloads, staff shortages, and endless report writing leave the supervising officer unable to perform all the tasks called for by casework. Coupled with the trend away from the medical model, probation and parole administrators have initiated both the brokerage approach and community resource management teams.

Brokerage

Almost diametrically opposed to the casework approach is the brokerage approach, in which the supervising officer is not concerned primarily with understanding or changing the behavior of the offender, but rather with assessing the concrete needs of the individual and arranging for the probationer or parolee to receive services that directly address those needs. Since the officer is not seen as the primary agent of treatment or change, there is significantly less emphasis placed on the development of a close, one-to-one relationship between the officer and the offender. With the brokerage

approach, the supervising officer functions primarily as a manager or broker of resources and social services that are already available from other
agencies. It is the task of the probation or parole officer to assess the service
needs of the offender, locate the social service agency that addresses those
needs as its primary function, refer the offender to the appropriate agency,
and follow up referrals to make sure the offender has actually received the
services. Under the brokerage approach, it can be said that the officer's relationship with community service agencies is more important than the relationship with an individual client. Both the brokerage and casework approaches share the importance of the offenders' participation in developing
their own supervision plans.

The National Advisory Commission on Criminal Justice Standards
and Goals (1973: 320) recommended that the probation system should "redefine the role of probation officer from caseworker to community resource manager." The Commission report (1973: 322–23) characterized
the new approach in the following way:

> To carry out his responsibilities as a community resource manager, the proba-
> tion officer must perform several functions. In helping a probationer obtain
> needed services, the probation officer will have to assess the situation, know
> available resources, contact the appropriate resource, assist the probationer to
> obtain the services, and follow up on the case. When the probationer encoun-
> ters difficulty in obtaining a service he needs, the probation officer will have
> to explore the reason for the difficulty and take appropriate steps to see that
> the service is delivered. The probation officer will have to monitor and evalu-
> ate the services to which the probationer is referred.

The Commission also addressed the problem of the individual probation officer's providing services that may be available elsewhere. They encouraged (1973: 32) the reliance of probation departments on other social
service agencies by suggesting that "Probation systems should not attempt
to duplicate services already created by law and supposedly available to all
persons. The responsibility of the system and its staff should be to enable
the probationer to cut through the barriers and receive assistance from social institutions that may be all too ready to exclude him."

With its emphasis on the management of community resources, the
brokerage approach requires intimate knowledge of the services in the
community and the conditions under which each service is available. It
may not be feasible for each officer to accumulate and use this vast amount
of information about all the possible community service sources. It has
been frequently suggested, therefore, that the brokerage of community services might be more easily handled if individual probation or parole officers were to specialize in gaining knowledge about and familiarity with an
agency or set of agencies that provide related services. For example, one officer might become extremely knowledgeable about all community agencies that offer services for individuals with drug-related problems, while

another officer might specialize in all agencies that handle unemployed or underemployed individuals. Regardless of whether officers decide to specialize or would prefer to handle all types of community agencies, the essential requirements under the brokerage approach are for the supervising officer to develop a comprehensive knowledge of the resources already available in the community and to use those resources to the fullest extent for the benefit of clients.

Closely related to the brokerage approach is the role of advocacy. Several authors have recently stressed the advocacy role for probation officers.[3] Recognizing the fact that some of the services the offenders need will not be available in the community, these authors suggest that, rather than trying to supply those needed services themselves, probation and parole officers should concentrate on working with community agencies to develop the necessary services. This will ensure that these services will be available not only to probation or parole clients, but also to other individuals within the community who might require them.

The essential tasks of the brokerage orientation to probation and parole are the management of available community resources and the use of those services to meet the needs of offenders. There is little emphasis on the quality of the relationship that develops between the officer and the offender; rather, more emphasis is placed upon the close working relationship between the officer and the staff members of community social service agencies. Counseling and guidance are considered inappropriate activities for the probation and parole officer; no attempt is made to change the behavior of the offender. The primary function of the officer is to assess the concrete needs of each offender and make appropriate referrals to existing community services. Should the needed service not be available in the community, it is the responsibility of the officer to encourage the development of that service.

In contrast to the medical model, the brokerage approach is based upon the reintegration model, which emphasizes the needs of correctional clients for specialized services that can best be provided by established community agencies. As a rehabilitation device, brokerage replaces the casework approach. The brokerage task requires the assessment of client needs and the linkage of available community services with those needs.

Obviously, the brokerage approach has its drawbacks. Besides the lack of a strong relationship between the probation or parole officer and the offender, community services may not be readily available. This is often the case in more rural communities, and these service agencies may not be willing to accept an offender population. The recent cutbacks in funding have reduced the number of social service agencies available, and have forced others to reduce services and referrals.

This discussion of casework and brokerage—the major orientations for probation and parole supervision and service provision—has highlighted the essential tasks of each approach and has emphasized their differences.

Another major issue in supervision is one of form. Should offenders be supervised by a single officer or would team supervision be more efficient and effective?

Single Officer Versus Team Supervision

The tasks of probation and parole supervision and service provision have traditionally been performed by a single officer who is solely responsible for the offenders on that caseload, a method that has been closely associated with the casework approach to supervision. In recent years, however, many probation and parole agencies have been experimenting with the team approach. This method involves the assignment of an offender caseload to a team of officers, with an emphasis on both the diversity of the needs of the offenders in the caseload and of the officer skills that can be assembled.

As mentioned, the traditional model of caseload management and supervision in probation and parole has been the single officer type. Under this model, a caseload comprised of a certain number of offenders is assigned, through some technique, to an individual officer. Regardless of the extent of homogeneity of the characteristics of the offenders in the caseload, the single officer is solely responsible for the supervision of and provision of necessary services to all the offenders in his caseload.

There are several reasons why this model has continued in use for so many years with so little modification. First, it is obviously the easiest and simplest method for a department to use in dividing up the tasks that the agency must perform. The number of presentence investigation reports that must be prepared can easily be divided among available officers and, similarly, new cases can quickly be assigned to an individual officer's caseload.

Another reason is the widespread acceptance of the casework approach to correctional supervision and its emphasis on the personal one-to-one relationship. This is, of course, consistent with the assignment of the offender to a single officer.

Finally, the issue of accountability for the performance of an offender under supervision is used as an argument in favor of single officer caseloads. The single officer arrangement facilitates the evaluation of the officer's effectiveness with respect to the performance of the cases under his or her supervision, and allows the agency administration to make comparisons of effectiveness among all officers in the agency.

But the use of single officer caseloads has other management implications for the agency. Among them being that since the model requires that each officer must be able to handle all of the tasks required by the agency as well as to supervise and provide services for a wide variety of offenders, each officer must not only be able to prepare competent presentence investigation reports and carry out routine supervision and surveillance procedures, but also must be able to accurately assess the needs of a great many different individuals and then provide the necessary services personally or make appropriate referrals. In order to perform this wide variety of duties, each officer must possess a broad range of abilities and specialized skills.

However, as a step in the direction of reorganizing probation and parole resources to more effectively and efficiently meet the needs of their clients and to most effectively utilize the talents of their personnel, many agencies are adopting the team approach to supervision. Under this approach, a caseload of offenders is assigned to a group of officers who function together as a small work unit. The team as a whole can operate under a generalist or a specialist model—that is, the team may supervise a broad range of clients (drug or alcohol abusers, property offenders, probationers with problems with employment, etc.) or each officer within the team may specialize in the provision of a specific service, or all officers may be expected to provide all necessary services. There are several arguments advanced for the use of the team approach.

The first argument generally presented in favor of the team model is that it is possible to offer the offender a broader range of expertise and skills than would be available from a single officer. The team can be composed of several officers, each possessing different but complementary skills and areas of interest, thus making available to each client in the caseload the widest possible array of problem-solving talents.

Closely associated with this position is the argument that the increasingly larger caseloads that agencies must handle can be better dealt with using team supervision. Instead of four officers each trying to handle a caseload of 80 probationers, a four-officer team can handle the 320 cases more efficiently. Proponents of the team model agree that several advantages occur with this arrangement. First, team members are familiar with most of the clients in the caseload, thus enabling supervision and service provision to clients to continue uninterrupted in the event of one team member's absence. Second, though advocates of the single officer model emphasize the importance of the positive relationship between the officer and the offender, advocates of the team model point out that the benefits of this relationship are lost if the officer and the client are not compatible. Using the team model, each offender has a greater likelihood of finding an officer with whom he or she is compatible and feels comfortable. Third, the members of the team can specialize by function, with one officer specializing in intake and, perhaps in conjunction with one or more other officers, handling most of the caseload classification. Another officer might perhaps specialize in routine supervision and surveillance checks, while others would handle the actual provision of services and the referrals to other social service agencies. Fourth, the officers who make up the team may wish to specialize by area of expertise and interest. Under this arrangement, one officer might deal with the drug or alcohol problems in the caseload, another officer with the employment problems or vocational training needs of clients in the caseload, and a third with clients who need assistance in obtaining educational advancement. Finally, the adoption of the team approach places accountability for the performance of the caseload on the team as a whole, rather than an individual officer. Thus, both the decisions about the appropriate supervision and service provision strategies for a particular offender and the responsibility for the offender's performance under supervision are shared among the members of the team.

The team approach also offers many opportunities for the agency to use volunteers and paraprofessionals. One or more volunteers or paraprofessionals can be assigned to a particular team, depending upon the needs of the team and the special skills and interests of the volunteer or paraprofessionals.

However, the team approach also has its shortcomings: The offender may feel "shuffled" around from officer to officer—and, because no one single officer is responsible for any one offender, no one officer can be held accountable. There are also the problems normally associated with teamwork: coordination, communication, everyone carrying their own load, and personality conflicts.

Overall, the team approach to supervision represents an innovative and efficient means of providing supervision to offenders. But there has been little systematic research on the effectiveness of the team approach versus the single officer approach.

The latest attempt to formally structure teams in probation and parole centers around the use of Community Resource Management Teams.

Community Resource Management Team

The Community Resource Management Team (CRMT), is defined by Dell'Apa and his associates (1976) as consisting of seven basic assumptions:

1. Probation and parole services are in need of improved delivery system models.
2. Most offenders are not pathologically ill; therefore, the medical (casework) model is inappropriate.
3. Most probation and parole officers are not equipped by education and experience to provide professional casework counseling even if it is needed.
4. Existing probation/parole manpower is not likely to be expanded. Consequently, these people must come to view their roles in different and perhaps radically new terms if they are to deal with the increasing numbers of offenders under supervision.

5. Services needed by the offender to "make it" in society are available in the community social service network, rather than in the criminal justice system.
6. Probation and parole staff must assume advocacy roles in negotiating appropriate community-based services for offenders. They must assume a community organization and resource development role for needed services that do not exist.
7. A team approach represents a powerful and viable alternative to the autonomous and isolated individual officer and "case" relationship.

The CRMT approach is based upon a growing disillusionment with the casework approach to counseling and the ability of the probation officers to focus their efforts within a team approach.

Under the CRMT approach, the PO avoids both the counseling and surveillance roles and becomes a "resource broker," matching clients' needs with available community services. As Wilson (1978: 49) has indicated, CRMT involves the synthesis of four major elements: needs assessment, resource brokerage, pooled caseloads, and team (participatory) management.

In addition to transforming the role of the PO, the use of CRMT calls for a restructuring of the operations of parole and probation departments. According to Wood (1978: 8), the key elements of the CRMT system are:

1. A greater investment of efforts during the initial period of each probation.
2. The formation of an orderly process of client problem identification and client identification.
3. Establishment of service categories corresponding to the needs of the clients and the protection of the community.
4. Individual case plan development utilizing the skills and interest areas.
5. The utilization of community resources as an integral part of the rehabilitative process.

The first tasks facing the PO under the CRMT method are the completion of an information-gathering interview, and the completion of a needs-assessment profile (see Figure 9–1). The needs classification involves an assessment of the offenders' needs, with point scores scaled across eight categories of need. This profile then serves as a basis for that offender's treatment plan. Since cases are pooled rather than assigned to an individual PO's caseload, the offender is referred to a particular PO to receive a reference or help with a particular problem. The POs then develop a specific expertise within a certain area, such as employment (Gasaway, 1977). The PO, therefore, operates like a "real estate broker" (Wilson, 1978), learning what programs and agencies exist in the community that deal with the problem area of interest to the client. One of the results of this approach should be a higher number of client contacts initially. In the latter months, the community agencies would provide the support the offender desires with a particular problem.

The CRMT approach has been adopted in a number of areas; however, one of the most thorough evaluations of this technique has been undertaken in Philadelphia. The ECTA Corporation (1981) conducted an evaluation of 292 CRMT clients in two parole units over a nine-month period. Their findings indicate some of the potential benefits and relevant problems associated with CRMT. With regard to the number of client contacts, it was discovered that the largest portion of agent time was devoted to the initial determination of the offender's needs. This occurrence was expected; however, the agents did not, with the passage of time, reduce their level of contacts. ECTA (1981: 7) believed that this lack of reduction in contact was primarily caused by an inability to actually involve clients with community services. Apparently, it is difficult to tie criminal justice clients into the traditional social service agency network.

Yet, this difficulty did not arise from a lack of referrals from CRMT agents. Over the nine-month period, the CRMT units made 454 referrals for the 292 clients. However, due to an apparent lack of interest on the part of the social service agencies, it was not possible to document whether or not the referral was an effective way of obtaining services for the parolee. For these reasons, the ECTA evaluators (1981: 30) concluded that the CRMT assumption that if community agencies exist, they are necessarily *anxious* and *able* to help, is not always true.

Contracting

As indicated in Chapter 7, recent events have called for a change in the role of the probation officer. In addition to the demands to increase the surveillance aspect of probation, other changes in this field have been geared toward enhancing the social service aspect of the probation officer's role. The use of various types of contracts is one example of this development.

One of the major issues in probation has been the provision of probation services from community organizations. Linquist (1980: 60) has reported the preliminary effects of a Florida law which provided that "Anyone on probation or parole shall be required to contribute $10.00 per month to a court approved public or private entity providing him with supervision and rehabilitation." In particular, this act authorized the Salvation Army (or other approved public or private entity) to utilize its community service as an integral part of any court-ordered probation program. This legislation made it possible for any court-approved organiza-

Figure 9-1 CRMT Needs Assessment Scale

First Iteration ——
Second Iteration - - - -

Category of Need

Degree of Need	Employment	Vocational Training	Academic Training	Physical Health	Mental Health	Legal	Substance Abuse	Housing
HIGH	Without work. No prospects.	No marketable skills.	Functional illiterate.	Incapacitated. Needs medical services	Unstable. Lashes out or retreats into self.	Habitual civil and criminal problems.	Needs detoxification and treatment.	Constant transient.
	Work unstable. Casual labor.	Laborer minimal skills.	Backward but able to function at basic level.	Chronically ill. Needs medical care.	Confused, anxious and/or self-deprecating.		Extensive substance abuse.	Moves often.
	Work part-time. Little promise for future.		G.E.D. and functions well.	Occasional incapacitation.	Rational but occasional confusion.			
LOW	Working near potential.	Achieved full potential for work.		In sound health. Seldom ill.				

Source: Frank Dell'Apa, et al. "Advocacy, Brokerage, Community, The ABC's of Probation and Parole," *Federal Probation* 40 (1976).

tion to provide probation services and to collect a $10-per-month supervision fee from each client.

As a result, the Salvation Army Misdemeanor Probation Program (SAMP) was developed. Linquist reports that SAMP provides over 90 percent of all probation supervision for adult misdemeanants in Florida and has served an average of 7,000 clients per month. Research revealed that the average SAMP client was a youthful first offender, sentenced to probation for a six- to twelve-month period for a conviction for petit larceny, possession of a controlled substance, or disorderly conduct. In addition, the clientele were employed, white urban males earning about $400 per month in a variety of jobs. They received the equivalent of what has been termed minimum supervision—one visit per month from SAMP.

Linquist examined a sample of 3,320 cases terminated in three major urban areas from December 1976 through April 1978. He discovered that the SAMP clients had a revocation rate of 6.3 percent and called this "exceptionally low, even for a nontraditional program." However, Linquist also discovered that one quarter of the SAMP clients were unable to pay supervision costs and raised some question over the cost effectiveness of the program.

The SAMP program represents an attempt to treat some offenders in a nontraditional fashion and provide close ties between them and community programs. Such an innovation could, when used with a particular type of client (such as misdemeanants), help the offender and relieve the burden of heavy caseloads upon a probation department. Its use could also permit a probation department to deploy its resources in a more efficient manner.

Another type of probation contract directly focuses upon the probationer and the department in an attempt to fully articulate the obligations of each party during the supervision period. As defined by Ankersmit (1977: 28), setting the contract simply means reaching an agreement with the offender as to what goals he or she will work toward achieving. The basic idea is to use this device as a central point in the planning process, specifically including the probationer in this process.

Ankersmit (1977: 31–32) identifies three possibilities when setting this contract. Each focuses upon the type and motivations of probationers and attempts to clarify their needs.

> 1. The "Barebones" Legal Contract. No counseling contract can be made because the probationer does not want counseling. His attitude is clear: "I have to be on probation. I don't like it, and there is nothing I want from you." If regular reporting is one of the conditions of probation, the client must still report. But it is explicit that no casework is offered. The client should be made aware that he must, as must all probationers, take the consequences of his behavior should he run afoul of the law.

2. The Counseling Contract. The probationer may want job counseling, e.g., to learn how to channel his anger in a less harmful way. The simple desire to stop breaking the law because of the unpleasant consequences is a very acceptable contract, and often the only one that can be set with a sociopathic personality. With such an offender, it is futile to moralize or preach. A hard-nosed approach about the discomforts of being incarcerated is best. Asking the probationer to talk in great detail about his personal experiences in jail or prison reminds him vividly of the unpleasant consequences of law breaking.

3. The Supportive Relationship. No verbal contract is set because the probationer is not capable of it, nor is he receptive to counseling in a goal-oriented sense. Nevertheless, he relies heavily on a supportive relationship. . . . The work here is mainly helping the probationer deal with his day-to-day crises. . . . The probation officer may be the only stable person in their lives.

Ankersmit asserts that the use of these contract categories will help probation officers set priorities within their caseloads, and help them more clearly realize what can and cannot be done with an individual probationer.

Scott (1978) reports the results of the implementation of probation contract programs in New York and Michigan. In New York, the Mutual Objectives Probation Programming program specifically identifies the clients' program plans in such areas as employment, education, vocational training, leisure time activities, dealing with financial problems, meeting health needs, or dealing with other problems. The plans are stated in the form of objectives (i.e., enroll in high school equivalency program within thirty days), and the agreement specifies the help that will be provided by the probation department to assist in the attainment of the objective. The New York contract also indicates the anticipated date of probation termination, which should provide additional incentive. Scott reports (1978: 57) that evaluations of this program have revealed that it was associated with the decreased use of the local county jails, decreased commitments to state prison, and shorter periods of probation supervision.

In Michigan, the Mutual Objectives Program focuses upon the establishment of contracts that closely resemble traditional special conditions of probation. Terms often outline payment of fines, court costs, or restitution; educational and vocational training; extra reporting agreements; or participation in drug, alcohol, or psychiatric treatment programs. Scott also reports preliminary evaluative evidence that the Michigan program has contributed to a reduced commitment rate to state prisons.

Scott clearly outlines some additional advantages, as well as disadvantages, associated with probation contracting. First, the probationer is intimately involved in supervision planning from the very beginning of this process. As a result, the sentencing judge is provided with additional information on program plans and on the motivations of the offender. Probationers have clear specifications of what is expected of them, including the possibility of early termination. In addition, the probation officer is provided with clearly specified objectives for supervision, and has a better idea of how to proceed with supervision plans. The hope is that contractual programming will result in a more efficient approach to probation management.

Some of the potential drawbacks of this approach include the issue of voluntarism. Is the convicted offender free to voluntarily negotiate the terms of a contract, and are such contracts truly legal? Will probation contracting become beset with all of the due process demons that have been raised by plea bargaining? Another question involves the role of the judiciary. Is the judge obligated to consent to the conditions of the probation contract? How should the prosecutor and the victim (if present) be involved? These questions indicate the necessity of entering negotiations with all relevant parties when establishing a probation contract. Scott indicates that it is possible to obtain the involvement of all important parties and arrive at a contract which meets the needs and concerns of all.

In short, it appears that contracting offers an opportunity to establish a system which fortifies and goes beyond the traditional standard special conditions of supervision. It can provide several benefits to both the offender and the department, and can lead to the efficient management of community services.

Supervision Planning

Regardless of the approach used by an agency to deliver services, an essential ingredient to successful supervision is planning. This includes the identification of the needs and problems of the offender, identifying the resources available and arranging for them, and evaluating the effectiveness of the supervision activities.

Needs Assessment

The recognition that a problem exists is essential if that problem is to be solved. Similarly, the supervising agent must assess the offender's needs and problems if an adequate resolution is to be made.

Most needs assessments are conducted by the individual probation or parole officer. Information from the offender, PSI, family members, or institutional records are common sources of information. The needs assessment can occur informally, which is usually the case, or it can be a formal activity required by the agency and involving various assessment materials. Figure 9–2 presents one such form from a county probation department, Here, needs are assessed by the probation officer, via the means dis-

Figure 9-2   Assessment of Client Needs

NEED AND CONTRACT INFORMATION

NAME _____

I.D. _____

OFFICER _____

Needs Data

Low need: This implies that a need exists, but that it is not severe enough to warrant special attention.

Moderate need: This could include upgrading in an area, or definite need that requires some attention.

High need: Obvious need exists. The client is so lacking as to require special attention to this area.

Initial Need Level

1. Vocational Training
   - (0) No need
   - (1) Low need
   - (2) Moderate need
   - (3) High need

2. Employment
   - (0) No need
   - (1) Low need
   - (2) Moderate need
   - (3) High need

3. Education Services
   - (0) No need
   - (1) Low need
   - (2) Moderate need
   - (3) High need

4. Budgeting and Financial
   - (0) No need
   - (1) Low need
   - (2) Moderate need
   - (3) High need

5. Drug Services
   - (0) No need
   - (1) Low need
   - (2) Moderate need
   - (3) High need

6. Alcohol Services
   - (0) No need
   - (1) Low need
   - (2) Moderate need
   - (3) High need

7. Mental Health Services
   - (0) No need
   - (1) Low need
   - (2) Moderate need
   - (3) High need

8. Medical Services
   - (0) No need
   - (1) Low need
   - (2) Moderate need
   - (3) High need

9. Legal Services
   - (0) No need
   - (1) Low need
   - (2) Moderate need
   - (3) High need

10. Welfare Services
   - (0) No need
   - (1) Low need
   - (2) Moderate need
   - (3) High need

11. Family Counseling
   - (0) No need
   - (1) Low need
   - (2) Moderate need
   - (3) High need

12. Individual Counseling
   - (0) No need
   - (1) Low need
   - (2) Moderate need
   - (3) High need

13. Group Counseling
   - (0) No need
   - (1) Low need
   - (2) Moderate need
   - (3) High need

14. Leisure Time
   - (0) No need
   - (1) Low need
   - (2) Moderate need
   - (3) High need

15. Housing
   - (0) No need
   - (1) Low need
   - (2) Moderate need
   - (3) High need

SOURCE: Adapted from the Lucas County Adult Probation Dept., Toledo, OH.

Figure 9-2   (*continued*)

Contract Information

When an area of moderate or high need is recognized, a contract may be
negotiated. This implies that the officer will attempt to secure the
necessary assistance whether internally or through an appropriate agency.
The contract is a <u>two-way street</u> -- the client is expected to honor the
conditions of the contract.

Needs Included in Contract

16. Contract Negotiated

   (0) No need

   (1) Low need

   (2) Moderate need

   (3) High need

17. Date of Contract

18. Vocational

   (1) Yes

   (2) No

19. Employment

   (1) Yes

   (2) No

20. Educational

   (1) Yes

   (2) No

21. Budgeting and
    Financial Services

   (1) Yes

   (2) No

22. Drug Services

   (1) Yes

   (2) No

23. Alcohol Services

   (1) Yes

   (2) No

24. Mental Health
    Services

   (1) Yes

   (2) No

25. Medical Services

   (1) Yes

   (2) No

26. Legal Services

   (1) Yes

   (2) No

27. Welfare Services

   (1) Yes

   (2) No

28. Family Counseling

   (1) Yes

   (2) No

29. Individual
    Counseling

   (1) Yes

   (2) No

30. Group Counseling

   (1) Yes

   (2) No

31. Leisure Time
    Activities

   (1) Yes

   (2) No

32. Housing

   (1) Yes

   (2) No

cussed above. This information becomes part of the offender's supervision
plan and allows periodic review of progress throughout the supervision period. This particular probation department also negotiates a "contract"
between the offender and the supervising officer. In this situation, a contract implies that the probation or parole officer will attempt to deliver the
necessary assistance, and that the offender will honor the conditions of the
contract.

    Needs assessments prepared by the supervising officer appear to be the
rule rather than the exception. In a recent survey of parole agencies, Latessa and Allen (1981: 11–12) found that twenty-five of the fifty-two jurisdictions surveyed reported that the parole officer to whom the parolee was
assigned prepared a needs assessment. Nineteen reported that these were in

conjunction with a formal needs assessment prepared by the agency. Two states had only the formal needs assessment, and six states reported only the parole officer's assessment.

Federal Supervision Planning Example

Perhaps the best example of supervision planning comes from the federal probation system, and is part of its overall classification process.[4] This process involves the establishment of an appropriate supervision level, defined as either high or low activity. Introduced in 1981, the Classification and Supervision Planning System determines the degree of risk of recidivism in an individual case and establishes an appropriate level of supervision activity.

The first step in this system is the classification of the offender into a supervision level. Two actuarial devices are used in the system—the risk prediction scale (which follows in this chapter), for persons on probation, and the salient factor score (see Chapter 6), for persons on parole. Here we will focus on the scale for probationers.

Using the risk scale in Figure 9–3, the probation officer determines the level of supervision from a choice of two: low activity and high activity.

Persons in the low-activity supervision level, as reflected in their histories, have usually experienced relative success in establishing personal stability. This level is analogous to minimum supervision where sustained control is seldom necessary. Persons in the high-activity supervision level have usually experienced difficulty in establishing and maintaining personal stability. Probation officers direct the greater proportion of their efforts toward persons in the high-activity supervision level. The federal system sets no upper limit on the number of contacts given a person in a month's time; however, a minimum of once a month is required.

With the approval of a supervisor, a probation officer may override the predicted supervision level from low activity to high activity. There are three conditions that justify an override:

I. Aggravated Offense Circumstances
   A. Violence
      1. present offense or prior record involving violence
      2. use of weapons in the commission of crime
   B. Notoriety of offense
      1. violation of trust by high ranking public official
      2. value of crime greater than $50,000
      3. crimes endangering national security
   C. Continuing criminal conspiracy
      1. wholesale drug distributor
      2. member of organized crime
      3. major corporate offender

Figure 9-3   Risk Prediction Scale

```
Automatic Component:   Automatically places an individual in low-activity
                       supervision if two conditions are satisfied.
```

```
    A.   Offender has a 12th-grade education or better;  and

    B.   The individual has a history free of opiate usage.

If the two conditions are not met, the remaining itmes are scored.

    C.   Twenty-eight years of age, or older, at time of
         offense (7 points)
         If not, score as 0.

    D.   Arrest-free period of five or more consecutive years (4 points)
         If not, score as 0.

    E.   Few prior arrests (none, one, or two = 10 points)
         If not, score as 0.

    F.   History free of opiate usage (9 points)
         If not, score as 0.

    G.   At least four months of steady employment immediately prior
         to arraignment for present offense (3 points)
         If not, score as 0.
```

Risk Score	Supervisor Level	Minimum Personal Contacts	Maximum Personal Contacts	Collateral Contacts
Automatic Assignment or 20–33	Low activity	1 per quarter	1 per quarter	Unlimited
0–19	High activity	1 per month	No maximum	Unlimited

SOURCE: Adopted from the Classification and Supervision Planning System, Probation Division, Administrative Office, U.S. Courts, January 1981.

II. Special Conditions
   A. Court or parole commission ordered special supervision
   B. Drug aftercare program ordered
III. Exceptional Case Circumstances
   (Exceptional case circumstances are significant social problems characterized by aggravated personal distress that, if left unresolved, would likely subject the community or offender to harm) [Classification and Supervision Planning System, 1981: 6].

The classification process is concluded with the establishment of an appropriate level of supervision activity.

The next step in this process involves the development of a supervision plan that identifies significant problems and the methods to be used in resolving these problem areas.

As with all good supervision planning, a critical element is the participation of the offender, since behavior changes only after there is perceived advantages to changing old behavior patterns (1981: 8).

The three basic interrelated components of the federal system are:

1. Identifying supervision problems
2. Setting objectives
3. Developing the supervision plan

Supervision problems can be defined as those circumstances that limit the offender's ability or desire to function within the requirements of probation and parole, and which the supervising officer anticipates are directly linked to supervision outcome. An example of a supervision problem from the federal probation system (1981: 9) is outlined in Figure 9–4.

After problems and objectives have been identified, the supervising officer formulates a plan for achieving those objectives. The methods selected are based on such considerations as the nature of the problem, the abilities and expertise of the officer, the availability of effective community resources, the attitude of the offender, and the exercise of authority necessary to insure the offender's participation.

The federal classification system requires that the plan specify whether a referral will be made to community resources, or whether the officer will be the primary provider of services. If community resources

Figure 9–4   Supervision Problem: An Example

```
Supervision Problems

Health:      This offender has a documented history of heroin
             addiction dating back 7 years and has two previous
             convictions for selling drugs to support a $100-a-day
             habit.
Family:      Recently separated from his wife and two children but
             would like to be reunited with them.  Several reports
             of wife abuse have been recorded.
Employment:  Unemployed — occasional construction laborer.
```

For each supervision problem, a corresponding supervision objective is developed.

```
Supervision Objectives

Assist offender to locate and maintain employment.  Abstain from
drug use, stabilize marital relationship.
```

were used, the officer must indicate how he or she intends to complement the work of that agency. The federal probation system does not allow an officer to delegate total responsibility for supervision of an offender to any other agency.

A well thought-out initial supervision plan is the cornerstone of supervision activities. The plan need not be lengthy, but it should specify actions to be taken by the supervising officer, the responsibilities of the offender, and the role of any community resources. Time frames for achieving the supervision objectives should be stated whenever it is reasonable to do so. Several examples of supervision plans from the Federal Classification Planning System (1981: 22) are as follows:

SUPERVISION PLAN

Although there are no significant supervision problems which can be clearly identified at this time, we do want to determine if Mr. Edward has a problem with compulsive gambling. Monthly personal contacts will be addressed to that end. Additionally, until we better understand his financial circumstances, monthly collateral contact will be made at his home and with relevant police officials.

SUPERVISION PLAN

Mr. Harris has a record of several minor convictions for drunk driving (3), and assault and battery (2), where the complainant was his wife. Although denied by Harris, alcohol abuse may be a significant underlying problem. Semi-monthly personal contact will explore the alcohol issue through direct confrontation and observation with Harris and interaction with the family. A referral to Alcoholics Anonymous may become necessary. The relationship of alcohol abuse to poor work performance and/or attendance will be explored with his employer, who is aware of Mr. Harris' probation status.

The payment of the court imposed fine of $2,000 may present a problem since considerable liabilities and pressing debts exist. This will be discussed in the next office visit.

SUPERVISION PLAN

Although a low-activity case, Mrs. Walters has a number of problems, most of which are economic in nature, including dependency on welfare, four residential moves in the past fourteen months, and two children experiencing school problems.

We have contacted the New Start Community Agency (637-2345), a United Way funded agency in her community. They are familiar with the family circumstances and are willing to assign a counselor to work with her and the family. We will discuss a referral to New Start with Mrs. Walters. The focus of this agency is to teach her a skill with the ultimate goal to enter her in the labor force, rendering welfare unnecessary. Two personal contacts will be made per quarter to encourage her involvement with New Start. Collateral contacts with the agency will be made as necessary.

SUPERVISION PLAN

Mr. Smith will be seen at the office once a month and at home or at his job twice a month for the purpose of monitoring his activities. Collateral contact will be made regularly with the intelligence division of the local police department to determine if he is associating with known criminals. Requests for travel outside the district will be thoroughly investigated before approval.

In addition to the supervision plan, the Federal Probation Division requires semiannual case reviews. This review includes an evaluation of the dynamics of the offender's supervision problems as they have emerged in the previous six months. The review highlights the degree of progress achieved in meeting previously established objectives and specifies the number and type of contacts during the period under review. Finally, the officer identifies new problems and revises the supervision plan to meet the current situation.

Undoubtedly, supervision planning varies from agency to agency, and often from officer to officer; however, the Federal Supervision Planning System presented above represents the "state of the art" in caseload management. Regardless of the process or format, there are common elements involved in supervision planning: recognizing problems, selecting objectives, developing a strategy, implementing that strategy, and, finally, evaluating the effectiveness of the entire process.

The final section of this chapter will examine one of the most important and controversial issues in correctional programming: differentiated levels of supervision.

Levels of Supervision

During the past two decades, probation and parole departments in the United States have devoted a great deal of attention to caseload sizes and their effectiveness. Often referred to as differentiated levels of supervision, varying caseload size can be seen as both a treatment and a management strategy. The major assumption behind differentiated supervision is that, while some offenders may require very little supervision, others will require intensive supervision (see Figure 9–5). Assignment to the different levels of supervision (generally minimum, regular, and intensive) is based upon an assessment of client risk and/or need, or a classification by type of offense.

The assumption behind intensive supervision is that decreased caseload size will lead to increased contact between the probation or parole of-

Figure 9-5   Revising Supervision Objectives

Supervision Problems and (Revised) Objectives

Mr. Johnson maintans steady employment and is current on his fine payments. No significant supervision problems are present. Case will be monitored for fine payment and for changes in social situations.

Supervision Problems and (Revised) Objectives

During the past 6 months, Mr. Little has exhibited problems of alcohol abuse. His wife reports he is not contributing enough money to support the family. Family arguments are frequent. Attendance problems at work have surfaced and his current employment may be in jeopardy. Since problems have reached near crisis proportions, intensive efforts to control alcohol abuse need to be initiated. Stabilizing the family situation and improving attendance at work are of paramount importance.

---

ficer and the client, resulting in improved service delivery and more efficient treatment, which in turn will effect a reduction in recidivism (Banks et al., 1976). For those who require few or no special services and pose little threat to community safety, minimum supervision has been used. This type of supervision is sometimes seen as "crisis intervention," since the contact between the probation or parole officer and the client may be limited to a monthly written report unless a specific request for services is made for a particularly stressful situation that the client might face.

Because there is a great deal of debate surrounding the use and effectiveness of differentiated levels of supervision, it is important to examine how the different levels translate into levels of contact and service delivery, to explore the definitions of levels of supervision, and to discuss basic management issues regarding this subject.

Intensive Supervision

At the conceptual core of intensive supervision services is the issue of caseload size. Behind the general interest in intensive supervision projects is the perceived failure of traditional probation and parole in which officer caseload sizes of one hundred to three hundred offenders are typical. Oversized caseloads are often identified as the obstacle to successful probation and parole; indeed, a very large caseload may have serious consequences for both the officer and the client. The probation or parole officer can easily feel overwhelmed in providing supervision and assistance to the offenders comprising this caseload if it is extremely large; this may, in turn, affect the quality of supervision and services rendered to each client.

There is no clear-cut consensus on what constitutes an adequate definition of intensive supervision. During the first phase of the well-known San Francisco project, conducted during the late 1960s, intensive supervision was operationally defined as:

> a twenty-five unit workload based upon an average of twenty cases for supervision, including probationers, parolees, and mandatory releases, and an average of one presentence investigation and report per month [Lohman et al., 1967: 1].

Clients are usually assigned to intensive supervision because of a high or specialized need, or high-risk factor; however, the actual caseload assignment for intensive projects varies considerably. While most report caseload sizes of twenty-five to fifty, there are some departments that consider eighty-five a reduced caseload. If, in fact, the regular officers are supervising 250 + clients, then there is some justification for this "intensive" label. In addition, consideration must be made for other duties assigned probation and parole officers. For example, presentence investigations will result in an increased workload, but will not necessarily be reflected in caseload size.

As expected, levels of contact are increased in intensive supervision. However, while contact data are available, there is some question as to the quality of the contacts that are being conducted. It is obvious that intensive supervision caseloads can double the number of contacts between the officer and client, and the amount of time spent in contacts. It is important, however, to point out that the difference between spending half an hour per month with a client and spending an hour per month is, relatively speaking, an extremely small difference considering the magnitude of treatment and service provision task that the officer is trying to accomplish. The major assumption with intensive supervision is that a multitude of benefits will flow from the increased contact between the officer and client, such as increased officer understanding, development of better skills in matching services to needs, better diagnostic assessments, and improved treatment judgments. Thus, the implied assumption is that the following causal link exists (Carlson et al., 1979: 68):

Decreased caseload size	→	Increased contact	→	Improved service delivery and more effective treatment	→	Reduction in recidivism rates

Recently, intensive supervision has been used for offenders who would otherwise be sentenced to prison. This not only saves money, but it has been an effective way to reduce prison overcrowding (Latessa, 1983). Perhaps the most extensive program in the country is the Intensive Probation Supervision (IPS) project in Georgia. The IPS is a statewide project in which a team of two probation officers are assigned caseloads of twenty-five probationers or less. They are required to see their clients at least five times per week, and everyone has a 7:00 P.M. curfew. This project is probably the most "intensive" attempt to increase supervision. Similar programs have begun in New Jersey and Washington (Gettinger, 1983: 7–8).

Minimum Supervision

It is a recognized fact that some offenders within the probation and parole agency caseload actually require little supervision. These clients may present very few concrete needs and pose little threat to community safety. It is believed that these individuals, who may comprise a large percentage of the total agency caseload, will perform acceptably and serve their probation or parole period successfully without even routine supervision.

These offenders are usually required only to check in periodically with their probation or parole officer, perhaps only in writing or by telephone. The officer, of course, is still available to provide support and assistance should the client request it. The minimum level of supervision is justified on two bases: first, the offender simply does not need any higher level of supervision or service provision; and second, the manpower resources of the agency can more effectively be utilized in concentrating on those who do present a variety of concrete needs or who appear to pose a threat to the safety of the community.

As Lohman (1969) indicates, minimum supervision can be termed "crisis supervision"—supervision that emerges only in a crisis situation and is brought to the attention of the officer by the client or another agency or person. Beyond this, the only contact between the officer and the client is the written monthly report.

A recent example of minimum supervision is the Administrative Caseload Project (Vito and Marshall, 1983). ACLP was developed in the Eastern District of Pennsylvania (federal) for offenders who were not viewed as a threat to the community and did not require a high level of supervision. Research indicated that the average ACLP client was:

A married, forty or older, white male with some dependents, who had a high school education or higher.

Employed full time at a professional occupation.

Considered a very good risk in terms of salient factor score.

Placed on probation as a result of a white-collar crime conviction and had no prior record.

Meets the conditions of supervision at the time of entry.

Had at least six months of supervision remaining.

Had to pay either fines or restitution.

Stable in terms of employment and finances, residence, domestic relations, and reporting.

In terms of service delivery, it was clear that the average case did receive minimum supervision. During his or her eleven months in the program, the average ACLP client received 3.2 telephone and 11.3 written but no home or collateral contacts while making a grand total of $140,155.38 of payments in fines or restitution. Of the ninety-three ACLP cases terminated from supervision over a two-year period, only two (2.2 percent) were recidivists. On this basis, it appears that minimum supervision, when used with the appropriate individual, can help deploy manpower in a more efficient fashion.

Effectiveness

The issues of how increasing or decreasing caseloads can affect performances of clients has received widespread attention and generated considerable controversy. Adams (1967: 48–57), discussing a decade of caseload research in California, stated that ". . . one is impressed by the fact that all the reduced caseload projects of the Los Angeles County Probation Department have shown small caseloads to be more effective. All have shown the experimentals to have significantly lower failure rates. . . ." The probation department succeeded in reducing failure rates, whereas the parole units that conducted reduced caseload projects did not have similar success. Adams concludes that ". . . probation and other open-community procedures will play far more important roles in the total correctional process." In the San Francisco Project, four levels of supervision were identified, classifying caseloads as "ideal" (fifty workload units), "normal" (a hundred workload units), "intensive" (twenty-five workload units), and "minimum" (self-reporting). After two years, an assessment was made of the project cases. The available data indicated that the number of contacts between an offender and the probation or parole officer is seemingly unrelated to success (Carter et al., 1967).

Adams and Vetter (1974: 333–43) concluded a thorough study of probation caseload effectiveness by indicating that there has not been an adequate assessment of the influence of caseload across the range of offender types. They found that in the few studies approaching methodological adequacy in which caseload size had been employed as an independent variable, results have been compounded by the influence of other variables.

Actually, we do not know what is operating when we provide "correctional treatment" in varying degrees of intensity; we do not know whether varying the caseload size leads to corresponding variation in intensity; and we do not know the differential effects of such manipulations on any number of potentially significant target variables. This chaotic state of affairs heavily underlies the necessity for research to be anchored in theory. . . . We must conclude that caseload size remains an open situation.

In an attempt to clarify some of the controversy surrounding differentiated levels of supervision, the National Institute of Law Enforcement and Criminal Justice of the U.S. Department of Justice recently funded a two-year study of intensive probation. This project selected Milwaukee as its test site to implement and evaluate the effect of intensive supervision with probationers. The following conclusions were obtained by this study (Executive Summary, 1982: 18–19).

The general characteristics of the probationers assigned to intensive service are: clearly high risk, a larger proportion with social service needs, high unemployment rates, significant earlier criminal histories.

Probationers assigned to intensive service for the first six months of probation had more face-to-face and phone contacts with their probation officers than their counterpart high-risk probationers in control groups receiving normal service levels.

Probationers receiving intensive service had higher referral levels to social community service agencies than other high-risk probationers. Intensive service probationers were referred more frequently, as well.

However, the rates of successful completion, revocation, new offenses, absconders for probationers receiving intensive service were no better than those receiving normal service.

On the other hand, the intensive service probationers performed significantly better than their counterpart high-risk normal-service probationers in all indicators of social adjustment.

It did cost approximately 50 percent more per probationer to provide intensive service levels.

The correctional caseload research that has followed the growing interest in intensive supervision has apparently fallen short of answering what seems to be the essential question: Do reduced caseloads have an appreciable effect on recidivism? It appears obvious that, within any intensive supervision project, a number of variables affect the supervision process, and the question of the effectiveness of reduced caseloads is perhaps misstated.

In actuality, intensive supervision could have any of a number of effects. The reduced caseloads could enable the officer to do a better job of keeping the client out of trouble, or it could lead the officer to increase surveillance and thus increase the possibility of probation or parole revocation. The client could find the added support, assistance, and services useful and make a more positive adjustment, or the client could react adversely to this increased contact and become more hostile toward those associated with the law.

Managerial Implications

A number of problems exist, the first of which is to determine the classification system utilized to place offenders in a certain caseload size. To date, these classification systems have been based upon a determination of risk or specific need. The major problem here is that no adequate "risk" classification system is known to exist. What type of offender will respond (i.e., refrain from further criminal behavior) to a particular type of program? Even if the classification issues were resolved, the problem of matching the offender and the officer must be confronted. A basis for selection is by no means clear. Personality characteristics have been suggested as a guide, but again, what kind of offender responds to what caseload size and type of officer has not been determined.

An additional shortcoming is that the treatment involved in intensive supervision has not been clearly stated beyond being described as "increased attention." As noted earlier, increased attention may actually be nothing more than spending one hour per month with each client rather than half an hour per month. The problem of lack of clarity is present in the concept of minimum supervision as well, since an adequate response by an officer to a crisis situation may actually require more attention than is normally given to a client in an intensive supervision caseload. There is clearly a need to isolate and identify factors in the officer/client relationship that define the quality of contact, rather than simply relying on the mere counting of contacts and contact time.

In addition to lack of direction, the probation or parole officer has no guarantee that reduction in caseload size will lead to greater personal job satisfaction. In fact, if intensive and minimum caseload sizes were implemented in the same office, hostility and dissension might result. Officers with the larger caseloads of minimum supervision cases may interpret their assignment as "more work for less pay," a morale problem that must be considered.

Given the fact that an oversized caseload could impede the delivery of needed services, reduced caseload size has its own particular set of problems for the officer, including the possibility of boredom, busy-work or supervision, "overkill" resulting in a subsequent increase in technical violations, or client-dependency engendered by the increased attention of the officer.

We know little about the budgetary implications of differentiated levels of supervision. It has been taken for granted that reduction in caseload size equals a savings by way of outcome effectiveness. It has also been assumed that increasing the size of minimum supervision caseloads would increase cost-efficiency. To date there are no adequate cost-benefit analyses of this subject.

Summary

This chapter has discussed one of the most important aspects of probation and parole: supervision of the offender. We have noted that assignment of offenders to a probation or parole officer for supervision can follow several models. Some offenders are randomly assigned to caseloads, others are assigned based on geography or special problems, while yet others are classified through the use of prediction devices.

Once assignment is complete, the approach or philosophy of supervision usually centers around casework and brokerage. Casework follows a belief that the supervising officers should be the primary agent of change and thus "all things to all people." The brokerage approach assumes that the best place for treatment is in the community, and that the primary task of the probation or parole officer is to arrange for and manage community resources. While casework is the norm, in reality most probation and parole officers and agencies use techniques from both approaches.

Perhaps due to the prevalence of the casework approach, the tasks of supervision have traditionally been performed by a single officer. This has begun to change, as many agencies begin to recognize the team approach as a viable alternative to the single officer model.

Perhaps the most innovative technique has been the development of community resource management teams in an attempt to more fully harness the resources of the community. Similarly, contracting for services has been suggested as one attempt to deliver more effective treatment and community involvement.

This chapter has also addressed supervision planning and provided an example of the latest strategy to accomplish the many facets of probation and parole supervision. These strategies will become more frequent and more sophisticated in the future.

Finally, this chapter presented a discussion of differentiated levels of supervision. Both intensive supervision and minimum supervision are designed to reallocate probation and parole department resources in a more responsive and effective manner, and while this chapter has attempted to present what is known about varying caseload size, debate and controversy exist. The question of whether intensive supervision reduces recidivism remains unanswered.

Notes

1. As before, parole board refers to all agencies (commissions, boards of charities, boards of prison terms, and so on) whose duty it is to release inmates to the community, under supervision, prior to the expiration of the original sentence length.
2. Much of this section was drawn from Eric W. Carlson, Evalyn C. Parks, and Harry E. Allen, *Critical Issues in Adult Probation, Issues in Probation Management*, (National Institute of Law Enforcement and Criminal Justice, Law Enforcement Assistance Administration, U.S. Department of Justice, September 1979), chapters III and IV.
3. For a good example of advocacy in probation and parole, see: Frank Dell'Apa, et al., "Advocacy, Brokerage, Community: The ABC's of Probation and Parole," *Federal Probation* 40 (1976):37–44; and Claude T. Mangrum, *The Professional Practitioner in Probation* (Springfield, Ill.: Charles C. Thomas, 1975), pp. 43–44.
4. Much of the material in this section is adopted from *Classification and Supervision Planning System* (Probation Division; Administrative Office of the United States Courts, January 1981).

Study Guides

1. What are the different ways in which probationers can be assigned to individual officers' caseloads?
2. Should an agency adopt a casework approach to probation supervision, or would a brokerage approach be more appropriate? Why?
3. What advantages are there for organizing the probation officer force into teams rather than utilizing the traditional single officer caseload model?
4. What are the fundamental steps in supervision planning?
5. What are the advantages and disadvantages of contracting in probation?
6. What are the basic concepts behind the CRMT approach? What problems does it attempt to solve?
7. What are the basic assumptions underlying casework? Brokerage?
8. Why does random assignment of offenders to caseloads pose problems to the supervising officer?
9. Why is social casework described as an art?
10. What are the major assumptions behind differentiated levels of supervision?
11. What are three of the reasons for reducing caseload size?
12. What are some of the possible effects of intensive supervision?
13. Describe the Classification and Planning System used by the Federal Probation System.
14. What are the basic functions a supervising officer can fulfill?

Key Terms

advocacy role	mutual objectives programming
brokerage	needs assessment
case review	override
casework	probation contracts
conventional model	SAMP
crisis intervention	supervision objectives
CRMT	supervision problems
high activity	team supervision
intensive supervision	tunnel supervision
low activity	vertical model
minimum supervision	

References

ADAMS, REED, AND VETTER, HAROLD. "Effectiveness of Probation Caseload Sizes: A Review of the Empirical Literature." *Criminology* 9 (1974):333–43.

ADAMS, STUART. "Some Findings from Correctional Caseload Research." *Federal Probation* 31 (1967):48–57.

ANKERSMIT, EDITH. "Setting the Contract in Probation." *Federal Probation* 41 (1977):28–33.

BANKS, JERRY, ET AL. *Issue Paper: Phase I Evaluation of Intensive Special Probation Projects*. Atlanta, Ga.: School of Industrial and Systems Engineering, Georgia Institute of Technology, 1976. Unpublished draft.

BOWERS, SWITUN. "The Nature and Definition of Social Casework." In *Principles and Techniques in Social Casework*, edited by C. Kasius, pp. 126–39. New York: Family Services Association of America, 1950.

CARLSON, ERIC, ET AL. *Critical Issues in Adult Probation: Issues in Probation Management*. Washington, D.C.: U.S. Department of Justice, 1979.

CARTER, ROBERT M., AND WILKINS, LESLIE T. "Caseloads: Some Conceptual Models." In *Probation, Parole and Community Corrections*, 2nd ed., edited by R. M. Carter and L. T. Wilkins, pp. 391–401. New York: John Wiley and Sons, 1976.

CARTER, ROBERT, M.; ROBINSON, JAMES; AND WILKINS, LESLIE T. *The San Francisco Project: A Study of Federal Probation and Parole, Final Report*. Berkeley, Calif.: University of California at Berkeley, 1967.

Classification and Supervision Planning System. Probation Division, Administrative Office, U.S. Courts, Washington, D.C., 1981.

DELL'APA, FRANK; ADAMS, W. TOM; JORGENSEN, JAMES D.; AND SIGURDSON, HERBERT R. "Advocacy, Brokerage, Community: The ABC's of Probation and Parole," *Federal Probation* 40 (1976):37–44.

ECKMAN, PAUL. *Impact Evaluation Report #26: Special Probation Caseloads for Impact Offenders*. Newark, N.J.: Essex County Probation Department, 1977: Page 1.

ECTA Corporation. *Final Report: Longitudinal Investigation of CRMT Normative Needs Clients*. Harrisburg, Penn.: Pennsylvania Board of Probation and Parole, 1981.

Executive Summary National Evaluation Program—Phase II Intensive Evaluation of Probation. Bethesda, Md.: System Sciences, Inc., March 31, 1982).

GASAWAY, DONALD D. "The Probation Officer as Employment Counselor," *Federal Probation* 41 (1977):43–44.

GETTINGER, STEPHEN. "Intensive Supervision: Can It Rehabilitate Probation?," *Corrections Magazine*, April 1983, 6–17.

HARDMAN, DALE G. "Authority in Casework—A Bread-and-Butter Theory," *National Probation and Parole Association Journal* 5 (1959):249–55.

LATESSA, EDWARD J. *The Fifth Evaluation of the Lucas County Probation Department's Incarceration Diversion Unit*. Cincinnati, Ohio: University of Cincinnati, 1983.

LATESSA, EDWARD J., AND ALLEN, HARRY E. "Parole and Probation: Predispositional Practices." Paper presented at the Annual Meeting of the American Society of Criminology, Washington, D.C., 1981.

LINQUIST, CHARLES A. "The Private Sector in Probation: Contracting Services From Community Organizations," *Federal Probation* 45 (1980):58–64.

LOHMAN, JOSEPH D., ET AL. *The Minimum Supervision Caseload: A Preliminary Evaluation: The San Francisco Project Series Report #8*. Berkeley, Calif. University of California at Berkeley, 1969.

———. *The Intensive Supervision Caseload: A Preliminary Evaluation: The San Francisco Project Series Report #11*. Berkeley, Calif.: University of California at Berkeley, 1967.

MANGRUM, CLAUDE T. *The Professional Practitioner in Probation*, p. 219. Springfield, Ill.: Charles C. Thomas, 1975.

MEEKER, BEN. "Probation is Casework," *Federal Probation* 12 (1948):51–52.

NATH, SUNIL B., ET AL. "Parole and Probation Caseload Size Variation: The Florida Intensive Probation Supervision Project," *Criminal Justice Review* (1976):61.

National Advisory Commission on Criminal Justice Standards and Goals. *Corrections*, pp. 320–23. Washington, D.C.: Government Printing Office, 1973.

President's Commission on Law Enforcement and Administration of Justice. *Corrections*. Washington, D.C.: Government Printing Office, 1967.

SCOTT, RONALD J. "Contract Programming in Probation: Philosophical and Experimental Bases for Building a Model," *The Justice System Journal* 4 (1978): 49–70.

STUDT, ELLIOT. "Casework in the Correctional Field," *Federal Probation* 17 (1954):24.

TRECKER, HARLEIGH B. "Social Work Principles in Probation," *Federal Probation* 19 (1975):8–9.

VITO, GENNARO F., AND MARSHALL, FRANKLIN H. "The Administrative Caseload Project," *Federal Probation* 46 (1983):33–41.

WILSON, ROB. "Probation/Parole Officers as Research Brokers," *Corrections Magazine* 4 (June 1978):48–54.

WOOD, WILLIAM. "Multnomah County Probation Teams," *Federal Probation* 42 (1978):7–9.

Recommended Readings

Banks, Jerry J., et al. *Evaluation of Intensive Special Probation Projects Phase I Report* (Washington, D.C.: U.S. Department of Justice, 1977). This report provides a summary of issues in intensive special probation and a framework for understanding project operations and impacts.

Carlson, Eric W., et al. *Critical Issues in Adult Probation, Issues in Probation Management* (National Institute of Law Enforcement and Criminal Justice, Law Enforcement Assistance Administration, U.S. Department of Justice, 1979). This comprehensive study of probation focuses on management issues common to both probation and parole. The chapters on caseload management and probation services are particularly relevant, and provide an excellent review of innovative programs and agencies practicing various strategies and techniques.

Latessa, Edward. "Community Supervision: Research, Trends, and Innovations." In *Corrections: An Issues Approach*, edited by M. D. Schwartz, T. R. Clear, and L. F. Travis, pp. 159–67 (Cincinnati, Ohio: Anderson, 1983). This article addresses the current research and innovations in the area of community supervision.

Linquist, Charles A. "The Private Sector in Probation: Contracting Private Services from Community Organizations," *Federal Probation* 45 (1980):58–64. Descriptions of the SAMP program in Florida. The author outlines the strengths and weaknesses of this approach.

Scott, Ronald J. "Contract Programming in Probation: Philosophical and Experimental Bases for Building a Model," *The Justice System Journal* 4 (1978):49–70. Scott provides a detailed description of several programs operating in this area and describes how the contracts are developed.

Wilson, Rob. "Probation/Parole Officers as Resource Brokers," *Corrections Magazine* 4 (June 1978):48–54. The purposes and uses of CRMT are presented in this article.

10

The Use of Paraprofessionals and Ex-Offenders

This chapter introduces the use of paraprofessionals and ex-offenders in probation and parole and gives special attention to the implementation and management of the paraprofessional program. In addition, some practical examples of programs that have successfully integrated this innovative approach to improve probation and parole effectiveness are presented.

A majority of volunteers are, in effect, paraprofessionals—that is, they generally do not have the experience or training of professional probation or parole officers. The discussions of volunteers and paraprofessionals are purposely separated, and the use of volunteers in probation and parole is examined in Chapter 11. Although many of the strategies and concerns in this chapter are generally applicable to volunteer programs, they essentially represent two diverse strategies and resources. Each varies on a number of dimensions, including the way in which they are employed, their roles, and their effectiveness.

Rationale

In the last decade, a movement to recruit auxiliary personnel from within the ranks of, or at least from within the same social class as, the population served by the probation and parole system, has gained increasing strength (Beless et al., 1972). Such individuals, often designated as indigenous paraprofessionals, are being used in a variety of social services, including corrections. While related volunteer programs are similarly designed to ease manpower shortages, the rationale for the indigenous paraprofessional in corrections differs somewhat from that of the volunteer.

Many professional corrections workers agree that a large segment of their clientele are, by virtue of their norms, values, and life-styles, alienated from the mainstream of society. Frequently, these persons are referred to as hard-to-reach, unmotivated, mistrustful, and resentful of authority. There exists, in other words, a marked social distance between many middle-class professional corrections workers and a large segment of their lower-class clientele (Grosser, 1966). Moreover, social distance by definition discourages client identification with the professional and often makes it very difficult for the professional to serve as an effective role model. The indigenous worker, conversely, has often experienced situations and problems similar to those that confront certain clients. The indigenous worker has the advantage of proximity in time and space, while typically the professional is limited to a nine-to-five, Monday-to-Friday schedule, living some distance from those served. The indigenous worker, living closer to a client has much greater familiarity with the client's environment, and has greater freedom to move about at times other than business hours. Interracial tensions in certain areas point out the need for nonprofessionals recruited from groups having an ethnic or racial affinity with certain offender populations. A communications gap resulting from social and cultural distance between middle-class professionals of any race and lower-class minority group members is a growing problem in client services.

Grosser (1966: 56–63) noted that indigenous persons bring to their staff positions unique qualities: an affinity with lower-class life, the folk wisdom of the urban slum, and the ability to communicate with and be accepted by the ethnic poor. He viewed the local resident worker as "a bridge between the lower-class client and the middle-class professional worker."

A logical extension of using indigenous paraprofessionals in corrections is use of the former offender. Drawing upon the experience of Alcoholics Anonymous, Synanon, and other self-help groups, this approach assumes that individuals who have experienced and overcome a problem have a unique capacity to help others with similar problems. The theory on which these self-help programs are based was first and perhaps best described by Cressey (1955: 116–20). The essence of the theory is:

1. If criminals are to be changed, they must be assimilated into groups which emphasize values conducive to law-abiding behavior and, concurrently, alienated from groups emphasizing values conducive to criminality.

2. The more relevant the common purpose of the group to the reformation of criminals, the greater will be its influence on the criminal members' attitudes.

3. The more cohesive the group, the greater the members' readiness to influence others and the more relevant the problem of conformity to group norms.

4. Both reformers and those to be reformed must achieve status within the group by exhibition of "pro-reform" or anti-criminal values and behavior patterns. As a novitiate . . . he is a therapeutic parasite and not actually a member until he accepts the group's own system for assigning status.

5. The most effective mechanism for exerting group pressure on members will be found in groups so organized that criminals are induced to join with non-criminals for the purpose of changing other criminals.

In addition, evidence exists which indicates that "role reversal" is a key method in rehabilitation of certain offenders. Riessman (1965: 27–32) characterized this phenomenon as the helper therapy principle and concluded: "Perhaps, then, social work's strategy ought to be to devise ways of creating more helpers, or, to be more exact, to find ways to transform recipients of help into dispensers of help, thus reversing their roles, and to structure the situation so that recipients of help will be placed in roles requiring the giving of assistance."

Expanding the role of paraprofessionals in probation and parole may be perceived by the system's professionals as a threat. However, if the manpower needs of corrections are to be met, expanding the role of the paraprofessional is a very realistic alternative. Some of the common rationales advanced for the use of paraprofessionals are: (1) there is a large pool of untrained, unemployed nonprofessionals from which to recruit; (2) it is possible to train nonprofessionals to perform significant reform roles; and (3) it would be economically efficient to use nonprofessionals in the correctional process.

Perhaps the most essential question to be addressed is whether paraprofessionals are in fact effective in performing the critical tasks of probation and parole. However, before that question can be addressed, it is important to understand the ways in which paraprofessionals are recruited, selected, trained, and utilized. The issues and strategies surrounding the use of paraprofessionals are essentially the same for volunteers. The following discussion represents a summary of prescribed techniques and strategies for introducing nonprofessionals into probation and parole.

Preparation of the Professional Staff

Before recruitment of paraprofessionals is even begun, it is very important to prepare the professional staff. Successfully integrating a paraprofessional program into an existing correctional organization depends upon adequate orientation of the professional staff to the purpose of the program and the role function of the paraprofessional vis-à-vis the professional. If the paraprofessionals are to have a chance of success, they must be accepted by the professionals. Summarizing from Clements (1972: 7–8), the following points for orienting the professional staff should be emphasized:

1. The professional and paraprofessional should work as a team.
2. The paraprofessional is not an errand boy.
3. Professionals should be willing to share their relationship with clients.
4. The workload of the paraprofessionals should be distributed among all the professional staff.
5. In-service training should be the responsibility of the professional.
6. Initial client meeting should include the professional and the paraprofessional.
7. The professional should notify external agencies of the paraprofessional's role.
8. The professional should assist the paraprofessional in goal setting and career expectations.

These simple, yet important points can reduce resistance and can, in part, help insure that the paraprofessionals will be given every opportunity to succeed.

Recruitment and Selection of Paraprofessionals

After the professional staff has been briefed as to the planned program, the recruiting stage can begin. The following types of sources for recruiting have generally been found to be most productive: professional probation/parole office recommendations, local social service agency referrals, word of mouth, neighborhood and community support, local media coverage, brochure and leaflet distribution, and newspaper advertising and employment office notices (Clements, 1972: 11–13).

Most paraprofessional applicants will have no previous work experience related to this field and little, if any, formal education along these lines. The selection criteria and process, therefore, should seek to determine their potential. Moreover, even after the selection criteria and processing have resulted in preliminary retention, employment should be offered on a probationary basis until the applicant has undergone the orientation and initial training program. Applicant response to the training sessions and early evaluation of on-the-job performance will test motivation and adaptability to the program and serve to fine tune the screening process to conform to the program's needs. This procedure should also tend to ease the applicant's transition into the new job, dispelling any misconceptions about probationers and parolees and minimize the possibility of counterproductive relationships between the paraprofessional and the client.

Selection Criteria

While selection criteria vary somewhat from program to program, there are many standard characteristics and requirements. The actual selection of paraprofessionals is perhaps the most crucial point. In a program aimed at reorienting offenders to an acceptable and constructive role in society, the applicants selected should have basic integrity that clients can recognize and trust.

Most programs suggest that the selection of paraprofessionals be divided into three stages: screening of written applications, interviews, and successful completion of an orientation and training program.

In addition, paraprofessionals recruited should: (1) be familiar with the community and neighborhoods of clients, (2) have a "common sense" understanding of human nature and society's basic values, (3) recognize one's own limitations, and (4) the capacity to accept individual differences (Beless and Rest, n.d.: 32–58). If the applicant is an ex-offender, he or she should be off parole or probation, and the type of offense should not be one that would exclude an applicant.[1]

Orientation and Training

The major objective of orientation is to establish a foundation for subsequent in-service learning in both group and individual supervision, and to serve as a final screening mechanism before case assignment. Every attempt should be made to keep orientation relatively informal while providing background information in such a way as to enable paraprofessionals to perform their tasks without, at the same time, neutralizing the "indigenous" qualities that make them valuable as paraprofessionals.

The expectations of orientation should not be high. Most of the training deemed necessary for minimal job performance should be designed to take place "in-service," during ensuing contacts with the supervisor and other paraprofessionals. There is a very real danger of overtraining the paraprofessionals. Too much formal training may threaten or bore the indigenous paraprofessionals or, equally undesirable, "bleed-out" the very qualities that make them desirable candidates in the first place.

Although orientation is followed by training, together they constitute a continuous process in which the paraprofessional is introduced to some of the basic concepts and contents of the field of corrections, and then is taught to develop skills necessary to help clients. Such orientation and training are primarily a supervisory responsibility, which enters into the continuing relationship between the supervising professional and the learning paraprofessional. At all stages of the orientation and training, paraprofessionals should be impressed with the fact that they are necessary and valuable team members who have an important role to play in the functions of the agency.

The orientation and training should help increase the paraprofessional's insight and sophistication, but not cancel out the nonprofessional qualities that make the paraprofessional a valuable asset. The skillful supervisor will not only help paraprofessionals develop their full potential, but will also help them recognize their own normal limitations in the helping process.

Since the orientation and training program can also be a screening out process, a probationary period should be established to weed out those applicants not meeting the requirements or duties expected of a paraprofessional.

Placement and Responsibilities

The delegation of responsibility to a paraprofessional should be a gradual and incremental process. In the initial stages, a paraprofessional may tend to be overly idealistic and assume more role functions than can be realistically fulfilled. The professional or training supervisor should attempt to delineate the paraprofessional's responsibilities and functions without unduly dampening natural enthusiasm. There may also be an element of bewilderment on the part of some new paraprofessionals that can be eased by graduating levels of responsibilities and functions as they progress in their in-service training. Paraprofessionals should be informed that their basic responsibility is to their clients and to their professional supervisor.

The caseload responsibility of the paraprofessional should initially be task-oriented. Surveillance and "listening" types of assignments should be given to them. As they progress (in four to six months), responsibilities should be gradually increased to include helping the client meet concrete or environmental needs, such as housing and employment. Between the first and second years, the area of responsibility should be gradually widened to include investigative and counseling responsibilities.

Although there will be some overlap, these responsibilities can be considered as four sequential categories that form the basis for the in-service development of the paraprofessional. These primary categories are (Clements, 1972: 33–46): (1) surveillance, (2) investigation, (3) concrete needs counseling, and (4) emotional needs counseling. Each of these categories is also considered an important part of the job of probation and parole officers.

Types of Caseloads

The assignment and size of caseloads vary from agency to agency; however, there are some basic rules in the area of assigning clients to paraprofessionals.

Optimally, the paraprofessional should be assigned "new" cases—that is, clients who have not been under the supervision of a "regular" probation or parole officer. This is recommended to avoid the possible reaction by the client that he or she is being unnecessarily "shuffled" from person to person, or that the quality of the supervision is being reduced. As far-fetched as it may seem, such feelings were manifested in the experimental POCA Project in Chicago (Beless et al., 1972: 10–15), and ranged from negative feelings toward a "new" man (i.e., the paraprofessional) to feelings by blacks that they were being "sold short" by having black paraprofessional supervising agents assigned to them. Once a paraprofessional program of this kind is firmly established, however, such reactions do not tend to recur.

The supervisor should then prepare a brief diagnostic summary of the offender, paying particular attention to his or her service needs (i.e., problem areas) and the area of residence plans. The case should then be staffed by the supervisor and the officer, and matched with the paraprofessional to whom the offender is to be assigned on the basis of such factors as race, the degree of harmony between client service needs and the paraprofessional's strengths and weaknesses, and residential proximity. For special problem cases, such as narcotics addiction or alcoholism, consideration should be given to assigning a paraprofessional who has experienced and successfully overcome such a problem.

The supervisor should expect paraprofessionals to vary markedly in their general approach to the role of change agent. The largest group of paraprofessionals will be most comfortable and skillful in providing concrete forms of services directly or through formal referrals. Some will be proficient at counseling. A few will function best in a surveillant capacity. All will be good at "rapping" or listening to clients, although they may be less verbal than regular officers in the office.

The supervisor or professional team member should capitalize on such differences in approach by matching the paraprofessional's talents with the client's needs. Matching along racial, ethnic, or residential dimensions is easily done; but other kinds of matching must be done by trial and error until experience reveals the range of skills possessed by each paraprofessional. The paraprofessional's ability to empathize and simply listen, however, is of paramount importance in accelerating the positive aspects of the rehabilitation process. A high degree of motivation, involvement, and enthusiasm may be characteristic of the paraprofessional, particularly when dealing with clients on a regular or weekly basis. If it is feasible, the number of clients assigned to paraprofessionals should enable them to make such weekly contacts; in any case, the number should not be overwhelming.

While paraprofessionals have gained widespread acceptance and use in probation and parole, their success is contingent upon meeting these concerns. The prescribed strategies for employing nonprofessionals serve to illustrate the operational implications that must be planned for in advance. Proponents of the paraprofessional concept have assumed that these individuals are able to contribute to the rehabilitation and reintegration of offenders at no greater risk than professional supervision. But the question still remains: How effective are paraprofessionals?

Effectiveness of Paraprofessionals

Probably the best designed study to date of paraprofessionals results from the Parole Officer Aide Program in Ohio (Priestino and Allen, 1975). This program, implemented in September 1972, utilized ex-offenders as quasi-parole officers. The goals of the project were to bridge the gap between the state parole agency and the parolees; facilitate communication between corrections, the community, and the state; engender trust and confidence in the correctional system; decrease recidivism; and reduce parole violations. While this program is no longer in operation (Scott, 1981: 225–38), the results of the evaluations illustrate the feasibility of using ex-offenders.

The use of ex-offenders to aid and assist with probationers or parolees is not unique to Ohio; however, two things were relatively novel. First, the authority, power, and trust given ex-offenders hired as aides were unique. Although the aides did not have the total autonomy of parole officers (or the authority to carry firearms), they did have their own caseloads for which they were primarily responsible. Second, the desire and commitment of the Ohio Adult Parole Authority to objectively evaluate the effectiveness of the program was exceptional. The Ohio Adult Parole Authority was attempting to capitalize on the resources of ex-offenders and to evaluate their effectiveness extensively.

It was discovered that the twenty-three parole officer aides employed by the state of Ohio during the first two years of the project performed as well as a control group of parole officers. As a result, the Ohio Adult Parole Authority hired additional aides and broadened their responsibilities. The third year's evaluation found very similar benefits. To determine the overall effectiveness of the parole officer aides, a number of research techniques were used, including the attitudinal questionnaire, in-depth interviews, field workers' reports, unit supervisors' ratings, a survey of inmates, and a survey of parolees supervised by aides and parole officers.

Results from the evaluations indicated that the aides' ability to relate to and aid parolees was higher than that of parole officers. Moreover, parolees indicated that aides were generally more concerned and sensitive about the types of problems they faced than were parole officers. Additionally, parolees felt that the aides maintained a higher level of contact than did parole officers.

Finally, the interaction between the aides and the parole officers provided a fertile setting for a new understanding of ex-offenders. This point is best illustrated by the experience of a senior parole officer assigned to supervise an aide (Blew and Carlson, 1976: 6):

> Initially, I was totally opposed to this program. I saw it as a high-risk venture with no returns. I was sure we were asking for big trouble by hiring our former clients. But, I guess, I've had to take it all back. The Aide in our office has helped me understand why parolees act like they do sometimes. It makes sense when an Aide explains why a parolee of mine can't seem to get his act together—to cope with day-to-day living. Also, the Aide helps the parolees understand why we have some of the rules we do.

In April 1976, the National Institute of Law Enforcement and Criminal Justice (NILECJ) designated the Ohio Parole Officer Aide Program one of seventeen "exemplary projects in the United States."

Ironically, as Scott (1981) has reported, the Ohio Adult Parole Authority had decided to scrap this project at roughly the same time this honor was bestowed. Apparently, the APA determined that the project was ineffective, largely because federal funding had been eliminated and the aides as a group had considerable trouble with the law. Of the original thirty-seven aides, fourteen were promoted to parole officer status (as of 1981, six were still with the APA), and six resigned or were terminated following an administrative investigation. Thirteen aides resigned or were terminated with criminal charges pending. Nine aides had been arrested for felonies. Thus, Scott's follow-up investigation of the Ohio program indicates that there were a number of problems surrounding this project.

Another widely publicized program was the Probation Officer Case Aide project conducted in Chicago in 1968 (Beless and Rest, 1969). Fifty-two part-time indigenous paraprofessionals were used in the federal probation system to provide services to "hard-to-reach" clients.

The central goal was to discover whether the indigenous paraprofessional could perform effectively as a rehabilitative agent in probation. Both recidivism rates and social adjustments of probationers assigned to paraprofessionals were examined. Examination of these measures revealed almost identical outcome patterns for each group. The aides showed a far greater frequency and regularity of contact with clients.

In the second phase of this program, twelve aides were selected to provide full-time supervision to caseloads of fifteen to twenty-five hard-to-reach clients (Witkowski et al., n.d.: 18). The evaluators concluded that, "It appears from the study that the employment of indigenous paraprofessionals in federal probation is operationally feasible and represents a promising adjunct to professional correctional supervision."

Almost all paraprofessional programs vary substantially from jurisdiction to jurisdiction (Latessa et al., 1979). Some use paraprofessionals as aides and supplements, while others incorporate them as full-time officers. In some cases, the part-time positions lead to career track opportunities. Many times paraprofessionals are recruited for "special" qualities other than those already discussed. For instance, one project in California (Langbehn et al., 1974) chose Mexican-American aides, since a large part of their clientele consisted of Spanish-speaking Americans.

In spite of the obvious advantages presented above, there is still a great deal of resistance to paraprofessional programs. As part of the Ohio ex-offender study, a survey of state parole agencies was conducted to solicit their attitudes concerning paraprofessionals. Tables 10–1 and 10–2 illustrate both the advantages and disadvantages cited by states for employing ex-offenders as parole or probation officer aides. Advantages included: greater rapport with clients; better understanding of problems, more capable of empathizing, and additional source of manpower. Among the disadvantages most often cited were: professional staff resistance, adverse publicity, corrupting parolees and probationers, and inability to find suitable candidates. While most of these constraints are symbolic, they can indeed be very real obstacles to the implementation and success of any paraprofessional program.

Table 10–1
Major Advantages Cited by States for Employing
Ex-Offender Parole/Probation Officer Aides

ADVANTAGES	NUMBER OF STATES*
Greater rapport with clients	33
Better understanding of client's problems	19
More capable of empathizing	14
Streetwise	9
Additional line of communication to the community	9
Resources and mediator	8
Unique support for professional staff	6
Stronger commitment to the job	5
Additional source of manpower	4
None	5

*Frequency of responses does not add to fifty because some states gave several advantages.
SOURCE: Joseph E. Scott, *The Parole Officer Aide Program in Ohio: An Exemplary Project*, p. 21 (Columbus, Ohio: [Ohio State University] Program for the Study of Crime and Delinquency, 1975).

Table 10-2
Major Disadvantages Cited by States for Not
Employing Ex-Offender Parole/Probation Officer Aides

DISADVANTAGES	NUMBER OF STATES*
Professional staff's resistance	16
Possible adverse publicity	12
Possibility of them corrupting their parolees or probationers	12
Difficulty of finding suitable candidates	10
Overidentification with client	4
Lack of career ladder	3
Expense in resocializing and training	3
Lack of information and experience in running such programs	2
Lack of most ex-cons education and intelligence	2
None	3

*Frequency of responses does not add to fifty because some states gave several disadvantages.
SOURCE: Joseph E. Scott, *The Parole Officer Aide Program in Ohio: An Exemplary Project*, p. 20 (Columbus, Ohio: [Ohio State University] Program for the Study of Crime and Delinquency, 1975).

In a recent survey of parole field agencies, Latessa, Travis, and Allen (1983) gathered information on the extent and usage of paraprofessionals and ex-offenders in parole. The information in Tables 10-3 through 10-7 is a summary of this survey.

There are currently eighteen jurisdictions that reported using paraprofessionals in parole. As Table 10-3 indicates, this survey revealed that qualifications for paraprofessionals varied from jurisdiction to jurisdiction. Thirteen jurisdictions listed one or more specific requirements for their paraprofessionals. Four states mandate having a high school diploma, and two have two-year college degrees in their list of employment requirements. Both Minnesota and the federal government use informal qualifications.

The information in Table 10-4 illustrates the functions that paraprofessionals perform in parole agencies. Almost half of the eighteen jurisdictions use paraprofessionals in support functions, and six report varying uses in direct supervision. Both Missouri and the federal government specialize the caseloads of paraprofessionals. One noteworthy exception is Vermont, which reported that its paraprofessionals collect fines and restitution.

Thirteen of the reporting jurisdictions provided information on starting salaries for paraprofessionals, and these data are displayed in Table 10-5. Starting salaries ranged from $450 per month in Idaho to $933 per month in Connecticut. The average monthly salary was approximately $713 per month.

This survey also reported finding eighteen jurisdictions using ex-offenders, see Table 10-6. Six states (Arizona, Illinois, Iowa, Kansas, Maryland, and Washington) report using volunteers and ex-offenders, but

Table 10–3
Qualifications for Paraprofessionals

Jurisdiction	GED/HS	Two-Year College Degree	Two or More Years of Experience	Other/Commentary
Delaware	—	X*	—	—
Florida	X	—	—	—
Idaho	—	—	—	Education in area
Minnesota	—	—	—	Informal qualifications
Mississippi	—	—	—	Student interns
Missouri	—	—	—	Some college
New Mexico	X	—	X	—
North Carolina	—	X	—	—
Ohio	—	—	—	Only use ex-offenders
Oregon	—	—	X	—
Pennsylvania	—	—	—	X†
Texas	X	—	—	Depends on function, up to three years of college
Vermont	X	—	X	—
Wisconsin	—	—	—	Eighteen years old
Federal	—	—	—	Informal qualifications

*Or experience.
†Knowledge of client life-style, interpersonal and oral skills, ability to read and write.
Source: Edward J. Latessa, Lawrence F. Travis III, Harry E. Allen, "Volunteers and Paraprofessionals in Parole: Current Practices," *Journal of Offender Counseling, Services and Rehabilitation* 8 (1983):97.

not paraprofessionals. One state (Virginia) reports use of ex-offenders, but does not report using either paraprofessionals or volunteers. Data on qualifications of ex-offenders were gathered, and in general, these were the same as for professional parole officers and agents (fifteen states). In addition, Iowa requires an ex-offender to have been off parole for a year, while Ohio also requires six months of steady employment, satisfactory completion of parole, release from disability (weapons), and no conviction for a drug-related crime. Reported use of ex-offenders ranged from a state high of sixteen (Ohio) to using only one. The federal government used the greatest number: forty. The average number of ex-offenders among reporting states was four in parole supervision services.

In 1974, Scott conducted a survey of correctional officials as part of the evaluation of the Ohio Ex-Offender Aide Project. Information from that survey indicated that sixteen states reported use of ex-offenders as pa-

Table 10–4

Functions Performed by Paraprofessionals Among Reporting Jurisdictions

Jurisdiction	Support Functions	Direct Supervision	Other Functions	Caseload Specialization
California	Yes	Limited	—	—
Idaho	Yes	—	PSI prep.	—
Michigan	Yes	—	—	—
Minnesota	Yes	Yes	PSI prep.	—
Missouri	Yes	Yes	PSI prep., counseling, employment	Employment needs
New Mexico	Limited	—	—	—
Vermont	—	Field contact, restitution	Collect fines	—
Wisconsin	—	Minimum	—	—
Federal	Yes	Yes	—	Ethnicity

Paraprofessional programs reported but no further details were available from: Connecticut, Delaware, Florida, Mississippi, Ohio, Pennsylvania, and Texas.

Source: Edward J. Latessa, Lawrence F. Travis III, Harry E. Allen, "Volunteers and Paraprofessionals in Parole: Current Practices, *Journal of Offender Counseling, Services and Rehabilitation* 8 (1983):100.

Table 10–5

Starting Salaries for Paraprofessionals

Jurisdiction	Starting Monthly Salary
California	$692
Connecticut	933
Delaware	899
Florida	538
Idaho	450
New Mexico	617
Ohio	752
Oregon	681
Pennsylvania	727
Texas	630
Wisconsin	832
Federal	876

Source: Edward J. Latessa, Lawrence F. Travis III, Harry E. Allen, "Volunteers and Paraprofessionals in Parole: Current Practices," *Journal of Offender Counseling, Services and Rehabilitation* 8 (1983):101.

role officer aides. The Latessa et al. (1983) survey found a total of 139 ex-offenders actually employed in parole, not including the federal system.[2] Interestingly, results from this survey revealed one additional state using ex-offenders, yet a total of only ninety-four employed. This includes the

Table 10–6
Jurisdictions That Reported Using Ex-Offenders, 1978

Jurisdiction	Number of Ex-Offenders Reported
Alabama*	2
Arizona	NA
Florida	3
Illinois*	—
Iowa*	1
Kansas*	1
Maryland*	—
Minnesota	5
Missouri	—
New Mexico	1
North Carolina	12
Ohio	16
Oregon	—
Pennsylvania	1
Texas	6
Virginia†	1
Washington*	5
Federal	40
Total	94

*Reported using volunteers only.
†Did not report using either volunteers or paraprofessionals

Source: Edward J. Latessa, Lawrence F. Travis III, Harry E. Allen, "Volunteers and Paraprofessionals in Parole: Current Practices," *Journal of Offender Counseling, Services and Rehabilitation* 8 (1983):102.

forty reported by the federal system. Excluding the ex-offenders in use in federal parole, there had been a 61 percent reduction in the total number of ex-offenders employed in parole. Perhaps the demise of LEAA has contributed to the decrease in ex-offender personnel, for as Scott (1974) noted, every ex-offender program started from 1970 through 1972 received LEAA funding.

While all of the jurisdictions that have started paraprofessional and ex-offender programs have not conducted evaluations, Latessa et al. (1983) found seven that did. The information in Table 10–7 illustrates that all the evaluations which have been completed have reported positive findings.

In spite of these studies, a great many questions still remain unanswered. For instance, do the paraprofessionals lose those qualities that make them special? When should they enter the promotion track? What is the best model: team or individual? Finally, we note that the evidence has not conclusively proven that paraprofessionals are more successful than professional probation and parole officers.

Table 10–7
Evaluations of Paraprofessionals and Ex-Offenders Programs

JURISDICTION	PARAPROFESSIONALS	EX-OFFENDERS
Idaho	Positive	—
Missouri	Positive	—
New Mexico	Informal	—
North Carolina	Positive	Positive
Ohio	—	Positive
Texas	In progress	—
Vermont	Positive	—
Federal	Positive	Positive

SOURCE: Edward J. Latessa, Lawrence F. Travis III, Harry E. Allen, "Volunteers and Paraprofessionals in Parole: Current Practices," *Journal of Offender Counseling, Services and Rehabilitation* 8 (1983):103.

Summary

Using those who have experienced and overcome a problem to help others with similar problems is not a new concept. The use of paraprofessionals in probation and parole represents an innovative attempt at increasing the delivery of services and the effectiveness of supervision. As a supplement to professional supervision, paraprofessionals represent a viable addition and a valuable aid in the rehabilitation and reintegration of offenders.

This chapter has presented some practical concerns associated with paraprofessional programs, and has illustrated some strategies for aiding in the implementation and operation of such programs. The key, as with most new projects, lies with adequate planning, preparation, and, most of all, cooperation.

In spite of the success demonstrated by several paraprofessional programs, a number of questions remain unanswered. While it appears possible to train nonprofessionals, there is still the question of the roles they should play, and how effective this innovation may prove to be. Finally, it has not yet been proven that it is more economically efficient to use paraprofessionals, and with today's concerns over cost-effectiveness (Love, 1981: 373), that could well be a critical question.

Notes

1. For example, in the federal system, a record of treason or bribery of a government official would automatically exclude an applicant.
2. The Scott study does not provide a list of the jurisdictions reporting ex-offenders. Only the total number was listed.

Study Guides

1. What are the reasons for using paraprofessionals?
2. What are the major objectives of orientation of staff and paraprofessionals?
3. What type of caseload should initially be assigned paraprofessionals?
4. Why was the ex-offender program in Ohio such a great success?
5. List the advantages and disadvantages of using paraprofessionals.
6. What are the reasons that paraprofessionals are initially resisted by professional probation and parole officers?
7. What are the frequent steps in screening paraprofessionals for probation or parole service?
8. How can paraprofessionals be assigned to clients without resistance by the clients?
9. What are the important considerations in matching paraprofessionals and clients?

Key Terms

"bleeding out"   paraprofessionals
"helper therapy principle"   role reversal
indigenous paraprofessionals   selection criteria
orientation

References

BELESS, DONALD W., AND REST, ELLEN. *Probation Officer Case Aide Project Final Report: Phase I.* Chicago: University of Chicago Law School, Center for Studies in Criminal Justice, 1969.

BELESS, DONALD W.; PILCHER, WILLIAM S.; AND RYSON, ELLEN. "The Use of Indigenous Nonprofessionals in Probation and Parole," *Federal Probation* 36 (1972):10–15.

BLEW, CAROL H., AND CARLSON, KENNETH. *An Exemplary Project, the Ohio Parole Officer Aide Program.* National Institute of Law Enforcement and Criminal Justice, Law Enforcement Assistance Administration: U.S. Department of Justice, Washington, D.C., 1976.

CLEMENTS, RAYMOND D. *Paraprofessionals in Probation and Parole: A Manual for Their Selection, Training, Induction and Supervision in Day-to-Day Tasks.* Chicago: University of Chicago Law School, Center for Studies in Criminal Justice, 1972.

CRESSEY, DONALD R. "Changing Criminals: The Application of the Theory of Differential Association," *American Journal of Sociology* 61 (1955):116–20.

GROSSER, C. F. "Local Residents as Mediators Between Middle-Class Professional Workers and Lower-Class Clients," *Social Service Review* 40 (1966):59–63.

LANGBEHN, ANITA, L.; PASELA, GUY E., AND VENEZIA, PETER S. *Yolo County, California Minority Probation Aides: An Evaluation of Mexican-American Probation Case Aide Project (1971–1973).* Davis, Calif.: National Council on Crime and Delinquency Research Center, 1974.

LATESSA, EDWARD J., AND ALLEN, HARRY E. Management Issues in Adult Parole. Unpublished draft. San Jose, Calif.: San Jose Research Foundation, 1982.

LATESSA, EDWARD J.; CARLSON, ERIC W.; AND ALLEN, HARRY E. "Paraprofessionals in Probation: A Synthesis of Management Issues and Outcome Studies," *Journal of Offender Counseling Services and Rehabilitation* 4 (1979):163–73.

LATESSA, EDWARD J.; TRAVIS, LAWRENCE F., III; AND ALLEN, HARRY E. "Volunteers and Paraprofessionals in Parole: Current Practices," *Journal of Offender Counseling Services and Rehabilitation* 8 (1983):91–105.

LOVE, KEVIN, G. "Paraprofessionals in Parole and Probation Services: Selection, Training, and Program Evaluation, *Journal of Criminal Justice* 9 (1981): 367–74.

PRIESTINO, RAMON, AND ALLEN, HARRY E. *The Parole Officer Aide Program in Ohio: An Exemplary Project.* Columbus, Ohio: Ohio State University, Program for the Study of Crime and Delinquency, 1975.

RIESSMAN, F. "The Helper Therapy Principle," *Social Work* 10 (1965):27–32.

SCOTT, JOSEPH. *A Follow-Up Evaluation of the Parole Officer Aide Program in Ohio.* Columbus, Ohio: Program for the Study of Crime and Delinquency, 1974.

———. "The dismantling of an LEAA Exemplary Project: The Parole Officer Aide Program in Ohio." In *The Mad, The Bad and the Different*, edited by Israel Barak and C. Ronald Huff, pp. 225–38. Lexington, Mass.: Lexington Books, 1981.

WITKOWSKI, GREGORY; REST, ELLEN; AND BUSIEL, GEORGE J. *Probation Officer Case Aide Project: Final Report: Phase II.* Chicago: University of Chicago Law School, Center for Studies in Criminal Justice, n.d.

Recommended Readings

Allen, H. E., et al. *Critical Issues in Probation Management* (Washington, D.C.: Law Enforcement Assistance Administration, National Institute of Law Enforcement Assistance Administration, 1979). This more recent study of probation practices presents a thorough examination of paraprofessionals in probation. Special emphasis is given the management implications.

Blew, C. H., and Carlson, K. *An Exemplary Project: The Ohio Parole Officer Aide Program* (Washington, D.C.: Law Enforcement Assistance Administration,

National Institute of Law Enforcement and Criminal Justice, 1976). This government document presents the findings of the Ohio experiment and is perhaps the best example of the use of ex-offenders in parole.

Scott, Joseph E. *Ex-Offenders as Parole Officers* (Lexington, Mass.: Lexington Books, D. C. Heath, 1975). This book analyzes the Ohio experiment with ex-offenders.

11

The Use of Volunteers

The probation and parole system operates under a basic philosophy of reintegration; connecting offenders with legitimate opportunity and reward structures, and generally uniting the offender within the community. It has become quite apparent that the correctional system cannot achieve this without assistance, regardless of the extent of resources available. Reintegration requires the assistance and support of the community.

This concept is certainly not a new one. The John Howard Association, the Osborne Association, and other citizen prisoners' aid societies have provided voluntary correctional-type services for many years. The volunteer movement developed in this country in the early 1820s, when a group of citizens known as the Philadelphia Society for Alleviating the Misery of Public Prisons began supervising the activities of inmates upon their release from penal institutions. This practice was later adopted by John Augustus, a Boston shoemaker, who worked with well over 2,000 misdemeanants in his lifetime (see Chapter 3).

Although considerably diminished by the early 1980s, the volunteerism movement has enjoyed a comeback over the past ten decades. Judge Keith Leenhouts of the Royal Oak (Michigan) Municipal Court resurrected the concept some twenty years ago, and continues to serve as a driving force behind this now relatively accepted, and still growing, movement. In addition to the many local programs in existence, such as the Lincoln (Nebraska) Volunteer Probation Counselor Program and the Ohio Parole Officer Aide Program (two of the first thirteen programs designated as "exemplary" by the Law Enforcement Assistance Administration), are several national programs supporting volunteerism, such as VISTO (Volunteers in Service to Offenders), and the American Bar Association–sponsored National Volunteer Aide Program. Recent estimates suggest the existence of more than 500,000 volunteers serving more than 3,000 jurisdictions nationwide.

Proponents of the volunteer concept consider it to be one of the most promising innovations in the field, claiming that it can help alleviate the problem of excessive probation and parole caseloads, and contribute to rehabilitation and reintegration goals for the offender.

Scope of Services

Volunteerism generally refers to situations where individual citizens contribute their talents, wisdom, skills, time, and resources within the context of the justice system, without receiving financial remuneration. Volunteer projects operate on the premise that certain types of offenders can be helped by the services a volunteer can offer, and that such services can be provided at a minimal tax dollar cost. It should be emphasized, however, that volunteer projects seem to present advantages and disadvantages to the community. While volunteer effectiveness will be discussed at length later in this chapter, it is important to note at this time that the principle behind volunteerism is to supplement, *not* replace probation and parole officer efforts by providing individualized special services. More specifically, volunteer programs in general have the ability to offer an amplication and diversification of services.

For example, consider the probation or parole officer who has one hour per month to spend with each client. The hour can be spent either directly with the client (where one hour of input leads to one hour of output), or to supervise a volunteer who will spend ten to fifteen hours with the client. A combination of the two systems seems to be the most logical, with the officer spending part of the time supervising the volunteer, and part of the time in direct contact with the client.

By drawing upon the time, talents, and abilities of volunteers to assist in service delivery, probation and parole officers can serve to broaden the nature of the services offered. Any community consists of persons who possess a diverse supply of skills and abilities that can be effectively tapped by volunteer programs. The National Center of Volunteers in Courts has reported that some 155 volunteer roles have actually been filled by volunteer persons in different jurisdictions. Scheier (1973) developed a list of more than two hundred potential volunteer services, including:

addiction program volunteer	intake volunteer
case aide	newsletter editor
clerical courtroom assistance	presentence investigator
diagnostic home volunteer	recreation volunteer
educational aide	test administrator and scorer
foster parent	vocational service aide
fund raiser	volunteer counselor

In addition to the direct services offered, volunteers can supply a number of support services. Volunteers often assist program operations in an administrative capacity. For example, the well-known Royal Oak, Michigan, program has been supervised by a full-time volunteer for quite some time. The VISTO program in Los Angeles County (California) has likewise utilized volunteers to fill some of its clerical needs, such as handling supplies, photocopying, answering recruitment correspondence, and routine office contacts, as well as participating in research projects. There can be little doubt that volunteers can thus serve as a means of amplifying time, attention, and the type of services given to clients by the system.

Care should be taken to articulate exactly what tasks the volunteers are expected to perform. The use of volunteer time can be maximized if the volunteer comes to work knowing exactly what they are to do. Furthermore, such a delineation can reduce some of the staff-volunteer conflict over the role and function of the volunteers, a number of which are contained in Table 11–1.

As volunteers provide services, they develop relationships with the clientele. The relationship between volunteer and client can be classified into several categories. Perhaps the most well known is the so-called *man-to-man* model. In this model, volunteers, on a one-to-one basis, seek to obtain the trust and confidence of the clientele and to help them maintain their existence, clarify social roles, and plan for the future. In the *supervision* model, volunteers work as a case aide to an officer and provide services to a number of clients. In the *professional* model, volunteers who possess specialized professional or semiprofessional skills provide these services to a number of clients. Occasionally, volunteers will be called upon to assist with program administrative functions and interact only indirectly with clientele. This is referred to as the *administrative* model. Obviously, each style has its place and is employed by volunteer program administrators when needs arise.

To assist in the delivery of these many services, and in the establishment of meaningful relationships, volunteers are encouraged to view their work from a broad, philosophical foundation. Horjesi (1973), for example, has developed a conceptual base from which volunteers can plan their in-

Table 11-1
Selected Volunteer Functions and Responsibilities

Identified Volunteer Use	Summary of Responsibility	Recommendations
1. One-to-one volunteer counselor	Serves as an extension to the adult probation officer. Provides servies to the client that the officer does not have time to give. Ideally, serves as support to a client in need of more comprehensive skills in the area of interpersonal development. Most popular method for use of volunteers in probation.	Necesssitate a valid and reliable screening technique. Volunteers should sign a waiver of liability release. A police check on potential volunteers is advisable. Strong orientation and in-service program should be developed. Assignment of volunteer to client should generally follow a period of observation of contracts between the probation officer and clients.
2. Presentence investigation	Assists probation officer in the investigative procedure used to consider an applicant referred by the courts for probation (e.g., contracting references, compiling data, and assisting in the preliminary write-up toward a presentence report).	Individual must have good communication skills Ideally suited to someone planning a career in social work or criminal justice. Retirees and nonworking women may be suited to this position. Volunteers should sign a waiver of liability release. Volunteers should not be allowed to make any personal contacts with neighbors, relatives, home visits, work visits, etc., except when accompanied by officer.

3. Clerical	Works in probation/parole office performing both routine and nonroutine clerical tasks (e.g., receptionist, answering phone, filing, typing, processing correspondence, etc.).	Draw from community volunteer action agencies, RSVP, volunteer bureaus, and all available volunteer clearinghouses. Assign varying duties, gradually increasing responsibility Volunteers should sign a waiver of liability release.
4. Courtroom assistance	Assists officers in filling out legal probation/ parole papers and referral slips. Handles any and all matters to facilitate court procedures for the officer-in attendance. Must be able to accurately record case materials.	Volunteers must possess good communication skills. Ideally suited to someone planning a career in social work or criminal justice. Retirees and nonworking women may be suited to this position. Volunteers should sign a waiver of liability release.
5. Auxiliary volunteers	Provide "specialized" services based on present or past professional training or resources. Utilized in an infinite number of ways to provide both direct and in-kind contributions to probation departments (e.g., money, materials, medical facilities). Services not directly related to duties of professional staff.	Use civic clubs, churches, philanthropic organizations, universities, volunteer agencies, fraternal and professional organizations as a base. Volunteer coordinator must possess good communication skills and have the ability to "sell" the merits of probation. Often requires the ability to create a job to fit the individual or organization. Represents a good alternative for rural departments. Volunteers should sign a waiver of liability release.

Table 11-1 (Continued)

Identified Volunteer Use	Summary of Responsibility	Recommendations
6. Volunteer probation/parole officer aid	Assists probation/parole officer in all facets of caseload management, including courtroom assistance, presentence investigation, interviewing, counseling, clerical, etc.	Necessitates a valid and reliable screening. A police check on potential volunteers advisable. Constant monitoring necessary. Volunteer should sign a waiver of liability release. Strong orientation and in-services programs should be developed. Should initiate as a "pilot program." Ideally suited to someone planning a career in social work or criminal justice, or anticipating a career change. Volunteers should first be assigned to misdemeanor unit. Volunteers should not be allowed to make any home visits unless accompanied by probation officer. Volunteer should possess good communication skills.

Source: Adapted from Patricia M. Shields, Charles W. Chapman, David R. Wingard, "Using Volunteers in Adult Probation," *Federal Probation* 47 (1983): 62–64.

tervention strategy. His framework is called Motivation, Capacity, and Opportunity, or the M-C-O approach, and it helps volunteers view clients' problems within the context of three interrelated factors: motivation, capacity, and opportunity. *Motivation* can be defined as what clients want and how badly it is desired. *Capacity* refers to various resources, skills, and abilities that clients possess. *Opportunity* refers to opportunities in clients' social environments, and those skills and services that volunteers bring to clients' life situations. As volunteers work with their clients, they need to keep all three factors in mind and relate them to their clients' perceived problems.

Funding and Costs

While the very term "volunteer" may imply that few costs are involved, this is not the case. Although the volunteers themselves receive little if any remuneration for their efforts, recruiting, screening, training, matching, and supervising of volunteers all involve a cost, as does the general operational maintenance of an office. Volunteer programs generally seek support from state and local government, federal grants, and private donations. Most programs seek funds from single sources; however, the trend may be to secure combinations of sources in order to assure their continued existence.

Eskridge (1980) reviewed the funding sources of twenty-one programs and found that twelve were apparently funded by the federal government, two received local support, nine received state funds, and three obtained private donations. Some 25 percent of the projects examined obtained financial support from combinations of sources, while the other 75 percent apparently looked to only one source for support.

The problem of program survival, from a financial perspective, may now be more acute than ever in light of the conservative fiscal trend that seems to be sweeping across the country. It should be pointed out that many volunteer programs began as privately funded operations and/or semidetached operations of the local court or probation department. Consequently, these programs will undoubtedly continue to expand on and develop the volunteer philosophy in an attempt to become adopted and funded by a government agency. This notion merits reiteration for, in practice, program survival may supersede all other operational objectives.

Organization

It appears that most volunteer projects are administered either through the local court, the probation department, or the department of corrections, even though they be administratively staffed entirely with volunteers. The important fact to remember is that ultimate control is usually maintained by the local government agency. One notable exception to this generalization is the state of Florida, where the volunteer program has been organized on a statewide, coordinated basis since 1968. Generally speaking, however, volunteer programs can be viewed as variations of one basic format (see Figure 11–1). Differences between programs are not so much within the structure of the organization, but rather in who fills the positions within the structure. As noted previously, volunteers may hold various positions within the organization, up to and including the chief administrator.

Notable exceptions to this general organizational chart are the volunteer programs run as nonprofit organizations. It appears that this is more common among *parole* volunteer programs than among probation programs. Obviously, in this case, the government agency is supplanted by a corporate board at the top of the organization. The relatively well-known man-to-man and woman-to-woman ex-offender assistance programs are examples of this nonprofit volunteer organization (Carlson et al., 1980).

Operations

The lack of proven success of a given volunteer project has often been seen as a function of poor management rather than a fault in the general volunteer philosophy. For example, the 1975 Southfield, Michigan, program reported an abundance of potential volunteers and clients, but the actual match rate was quite low because of operational inadequacies (City of Southfield, 1975). A 1976 study of fourteen volunteer projects in the state of Indiana found that all programs were experiencing insufficient communications between probation officers and volunteers, resulting in a subsequent lack of coordination of efforts (Hume et al., 1976). The Santa Barbara, California, project also reported a lack of communication between volunteers and probation officers and insufficient general managerial support as major drawbacks to project operations (Santa Barbara County, 1973). Such difficulties must be viewed in the context of operational problems, but not as a disparagement of the volunteer concept. The future of volunteerism in this country will depend upon the ability of volunteer program managers to effectively deal with the following operational components.

Community Support

To operate as a viable entity, volunteer programs must obtain and maintain the support of the public at large, the media, local political officials,

Figure 11-1 Organization of VIP Programs

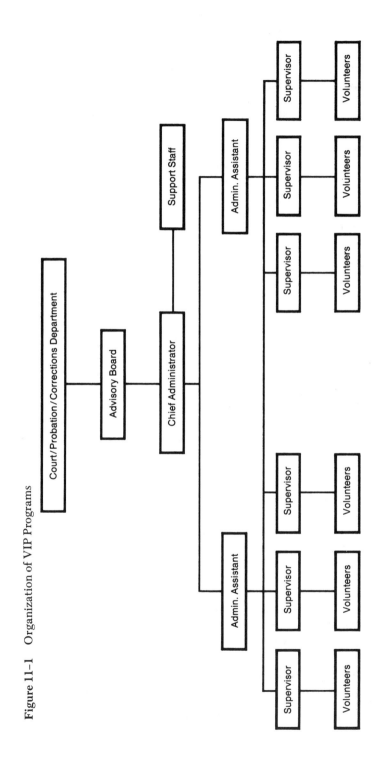

the local court, and the probation department. Lack of support from any one of these components will jeopardize the existence of any volunteer program. Engaging in activities that serve to alleviate friction and promote cooperation and understanding is essential to the establishment and continuance of a volunteer project. While it is not the purpose of this chapter to delve into the political ramifications of developing and maintaining a volunteer project in a community, it is important to note that complex political realities do exist and must be dealt with in order to facilitate continued program stability. This activity may very well be the foundation of successful operations and continued project stability.

Recruitment

A successful volunteer program requires an adequate supply of volunteer workers. In general, it is not difficult in most communities to attract a pool of qualified applicants. Reports have generally shown today's volunteer to be successful, mature, and well educated (Scheier, 1970).

Ku's report (1976) of the Lincoln, Nebraska, program noted that the mean age of its volunteers was twenty-seven and 60 percent were married. The average educational level was a little over fourteen years, and over 90 percent of the volunteers expressed a religious affiliation.

Kratcoski's (1982) sample of 545 volunteers also revealed an above high school educational attainment. In addition, he discovered a virtually equivalent distribution of males and females, and that the volunteers were predominantly white. The volunteers tended to be rather young with 40 percent under the age of thirty. While no figures were given, Kratcoski further reported that a "desire to help others" played a major role in motivating the volunteers to participate.

In their review of the Franklin County (Ohio) program, Seiter et al. (1974) reported volunteerism to be generally a middle-class phenomenon. The mean age of the volunteers was found to be almost thirty-two, with about 70 percent of the volunteers being males and more than 65 percent married. The average volunteer had some college experience. Two-thirds of the volunteers had had no prior experience in the criminal justice system.

Churches and religious organizations are prime sources of volunteers, as are graduate and undergraduate students of a local university or college. Community service groups and professional organizations representing occupations—such as teachers, accountants, businessmen, and social workers—have often been sources of volunteers. Many volunteers have been referred by program staff, and court and probation department personnel. In particular, judges have served as excellent recruiters. The volunteers project in Eugene, Oregon, found that most persons will volunteer their services if they are personally asked the question: Will you please give the Juvenile Department a hand with a delinquent boy or girl who needs a friend?

Another widely used source of volunteers is the volunteer bureau. These bureaus act as clearinghouses to which interested persons can apply as volunteers by stating their interests and preferences for the type of program with which they would like to work. The volunteer program then approaches the bureau with its particular needs, and a volunteer is matched with the program most suitable for him or her.

As a supplement to each of these sources, individual word of mouth has been an indispensable means of recruiting. Communications among friends an acquaintances regarding a specific program have and will continue to assure a solid source of volunteer applicants.

Distribution of promotional materials by way of the mail, the press, radio, and television are other recruitment means often undertaken. While these latter sources are recruiting techniques aimed at selected individuals, such methods are an attempt to inform a large, public audience of the program. Such mass approaches are then followed by more personal interviews for discussions of the program and more selective screening.

Screening and Selection

A key element in a successful volunteer project is the care the program takes in screening applicants, and the opportunity afforded the applicants to screen the project. There are basically six methods used in this two-way screening process: the application form, the personal interview, letters of reference, police background checks, self-screening, and performance during training.

The application form itself can provide a wide variety of relevant information for administrative use. Many volunteer programs personally interview potential volunteers. These interviews provide the applicant with more information about the project while allowing the agency to determine if the applicant can work well in its particular program. Letters of reference provide an outsider's opinion of the applicant's ability to relate to and assist others.

Which technique is used varies from agency to agency. For example, Latessa, Travis, and Allen (1983) surveyed fifty-two parole jurisdictions and found thirty-five that used volunteers. Of those, fourteen did not have any formal qualification requirements. The most frequent specific requirement was passing a background check (seven jurisdictions), closely followed by a "desire to help" (six jurisdictions). (See Table 11–2.)

Some work has been done in an attempt to identify the most effective volunteer. Pus (1975) found housewives to be the most successful volunteer

Table 11-2
Qualifications for Volunteers

Jurisdiction	None	Training	Interview	Background Check	Desire to Help	Other/Commentary
Alabama	—	X	X	X	—	—
Arizona	—	—	—	X	—	—
Arkansas	—	—	—	—	—	Same as field officer
Delaware	X	—	—	—	—	—
Florida	—	X	—	—	—	—
Georgia	X	—	—	—	—	—
Idaho	X	—	—	—	—	—
Iowa	X	—	—	—	—	—
Kansas	X	—	—	—	—	—
Kentucky	—	—	—	X	—	—
Maine	X	—	—	—	—	—
Maryland	—	—	X	—	—	—
Massachusetts	X	—	—	—	—	—
Mississippi	—	X	—	—	X	—
Missouri	X	—	—	—	X	—
Montana	—	X	—	—	—	—
Nevada	—	—	—	—	—	Experience
New Jersey	—	—	—	—	—	Counseling skills; orientation

State						Notes
New Mexico	—	—	—	—	X	
North Carolina	—	—	—	X	—	
North Dakota	—	—	—	X	—	Reliable
Ohio	—	—	—	—	X	
Oregon	—	—	—	X	X	Application; 1-year commitment; orientation
Pennsylvania	—	X	—	—	—	
Tennessee	—	X	—	X	—	
Texas	X	—	—	—	—	
Utah	—	—	X	X	—	Contractual agreement
Vermont	X	—	—	—	—	
Washington	X	—	—	—	—	
Wyoming	X	—	—	—	—	
Washington, D.C.	X	—	—	—	—	
Federal	—	—	—	—	X	

Missing or no information: Alaska, Connecticut, Illinois.

SOURCE: Edward J. Latessa, Lawrence F. Travis III, Harry E. Allen, "Volunteers and Paraprofessionals in Parole: Current Practices," *Journal of Offender Counseling, Services and Rehabilitation* (1983):96.

across occupational categories. Contrary to a number of earlier hypotheses, younger volunteers were found to be just as successful as older ones. The study concluded that a wide variety of volunteers could be used without lowering the success rate of the program. Vito et al. (1980) found that volunteers' race was a factor impacting upon parole success. Nonwhite volunteers were less successful, measured in terms of client rearrest, than white volunteers, especially when nonwhites were matched with nonwhite clientele.

Some programs require a preservice training exercise for potential volunteers. A volunteer's training-exercise performance is often reviewed and compared to a minimum standard. Those who fall below the standard are often not selected. Self-screening, when the applicant per se examines the program and his or her own capabilities, resources, and motivation and decides whether to make the commitment to be a volunteer, is a vital element in the screening process. Applicants also must be given the opportunity to screen a project. The screening and selection process then becomes a two-way street as administrators seek information to make judgments on the selection of volunteers and the volunteers seek information to make a judgment on whether to become a participant in a specific program.

Matching volunteers with clients is, obviously, the crux of the volunteerism philosophy. The basic principle of sound matching is to identify the important needs of the client and, subsequently, to make a match with the volunteer who is most likely to make a significant contribution to meeting these needs.

Most programs seem to have identified a set of matching criteria to effect this more solid relationship. Elements generally considered are: gender, prior volunteer experience, age, ethnic background, education, intelligence, occupation, community contact, interests, socioeconomic level, and counseling skills. As can be expected, the relative importance of each characteristic varies from program to program, and its significance also varies *within* programs as different types of match relationships are sought. For example, it has been noted that some programs tend to match volunteers with clientele whose criminal histories seem to indicate that they are more likely to recidivate than the probationer or parolee population as a whole. This interesting observation by Sternback (1971) has been independently confirmed by Ku (1975) and Cropper (1977). Ku (1976) reported that the Lincoln, Nebraska, program deliberately targets high-risk offenders from the general population for assignment into the volunteer program. As Sternback (1971: 10) notes, the Philadelphia project administrators concur in this philosophy, assigning volunteers to high-risk probationers because they are more inclined to violate probation and are perceived as needing more attention. On the other hand, other programs—such as the Alameda County, California, program (Norris and Stricklin, 1976); the Wilmington, Delaware, program (Metz, 1975; and the San Francisco volunteer program (California Youth Authority, 1976)—tend to focus their volunteer time upon low-risk cases.

Beless et al. (1972) have suggested that matching volunteers with the same socioeconomic background as the client seems to reduce social distance and encourages client interaction with the volunteer. Berer and Zautra (1974) found that middle-class volunteers were considered more helpful than staff officers by middle-class probationers, while line officers and lower-class volunteers were considered more helpful by working-class and less-educated clients. On the other hand, Hume et al. (1976: 25) pointed out that while using such socioeconomically "suitable" personnel may facilitate communication during the course of the match, in everyday life clients will be forced to deal with persons from other social classes, and will need to learn how to cope with such relationships. Volunteer programs will not serve to improve long-term clientele behavior by isolating them from world realities.

One additional matching criterion of interest is that of gender. Eskridge and Carlson (1979) found mixed reviews of the role of this variable. At this point in time, it looks as if male and female clients can probably perform equally as well in a volunteer relationship, all else held constant.

It does appear that most programs have, at least initially, experienced difficulty in effecting good matches. Some programs claim a successful match-relationship rate of as high as 75 percent (Ku, 1976), while others have low success rates and therefore purposely do not report. It is rarely possible to achieve the "best" match for all clients. When it is not possible to identify the best match, the decision must be made whether to delay assignment or assign the client the next best available match. The ability of a project to make effective best-available matches is the cornerstone of successful operations and continued project suitability, second only to the maintenance of solid community support. To facilitate solid "second best" matches, projects seek to maintain an adequate supply of volunteers with the skills necessary to meet clients' needs. Selective recruitment of volunteers at the presentence investigation stage, and prompt reassignment of current volunteers to new cases, can serve to increase the probability of effecting good matches.

Other matching problems have also arisen. Some programs are evaluated on the basis of the gross number of matches made. One result is an emphasis on the quantity of match making, with little emphasis on the *quality* of the matches. Often, volunteers insist on being assigned to certain kinds of clientele, even though the matching rules may indicate that the match would not be a good one. It appears that those programs which are short of volunteers will allow the match to take place, while those programs seeking to maintain high efficient ratings will not.

The general inefficient use of volunteer resources due to poor program management has been frequently noted. While it is to be expected that, at any given time, a certain percentage of a program's volunteers are awaiting assignment (either an initial assignment or a reassignment), some programs report the figure to be as high as 40 percent (City of Southfield, 1975). This is a matter of some concern, for it has been found that when persons seek to become involved as volunteers, the passage of time serves to dampen enthusiasm. In response to this reality, volunteer programs seek to minimize the match assignment time lag or "down time." Eskridge (1980) found extensive variation in this effort among existing programs. He found that some programs reported a time lag of less than thirty days, while others reported the gap to be as long as eleven months. One program reported that some of their volunteers were never assigned a client, and another reported that the delay was so extreme that, at times, offenders were already dismissed from probation before volunteers were assigned. In a related study, Pus (1975) found that programs which were able to affect a volunteer-client match and keep it active for more than six months had a significantly higher success rate among clientele than those who were with volunteers for less than six months. In other words, it appears that a significant criterion for success is length of time a volunteer works with a client. Again, inordinate match assignment time lags can serve to impact negatively upon overall program performance.

Supervising the Match

Once a relationship model has been chosen and the match made, the supervision phase becomes important. While the nature and degree of supervision varies from program to program, it is possible to classify the broad nature of supervision techniques into five categories:

1. Supervision of volunteers
2. Written reports obtained from volunteers
3. Verbal reports obtained from volunteers
4. Periodic meetings between volunteers, program administrators, and probation/parole officers
5. Feedback from clientele obtained by program administrators and probation/parole officers

As with any superior-subordinate relationship, volunteer program operations involve a trade-off between volunteer discretion in working with the clientele and accentuating individual volunteer personalities. This trade-off must be tempered in such a way so as to meet the philosophical framework and general goals of the program. Indeed, working with offenders is a sensitive matter, and controls on the use of discretion by volunteers are essential. Many programs report initial, and occasionally continual, animosity between volunteers and probation/parole officers. This is due in large part to a parole/probation officer's perception that volunteers have violated a program's philosophy and guidelines. Indeed, instances have been reported of volunteers siding with their clients in an adversary relationship with probation/parole officers. Such instances are not generally constructive for the client, the volunteer, or the program, and they do not meet with the broad philosophy of supplementary probation and parole services.

Within, and perhaps superseding, this entire matter of supervision is the issue of communication. As has been noted previously, poor communication patterns have repeatedly surfaced in programs as primary obstacles to efficient volunteer program operations. In the future, program administrators will need to increase the flow of accurate information between themselves, volunteers, and probation/parole officers, in order to maximize service delivery.

Training

A significant aspect of any volunteer program is training. More than a desire to serve is needed to be effective in volunteer service. A multitude of training techniques are utilized. Slide shows, movies, large and small group discussions, role playing, one-to-one discussions, and lectures represent a few of the techniques. Training can be conveniently categorized in a time sequence, namely training prior to a case assignment and training subsequent to and concurrent with a case assignment.

Volunteer program training sessions generally focus upon more general approaches in working with the clientele rather than dealing with specific skills development. Emphasis is placed on what to expect from a relationship with a client and on an examination of volunteer reactions to certain situations. In addition, some time is usually spent in orienting the recruit to the program's purposes and procedures.

The extensiveness of the training differs from program to program. The Macomb County, Michigan, program requires some twenty-four hours of precase assignment instruction, while the Jackson (Indiana) Circuit Court program apparently offers no training at all for its volunteers. Kratcoski (1982) found that 81 percent of the volunteers he sampled had received some training, although only half of those polled felt the training was "adequate." Latessa et al. (1983) found that only five of the thirty-five parole agencies that have volunteer programs conducted any training, and only two (New Jersey and Pennsylvania) required the volunteers to actually complete orientation training. Eskridge (1980) found that approximately 90 percent of the studies reviewed offered at least some form of training to volunteers.

Evaluations and Effectiveness

Proponents of the volunteer concept have assumed that volunteers are able to contribute to the rehabilitation/reintegration of offenders at no greater risk to society than the traditional system, and at a cost less than that of the traditional system. Evaluations to date tend to bear this out. One particular study of interest is the M-2 parole volunteer evaluation (M-2 Sponsors, Inc., 1978). In this two-year experimental study, parolees matched with volunteers had a favorable parole outcome of 80.5 percent, while parolees not matched with a volunteer had a favorable parole outcome of 66.2 percent, or approximately 14 percent less. Scioli and Cook (1976) conducted a review of a large number of volunteer programs and, after screening out all but ten because of methodological deficiencies, concluded that there was evidence suggesting that volunteers performed at least as well as, and perhaps at times better than, the program alternatives. Eskridge and Carlson (1979) were able to identify thirty-eight methodologically sound research efforts and came to a similar conclusion. In the most recent evaluation synthesis, Sigler and Leenhouts (1982: 28) concluded: "All evaluations to date, that we know about, indicate the positive impact of volunteers on criminal justice clients." Sigler and Leenhouts did state, however, that the methodological quality of the evaluations they reviewed were rather weak, and they called upon future researchers to adopt a more methodologically rigorous design. The matter of cost saving, though, was not adequately covered in any of these reviews and continues to be an issue of some concern.

A cost-benefit analysis is a comparative listing and measuring of the economic "pros and cons" of a program reduced to a single monetary dimension.[1] Cost-benefit calculations of volunteer programs will clearly differ depending upon the point of view chosen, be it government, society, client, or volunteer. Furthermore, such analyses become even more methodologically hazardous when attempting to measure nonmonetary factors (satisfaction, self-esteem) from a quantitative perspective. When reviewing volunteer programs in a cost-benefit framework, it should be emphasized that, without standardization, cost-benefit comparisons can become confusing and subjective exercises. Nonetheless, several attempts have been made to bring cost figures to the public's attention. One project that has sought to ascertain its value to society is the well-known Royal Oak project. In 1975, the Royal Oak (Michigan) Municipal Court project claimed to be operating on an annual budget of $50,000, and providing the community with $300,000 worth of services, for a gross direct savings of $250,000 (National Council of Crime and Delinquency, 1976). In 1974, the Macomb County, Michigan, project determined that it had donated some 7,429 hours of services worth $37,145 to the community. The actual cost of $21,765 was encumbered by the project, leaving a gross direct savings of some $15,000. The total dollar amount for 7,429 hours of service at the then-current probation officer salary of $7.50 per hour would place the gross direct savings at $32,000, or an adjusted savings of about $10,250 (Amboyer, 1975). The Macomb County Volunteer Counseling Project reported a gross direct savings of some $9,000 to the community in 1975 (Macomb County, 1975).

As noted earlier, caution should be used in interpreting these data, for each volunteer program is different in terms of operations and cost-benefit computations. Even if it were possible to equate the various program operations and the fiscal methodology used to compute costs and benefits, the figures would be difficult to interpret. For example, a new system savings of $10,000 in the operation of a larger program in a metropolitan area does not have the same impact as a $10,000 new system savings in the operation of a small program in a small town. The most significant figures would be those that demonstrate the net system costs and savings, and the net *individual* costs and savings. There does not appear to be such information available at this time. From the information available, however, it appears that volunteer programs are capable of providing services at a cost less than that of the traditional system.

To stop at this point and imply that volunteer projects have had no other impact upon the system would be misleading. The operationalization of volunteer projects has resulted in a number of collateral impacts. Hill's study (1972) of the Anchorage and Fairbanks, Alaska, programs found that the majority of the adult offenders in the volunteer programs were misdemeanants referred by the district court, and that many and perhaps a majority of them would not have been on probation at all had the volunteer project not existed. These individuals, prior to the incorporation of the volunteer project, would have been judged as not needing probation officer supervision. With the advent of the volunteer project, they found themselves subject to both a volunteer's and a probation officer's supervision. This is an example of the so-called widening of the net phenomenon.[2]

Volunteerism proponents have long held that caseloads would be reduced as a direct result of volunteer programs. Eskridge and Carlson (1979) found this to be the case in some jurisdictions, but also found programs where there was a tendency to increase officer responsibility. Officers in some jurisdictions are apparently required to not only maintain their present caseload, but also to monitor and, at times, supervise the activities of several volunteers. Hume et al. (1976: 40) concluded that contact time with probationers could be purchased more efficiently by hiring another probation officer, rather than establishing a volunteer program.

A series of issues have arisen from the probation/parole officer–volunteer relationship. The fact that some officers feel volunteers are a threat to their jobs has surfaced in various programs. This element of the officer-volunteer relationship cannot be eliminated unless officers can be convinced that they will not lose their jobs, grossly alter their roles, or diminish their potential vertical mobility within the department because of the volunteers. One way to overcome this problem is to develop very clear volunteer job descriptions in conjunction with the officers (see Table 11–1). Hiring volunteers as probation officers is a common practice in some departments and will not likely change. But it must be undertaken in such a way that minimizes the threat to the existing probation officers. The 1976 report of the statewide volunteers effort under way in Nebraska noted that some initial resistance to the volunteer program was felt from probation officers, but abated when the officers were assured that the program would not adversely affect them (Nebraska State Probation Administration, 1976). Others have noted an increase in job-role resentment. While probation and parole officers serve as enforcers, the volunteer is allowed and encouraged to participate in enjoyable activities with the client. This resentment on the part of the officer must be minimized. Volunteers going to bat, so to speak, for their clients in court and revocation hearings, despite the officers' feelings to the contrary, has been an area of great concern for many programs. Due in large part to these forces, many programs are continually undermined by apathetic and/or resentful department personnel. For example, the 1976 San Francisco program reported that almost 50 percent of the department staff surveyed felt that the program did not have the department staff support or the administration support it needed to be successful (California Youth Authority, 1976: 91–94). Gosselin (1974: 5) reported that only about half of the probation officers in the New Hampshire program truly believed in the volunteer project and actively worked for its success.

Summary

Volunteer programs have been explored here because of the assumption that probation and parole services can be upgraded by utilizing volunteers. While there is no clear-cut evidence that volunteer programs are any more or any less successful than other program alternatives, it generally seems that volunteers can provide enhanced services at a relatively cost-beneficial rate. Efforts must be made, however, to enhance the quality of research undertaken. One particular improvement would be the development of a standardized set of evaluation criteria. While such adjustments are desirable, and although all individual projects are certainly not successful, it should again be noted that from the available evidence, volunteer programs in general seem to be able to offer at a reduced cost, an increase in the quality of probation and parole services. Still, Eskridge and Carlson (1979) note, there are some concerns relative to the longevity of the program impact. It may well be that involvement in volunteer relationships has only a short-term, cosmetic impact upon clients' behavior patterns. Furthermore, volunteer programs are fraught with a number of operational pitfalls, and should be undertaken with care and advance planning. Care should be taken in any attempt to obtain probation and parole officers' support for such a program, and an effort made to insure their continued assistance. Operations must be streamlined in order to facilitate prompt processing, assignment and reassignment of program applicants, and clearly delineated communication lines established and kept operable. Volunteers must receive adequate training and suitable matches must be made. Indeed, it appears that volunteerism is a sound concept, but programs experience some difficulties in their operations.

While a number of concerns and criticisms of volunteerism have been aired, it appears to be an extremely viable alternative, especially for the cost-conscious 1980s. It is important to emphasize that many of the objections to volunteerism that have been raised can be dealt with in a constructive manner through continued community support and a commitment on the part of the many volunteer program administrators to improve operations. Volunteers pose a definite promise in probation and parole practices and services. However, at present, it is but a promise still largely unfulfilled. Volunteer programs really have not been wholeheartedly embraced by probation and parole agencies. In fact, volunteer programs face the challenge of successfully selling themselves to a public and to criminal justice managers who have grown somewhat suspect of the promise. Kratcoski (1982) reports that half of all volunteer programs now fail within two years. The promise of success is unmistakably there, and it is now incumbent upon the volunteer programs to actually deliver in a visible fashion.

Notes

1. For a more complete view of cost-benefit analysis from a correctional perspective see: Carl W. Nelson, "Cost-Benefit Analysis and Alternatives to Incarceration," *Federal Probation* 39 (1975):45–50; and Carl W. Nelson, and Jeffrey I. Chapman, *A Handbook of Cost-Benefit Techniques and Applications* (Washington, D.C.: American Bar Association Correction Economics Center, 1975). As these authors note, methodologically sound cost-benefit reviews are extremely complex matters involving the collection and analysis of primary, sec-

ondary, and tertiary cost and benefit data. Such data are simply not available in most correctional settings; subsequently, most cost-benefit analyses undertaken in the correctional system are exercises in subjective quantification resulting in endless dispute and debate.

2. "Widening of the net" has actually come to have two interpretations. First, and perhaps most commonly understood, is the *overreach* phenomenon, where more persons are brought into the system than before because certain types of programs came into existence, as the example noted in the text. The second category is the *overthrust* phenomenon, where persons are pressed further and further into the system so as to take advantage of certain types of programs. For example, see the findings of the overthrust impact of shock probation in Joseph Scott, Simon Dinitz, and David Shichor, "Pioneering Innovations in Corrections: Shock Probation and Shock Parole," *Offender Rehabilitation* 2 (1977): 113–22.

Study Guides

1. What information should be used to determine who should be accepted as a volunteer?
2. What information should be used to determine which clientele should participate?
3. How much discretion should be given to volunteers in their dealings with clients?
4. What can be done to minimize the friction between volunteers and probation/parole officers?
5. What can be done to maximize the amplification and diversification of volunteer services, while minimizing societal risk and operational costs?

Key Terms

administrative model
cost-benefit analysis
Keith Leenhouts
M-C-O
one-to-one model

professional model
supervision model
volunteerism
widening the net

References

AMBOYER, DONALD J. *Volunteer Probation Aides Project Evaluation of 1974.* Mt. Clemens, Mich.: Macomb County Probation Department, 1975.

BELESS, DAVID; PILCHER, WILLIAM; AND RYAN, ELLEN. "Use of Indigenous Nonprofessionals in Probation and Parole," *Federal Probation* 36 (1972):10–12.

BERER, J., AND ZAUTRA, I. *The Evaluation of the Effectiveness of Volunteers and Probation Officers Misdemeanant Services.* Unpublished manuscript. Salt Lake City: University of Utah, 1974.

California Youth Authority. *Citizens in Corrections: An Evaluation of 13 Correctional Volunteer Programs.* Sacramento, Calif.: California Youth Authority, 1976.

CARLSON, ERIC W.; VITO, GENNARO F.; AND PARKS, EVALYN. "Race as a Factor in Volunteer Assistance to Parolees," *Evaluation Review* 12 (1980):323–38.

City of Southfield. *Probation Improvement Program-Subgrant Final Evaluation Report.* Southfield, Mich.: City of Southfield, 1975.

CROPPER, CABELL C. *Evaluation of Probationer Volunteer Programs in the 9th, 11th, 12th, 18th and 19th Districts.* Denver, Colo.: Colorado Judicial Department, Research and Evaluation Unit, 1977.

ESKRIDGE, CHRIS W. "Issues in VIP Management: A National Synthesis," *Federal Probation* 44 (1980):8–18.

ESKRIDGE, CHRIS W., AND CARLSON, ERIC. "The Use of Volunteerism Probation: A National Synthesis," *Journal of Offender Counseling, Services and Rehabilitation* 4 (1979):175–89.

GOSSELIN, IVETTE L. *An Evaluation of Coordinators of Volunteers.* Concord, N.H.: New Hampshire Probation Department, 1974.

HILL, MARJORIE. *Project Evaluation: Partners—Community Volunteers in a One-to-One Relationship.* Juneau, Alas.: Alaska Department of Health and Social Services, Division of Corrections, Systems and Research Unit, 1972.

HORJESI, CHARLES R. "Training for the Direct Service Volunteer in Probation," *Federal Probation* 37 (1973):38–41.

HUME, REX D., ET AL. *Evaluation of Probation Services and Volunteers in Probation Programs: Final Report.* Bloomington, Ind.: Indiana University, School of Public Environmental Affairs, Institute for Research in Public Safety, 1976.

KRATCOSKI, PETER C. "Volunteers in Corrections: Do They Make a Meaningful Contribution?," *Federal Probation* 46 (1982):30–35.

KU, RICHARD. *The Volunteer Probation Counselor Program, Lincoln, Nebraska: An Exemplary Project.* Washington, D.C.: LEAA, NILECJ, 1976.

LATESSA, EDWARDS J.; TRAVIS, LAWRENCE F., III; AND ALLEN, HARRY E. "Volunteers and Paraprofessionals in Parole: Current Practices," *Journal of Offender Counseling, Services and Rehabilitation* 8 (1983):91–105.

Macomb County Probation Department. *Final Evaluation Report: Volunteer Counseling.* Mt. Clemens, Mich.: Macomb County Probation Department, 1975.

METZ, HAROLD. *Volunteers in Probation: A Project Evaluation.* Wilmington, Dela.: Delaware Council on Crime and Justice, Delaware Department of Corrections, 1975.

M-2 Sponsors, Inc., of California. *Successful Habilitation of Ex-Offenders.* Haywood, Calif.: M-2 Sponsors, 1978.

National Council on Crime and Delinquency. *Citizens Participation in a Probation Department*. Royal Oak, Mich.: National Council on Crime and Delinquency, 1976.

————. *Volunteers in Prevention. Royal Oak, Mich.: National Council on Crime and Delinquency, 1977.*

Nebraska State Probation Administration. *Thirty-Sixth Monthly Report for the Statewide Volunteers in Probation*. Lincoln, Neb.: Nebraska State Probation Administration, 1976.

Norris, Robert O., and Stricklin, Margaret B. *Volunteers in Probation Annual Report (December 1976)*. Oakland, Calif.: Alameda County Probation Department, 1976.

Pus, Susan. *Assessment of Probation Programs in Metropolitan Toronto*. Toronto: Ministry of Correctional Services, 1975.

Santa Barbara County. *Santa Barbara County Probation Department Volunteer Coordinator Grant Program: An Evaluation of Its Effectiveness*. Santa Barbara, Calif.: Santa Barbara County Probation Department, 1973.

Scheier, Ivan. "The Professional and the Volunteer: An Emerging Relationship," *Federal Probation* 34 (1970):8–12.

————. *National Register of Volunteer Jobs in Court Settings*. Boulder, Colo.: National Information Center on Volunteerism, 1973.

Scioli, Frank P., and Cook, Thomas J. "How Effective Are Volunteers?," *Crime and Delinquency* 22 (1976):192–200.

Seiter, Richard P.; Howard, Sue A.; and Allen, Harry E. *Effectiveness of Volunteers in Court: An Evaluation of the Franklin County Volunteers Probation Program*. Columbus, Ohio: Ohio State University Program for the Study of Crime and Delinquency, 1974.

Shields, Patricia; Chapman, Charles W.; and Wingard, David R. "Using Volunteers in Adult Probation," *Federal Probation* 47 (1983):57–64.

Sigler, Robert T., and Leenhouts, Keith J. "Volunteers in Criminal Justice: How Effective?," *Federal Probation* 46 (1982):25–29.

Sternback, Jack C. *Evaluation Report: Community Resources and Volunteer Unit*. Philadelphia, Penn.: Philadelphia Probation Department, 1971.

Recommended Readings

Barker, Gordon H., and Matson, Ronald R., *Volunteers in Court: Collected Papers* (Washington, D.C.: Youth Development Delinquency Prevention Administration, 1971). Complete review of the advantages and disadvantages of volunteer programs. Includes a section that is a volunteer probation officer's handbook or operation manual.

Ku, Richard. *The Volunteer Probation Counselor Program, Lincoln, Nebraska: An Exemplary Project* (Washington, D.C.: LEAA, NILECJ, 1976). Detailed description of the operations of this program, in which carefully screened and trained individuals assist salaried probation staff with one-to-one counseling of high-risk misdemeanant probationers.

National Council on Crime and Delinquency. *Volunteers in Prevention* (Royal Oak, Mich.: National Council on Crime and Delinquency, 1977). Thorough review of the present and potential uses of volunteers in the justice system.

Smykla, John O. *Community-Based Corrections: Principles and Practices* (New York: Macmillan, 1981). Examines the interrelationships of community-based alternatives, including volunteers, with the justice system as a whole.

12

Probation and Parole Effectiveness

The effectiveness of probation and parole is a hotly contested issue, and final word on this most important question is not clearly available.[1] Many critics of both probation and parole point to discretionary abuses, the arbitrary nature of the indeterminate sentence, the disparity in sentencing practices by judges, the failure of rehabilitation and supervision, and the inadequate delivery of services. In an attempt to offset some of these criticisms, mandatory and determinate sentencing systems have been imposed, sentencing tribunals have been formed, parole boards have begun to adopt and implement decision-making guidelines, and probation and parole departments have tested new and innovative service delivery strategies. But these, too, are open to attack and are frequently criticized.

Much has been written about probation and parole effectiveness. We know that over 67 percent of all released felons re-enter society on parole[2] and that the number of individuals on probation is two and one-half times the number in prison and on parole. We also know that there is an acute shortage of trained professional probation and parole officers, resulting in large caseloads and workloads for probation and parole departments. We continually experiment with service systems—such as brokerage, team, casework, intensive or specialized caseloads, and volunteer-paraprofessionals—but, again, we know little about the actual effectiveness of these strategies in probation and parole. In short, there have been nearly as many innovative programs and reported results as there are persons under supervision. The question of effectiveness remains, and since it is so essential, it must be closely examined.

Effectiveness

While the debate over correctional effectiveness will surely continue for some time, those attempting to evaluate and measure the worth of various strategies found in corrections face a most difficult dilemma—defining "effectiveness."

A large part of the problem lies in the desire on the part of researchers and practitioners alike to define failure or success in clear-cut, either/or terms. There is a strong need to view success or failure on a continuum, rather than as a win or lose dichotomy. For example, an offender may complete a sentence of probation yet have erratic employment and numerous technical violations. This individual is certainly not as successful as one who finishes probation, gains upward mobility in a job, makes restitution, supports a family, and incurs no new charges of any type; still, both these cases may be classified as successes. There is also a great deal of difference between the offender who is caught on a minor charge or a technical violation, and one who commits a serious new felony.

In addition to this problem, there is no agreement on the indicators of effectiveness. While most agree that recidivism should be a primary performance measure, there is no agreement on its definition nor on the indicators to be used for its measurement. Indeed, a recent study of parole supervision found that the nature of the outcome criteria had a significant effect upon the interpretation of results (Gottfredson, Mitchell-Herzfeld, and Flanagan, 1982). Researchers tend to define recidivism in terms that fit the available data, yet we know that official sources are inadequate at best. Community follow-up and appropriate comparison groups are the exception rather than the rule when examining the recidivism of probationers and parolees. There is also some evidence that the amount of time given to the follow-up period may have a significant effect on the reported recidivism rates (Hoffman and Stone-Meierhoefer, 1980).

Perhaps the most limiting aspect of effectiveness studies has been the neglect given to other performance measures. By simply comparing recidivism rates, researchers have ignored some of the main effects that probation and parole are designed to achieve. The number and quality of contacts and services provided the probationers and parolees need to be adequately defined and gauged. There are few good cost-benefit or cost-effectiveness studies.[3] The importance of this type of information cannot be sufficiently stressed. These types of studies can help probation and parole agencies make more efficient selections in terms of the resources they will employ and the strategies to be used to deliver those resources.

Finally, a list of effectiveness indicators should include the degree of *humaneness* that community supervision affords the offender, and the impact of these alternatives on reducing prison populations and overcrowded conditions in jails and prisons.

There is little doubt that recidivism, no matter how it may be defined, should remain a main criteria; however, the need to measure additional outcome indicators appears obvious. Indeed, there has been a great deal of criticism directed at the research conducted in the area of correctional programming.

Parole Effectiveness

What is actually known about the effectiveness of probation and parole, and what should future research priorities be? The next section summarizes what is generally concluded about selected topic areas of interest in parole effectiveness. This discussion of topic areas is basically organized along the general flow of criminal justice decision points as they relate to parole; however, most of the findings also pertain to probation, particularly those on supervision and innovative programs.

Preinstitutional Factors

For at least four decades, researchers have attempted to distinguish the factors that relate to parole success. The rationale offered for such ambitious endeavors vary but, for the most part, they represent attempts to develop prediction instruments and to provide decision-makers (especially parole boards and judges) with information for more successful judgments.

After reviewing all available literature, one is immediately aware of the confusion and contradictions that such research has generated. For almost every study and factor presented as a "successful indicator" or "stable predictor," there is another refuting the finding. The folly of presenting the "ideal" parolee as a "middle-aged white male with no prior record and an annual income over $20,000" is obvious. The studies that have identified significant factors are often methodologically flawed, or limited in their generalizability.

Some studies have attempted to relate supervision success to such nebulous concepts as "self-esteem" or to other equally unmeasurable personality constructs. One study (Syrotvik, 1978) attempted to correlate birth order with parole success. The author concluded that a firstborn was more likely to succeed. We do not know if this applies to both males and females, if the results differ with family size, or if "only child" has an effect on outcome. It also suggests little if any policy direction.

Studies showing race to be a significant factor are refuted by others showing no racial differences in outcome. The only two variables that appear to be consistently associated with parole effectiveness are *age* (the over forty group does better) and *type of offense* (with repeat property offenders more likely to fail than personal offenders, especially murderers).[4]

Recently, prediction in criminal justice has increasingly used more statistically sophisticated methods, especially multivariate statistical techniques. In spite of these advancements, there is little evidence that more sophisticated techniques improve the predictability of parole success beyond that achieved by simpler methods (Van Alstyne and Gottfredson, 1978).

In spite of the difficulties posed by predictive instruments, the Federal Parole Commission and a number of states have begun to develop and implement decision-making guidelines designed to limit discretion, structure decision making, and provide more equity in sentencing. The underlying assumption is that more "objective" criteria will lead to better predictions in future success or failure. (For a more thorough discussion of these guidelines, see Chapter 6.)

Institutional Factors

Several aspects of the institutional experience are thought to be related to parole and its effectiveness, such as length of time incarcerated, institutional programs, and parole conditions imposed as conditions of release.

Research that has examined the effects of the amount of time served on parole have generally concluded that the shorter the amount of time served, the greater the likelihood of successful parole (Gottfredson, Gottfredson, and Garofalo, 1977; Eichman, 1965). Although none of these studies found a "magic" number for time served, most studies centered around a two-year incarceration period as a cutoff point.

Most researchers concluded that longer prison terms had an adverse effect upon parolee chances of success, implying that the negative aspects of prisonization seem to intensify with time. For example, in his study of shock probationers, Vito (1978) concluded that even a short period of incarceration had a negative impact. The question that remains unanswered by this research is: Are there any characteristics of inmates who have served more time that are also associated with an unfavorable parole outcome?

Existing research on the effectiveness of institutional programs is dismally inadequate (Robison and Smith, 1971). Most such programs are analyzed in relation to institutional adjustment, disciplinary problems, and impact of program participation on the parole-granting process. The few evaluations that included a parole period usually show little if any positive effects with regard to recidivism.

Some of the most insightful findings about institutional effects on parole were presented by Glaser (1964: 3–6). In his examination of the federal correctional system, 250 parole successes were compared to 308 failures. The highlights of his findings were:

1. Inmates are most concerned with avoiding trouble with other inmates than in maximizing inmate friendships.
2. Most inmates have a sincere interest in self-improvement and conforming to staff expectations while in prison.
3. The influence of criminalistic inmates on other inmates seems to be a direct function of the isolation of staff from inmates.
4. Training and education programs in prison are not geared to the reality of work life out of prison.
5. A combination of education programs in prison is favorably related to parole outcome.
6. Parolees often have unrealistic expectations of rapid occupational movement, and suffer from frequent unemployment.
7. Inmate expectations of postrelease difficulties in terms of police harassment seem to be overrated.
8. Family discord is an aggravating factor in adjustment while on parole.

Even though this study is somewhat dated, it tends to illustrate the adverse effects of institutionalization.

In a recent survey of fifty-two parole field supervision agencies (Allen and Latessa, 1980), forty-nine had residency requirements as a condition of parole, and forty-seven had an employment requirement. The literature produced only two studies that were directly related to the imposition of these conditions and parole effectiveness. Although one study (Beasly, 1978) showed a relationship between stability of residency and parole success, the lack of research in this area makes generalization impossible.

Release

Primarily in response to the determinate sentencing advocates, researchers have increasingly turned their attention to evaluating the success of parole supervision.

Critics of parole supervision rely on two basic arguments to support their views. The first is that parole supervision simply is not effective in reducing recidivism. The second, more philosophical argument is that supervision is not "just" (von Hirsch and Hanrahan, 1979). A more plausible conclusion is that the evidence is mixed that parole supervision is effective in reducing recidivism rates among parolees.

Several studies have compared parolees to mandatory releases, but they've failed to control for possible differences in the selection of the groups (Martinson and Wilkes, 1979). Other studies that have been controlled for differences have reported favorable results (Gottfredson, 1975), and yet other studies have reported less positive results (Waller, 1974; Jackson, 1983). The 1979 Uniform Parole Reports also compared parolees with mandatory releases. The existing evidence seems to be in favor of parole supervision (see Chapter 1).

Even the most outspoken critics of parole agree that the agencies responsible for the task of supervision are often understaffed, their officers undertrained, underpaid, and overworked. They are inundated with excessively large caseloads, workloads, and paperwork. Community services are either unavailable or unwilling to handle parolees, and as a consequence parole officers are expected to be all things to all people. As indicated in Chapter 7, they are also expected to perform the paradoxical function roles of surveillance-policeman and rehabilitator-treatment agent.

There is some evidence that, by shortening the amount of time on parole, we could save a considerable amount of money and time, and not seriously increase the risk of failure. Most data seem to indicate that the majority of failures on parole occur during the first two years (Hoffman and Stone-Meierhoefer, 1980) and drops significantly thereafter. There is also some evidence that early release into the community and from parole incurs no higher risk to the community and, in fact, is justifiable on cost considerations (Holt, n.d.).

In a summary statement, we have selected some findings from a Washington State (1976) ten-year follow-up of parolees. Most of these findings are consistent with other, less comprehensive studies. It was found that the first year of parole was critical, with over half of those paroled returning to prison during this time period. In this study, there were more failures in the second than the first six months after release. It was also found that those convicted of murder and manslaughter were less likely to recidivate, and that property offenders—especially those convicted of burglary, auto theft, and forgery—had the highest failure rate. As expected, younger parolees did significantly worse than those over forty years of age. Blacks did slightly worse than whites after the first six months, and Native Americans did significantly worse than all other groups.

It is not surprising that many of these same findings can be both supported and refuted in the literature. One should consider this information in light of the fact that the Uniform Parole Reports notes that the bulk of parole failures are for technical violations. It is important to understand that there are distinct differences between technical violations and commitment for new offenses.

Special Topic: Women

In spite of the recent focus on and attention given to the female offender, research on women on parole has been relatively sparse (Florida State, 1976). One study compared three samples of female parolees, each released at different times. The only possible conclusion was that the failure rates of the three study samples were significantly different, perhaps indicating changes in social structure and policy with respect to female criminality.

Findings from other studies were not surprising: Female property offenders do worse on parole, and first offenders do better; nonalcohol users do significantly better; black female offenders committed more personal offenses than did their white counterparts; and males (especially blacks) were more likely than females to recidivate. An interesting finding was that males, when compared to females, were more likely to *receive* parole. One reason offered for this is that females tended to be incarcerated for more serious offenses than were males.

The problem with most of these findings is that they tell us little, if anything, about the effectiveness of parole with women. All of the studies had methodological weaknesses; in addition, they lacked a strong conceptual base. Further, these studies give little indication of how to deal more effectively with female parolees. While female parolees represent a small percentage of the total parole population, all indications are this figure is growing dramatically.

Special Topic: Murderers

Murderers, like female parolees, represent a small percentage of the total parole population. Unlike females, however, murderers on parole have been the focus of a great deal of research over the years.

Studies of parole success by type of offense repeatedly indicate that those who commit murder are among the best parole risks (Neithercut, 1972). The reasons for this conclusion vary; the explanation most frequently offered is that most murderers tend to be first offenders who have committed crimes of passion and emotion. Another reason cited is age; since most convicted murderers spend a great amount of time incarcerated, they tend to be older when released, usually after the high-crime-risk years of sixteen to twenty-nine.

Other studies analyzed "dangerous" parolees and found that they are more likely to be returned to prison on technical violations and that personal offenders react more negatively to intensive supervision than do repeat property offenders. One possible explanation for this may be because they are kept under closer surveillance than other types of offenders.

Overall, studies examining violent offenders and murderers were found to present consistent findings and conclusions over time.

Special Topic: Contract Parole

One of the most recent innovative programs is contract parole (see Chapter 9). This involves the inmate, prison authorities, and the parole decision-makers in developing a viable plan to prepare an inmate for release to the community. As a systematic program, this technique has been implemented and evaluated in several states.[5] Although it is premature to speculate about the effectiveness of contract parole, it has not yet demonstrated a significant impact. Most of the studies conducted to date are still in the experimental stages, or the program was abandoned with mixed or negative reviews.[6] The inherent contribution of contract parole seems to lie in its effectiveness in forcing correctional authorities to closely examine the programs and services they offer. By strengthening promising programs and abandoning weaker ones, the long-term effectiveness of contract parole might be impressive. For now, however, legal complications coupled with financial considerations present an immediate obstacle for contract parole.

Special Topic: Determinate Sentencing

As suggested previously, parole has been attacked on a number of fronts, including its ineffectiveness in presenting recidivism and as undermining the deterrent effect of incarceration. Central in the criticisms of parole is concern with the parole-granting process, and the arbitrary and capricious manner in which decision making occurs. Because of its association with the indeterminate sentence, and the widely publicized failure of the medical model, a number of states have enacted legislation either to abolish or severely curtail the function of parole.[7]

The two basic alternatives have been to replace the indeterminate sentencing entirely, or to reform it. Thus far, most legislation has focused on the former. The type of sentencing legislation selected has varied from state to state, but generally includes presumptive sentencing, determinate discretionary sentencing, or use of sentencing guidelines.[8] Several states that have moved toward presumptive sentencing still include parole as a component of the system, most notably California (see Chapter 1), which has mandatory periods of parole supervision. The California statute has been termed the "purest determinate sentencing scheme yet adopted," and the statute clearly states that the purpose of sentencing is imprisonment, not rehabilitation.[9] Although the statute abolished the parole-release function of the parole board, parole supervision was retained. Other states adopting this type of legislation, such as Indiana, have also retained parole supervision, but with a one-year maximum for supervision. Unfortunately, very little data are yet available to measure the effectiveness or impact of the new determinate sentencing acts. Preliminary research, however, has revealed some interesting and somewhat contradictory findings.

One of the predicted effects of the determinate sentence is an increase in existing prison populations. A report of the California Department of Corrections reveals that the number of male felons received from court in January-June 1978 under the new determinate sentencing statute increased 22 percent over the same period in 1977. In addition, the number of male felons received during fiscal year 1977–78 was the highest ever received during the entire history of the California Department of Corrections (Ryan and Pannel, 1979).

In a more recent study, Brewer, Beckett, and Holt (1981: 200–31) found that while the commitment rates increased dramatically, the result has been a moderation in the overall length of prison terms. They also cautioned that political efforts could eventually result in much longer penalties.

There are some preliminary data on Maine's determinate sentencing and abolition of parole. Kramer and Katkin (1979) found that criminal punishments have actually become less severe in Maine since the enactment of the new code. Although these researchers only looked at the first year, they found that there was an increase in the use of probation for all classes of offenders. They also found that instead of decreasing the sentencing disparity, as many had anticipated, the change led to an increase in sentence disparity. This was not explained away by relevant variables, and it led the researchers to conclude that much of the postcode variations could be attributed to differences between judges. There was also little preliminary evidence to show that certainty of punishment had actually increased.

In sum, it appears that the attacks on parole will continue. There seems to be a belief on the part of many practitioners and legislators, when faced with the possibility of abolishing parole, that release under supervision is more palatable than release without it. Even Martinson and Wilks (1979: 26–27), outspoken opponents of the rehabilitative model, have concluded that "The evidence seems to indicate that the abolition of parole supervision would result in substantial increases in arrest, conviction, and return to prison."

Probation Effectiveness

As with parole, the quality of probation research is dubious. Unlike parole, which is found on the state and federal level, probation still remains primarily a local governmental function. The fact that probation can be found at local, state, and federal levels; that there are municipal and county probation departments; and that probation serves both misdemeanants and felons, combined with the problems discussed previously, make research in probation very difficult to conduct. Indeed, much of the research has been limited to only the several probation departments to which researchers have been welcome. This event gives us a limited sense of the true picture of probation.

As with parole, the research on probation effectiveness will be divided into sections.[10] However, unlike our presentation of parole, the research on probation will be divided into four groups: studies that compare the performance of offenders receiving alternative dispositions; studies that simply measure probation outcome without comparison with any other form of sanction; studies that measure probation outcome and then attempt to isolate the characteristics which tend to differentiate between successful and nonsuccessful outcomes; and studies that examine the cost effectiveness of probation.

Probation Versus Alternative Dispositions

To examine the effectiveness of probation compared to other dispositions we looked at five studies. Three of the studies compared recidivism rates of individuals placed on probation with individuals sentenced to incarceration. Babst and Mannering's study (1965) compared similar types of offenders who were imprisoned or placed on probation. The sample consisted of 7,614 Wisconsin offenders who were statistically comparable in original disposition, county of commitment, type of offense committed, number of prior felonies, and marital status. Parolees were followed for two years, and probationers were followed for two years or until discharge from probation, whichever came first. Violations were defined as the commission of a new offense or the violation of probation/parole rules. The findings of this study showed that, for offenders with no prior felony convictions, the violation rate was 25 percent for probationers and 32.9 percent for parolees. For offenders with one prior felony conviction, violation rates were 41.8 percent for probationers and 43.9 percent for parolees; for offenders with two or more felonies, the rates were 51.8 percent for probationers and 48.7 percent for parolees. With respect to the difference in violation rates for first offenders (which was statistically significant at the .05 level), Babst and Mannering note that this finding could be a result of the fact that parolees are a more difficult group to supervise or could actually show that, at least for first offenders, incarceration does more harm than good.

Another study done in Wisconsin (Wisconsin Division of Corrections, 1965) compared the performance of burglars, who had no previous felony convictions, sentenced to prison or placed on probation. While this study also attempted to investigate the characteristics associated with successful and nonsuccessful probationers and parolees, we will simply report at this point that the violation rate (based on a two-year follow-up, using the same definition of violation rate as Babst and Mannering, above) for burglars placed on probation was 23 percent, and for burglars who were incarcerated and then placed on parole was 34 percent. Thus, it appears that, as with the Wisconsin study, probation was more successful than parole.

The Pennsylvania Program for Women and Girl Offenders (1976) compared recidivism rates between all women placed on state probation or released on state parole during a two-year period. Recidivism was defined as any technical violation of probation or parole or any new criminal charge. The findings showed that, overall, women placed on probation had a 35.6 percent recidivism rate, while women sentenced to prison and then placed on parole had a 31.5 percent recidivism rate. When only women with no prior convictions were considered, the probationers had a 24 percent recidivism rate, and the parolees had a 23.1 percent rate. The differences between these rates were not statistically significant.

Whereas these three studies compared probation with incarceration, a California study (California Department of Justice, 1969) compared violation rates among offenders placed on probation, offenders sentenced to probation following a jail term, and offenders given straight jail sentences. The study examined the performance of a cohort of offenders, all of whom had an equal exposure of one full year in the community. For the probation group, cohort status was gained on the date of the beginning of the probation period; for the group receiving jail sentences, cohort status began on the date of release from jail. To evaluate the relative effectiveness of these dispositions, three violation levels were used: "none" signified no known arrest for a technical violation or a new offense, "minor" signified at least an arrest and perhaps a conviction resulting in a jail sentence of less than ninety days or probation of one year or less, and "major" signified at least a conviction resulting in a jail sentence of not less than ninety days or a term of probation exceeding one year. Since each case was followed for only a year, the final outcome of a violation occasionally did not occur until after the year was over. If it could be inferred that the disposition or sentence was the result of an arrest that did occur within the follow-up year, the action was included in the violation rate.

The findings of this major study are presented in Table 12-1. Those offenders receiving jail sentences without the benefit of probation services had the worst record of recidivism.

These studies illustrate that as a disposition, probation appears to be more effective than incarceration, even for a short period of time. This may be due, in part, to the fact that probationers immediately return to the community, their jobs, and their families.

Table 12–1
Violation Levels of Sentenced Offenders in California

	VIOLATIONS		
SENTENCE	*None*	*Minor*	*Major*
Probation only	64.7%	23.7%	11.6%
Jail, then probation	50.3%	31.7%	18.0%
Jail only	46.6%	29.5%	23.9%

SOURCE: California Department of Justice (1969).

Finally, an Alaska study (Alaska Department of Health and Social Services, 1976) utilized an experimental design to compare the performance of misdemeanant offenders receiving probation supervision with offenders officially on probation but not required to report to the probation unit. The groups were created by random assignment to the experimental group (under supervision) or the control group (no supervision) and were followed for periods ranging from two months to slightly more than two years. Performance was assessed by means of recidivism, defined as the conviction for a new offense. The findings of the study showed that 22 percent of the experimental group members and 24 percent of the control group members had been convicted of new offenses during the follow-up period.

Given the paucity of research and the caution with which recidivism data must be approached, it is nearly impossible, not to mention inappropriate, to attempt to draw any conclusions from these studies about the effectiveness of probation compared to other alternative dispositions. Of the studies that compared probation to incarceration, it tentatively appears that probation may have a significant impact on first offenders. It may also be suggested that the severity of violations appears to increase in proportion to the severity of the disposition. It does not appear that the provision of probation supervision for misdemeanants is more effective than an unsupervised probation period.

Probation Outcome

There were a number of studies that reported recidivism rates only for probationers. Ten of these were reviewed, but one should remember that definitions of failure, follow-up periods, and the types of offenders differ significantly from one study to another. Table 12–2 includes the author, types of instant offenses committed by the probationers in the study, the definition of failure used in the study, the length of follow-up, and the failure rates.

Table 12-2
Studies Reporting Recidivism Rates for Probationers

Study	Instant Offenses	Failure	Follow-Up	Failure Rate (Percent)
Caldwell (1951)	Internal Revenue laws (72%)	Convictions	Postprobation: 5½–11½ years	16.4
England (1955)	Bootlegging (48%) and forgery	Convictions	Postprobation: 6–12 years	17.7
Davis (1955)	Burlary; forgery and checks	2 or more violations and revocations (technical and new offenses)	To termination: 4–7 years	30.2
Frease (1964)		Inactive letter, bench warrant, and revocation	On probation: 18–30 months	20.2
Landis (1969)	Auto theft, forgery and checks	Revocation (technical and new offenses)	To termination	52.5
Irish (1972)	Larceny and burglary	Arrests or convictions	Postprobation: Minimum of 4 years	41.5
Missouri Division of Probation and Parole (1976)	Burglary, larceny, and vehicle theft	Arrests and convictions	Postprobation: 6 months–7 years	30.0
Kusuda (1976)	Property	Revocation	To termination: 1–2 years	18.3
Comptroller General (1976)		Revocation and postrelease conviction	Postprobation: 20-month average	55.0
Irish (1977)	Property	Arrests	Postprobation: 3–4 years	29.6

Source: Harry E. Allen, et al., *Critical Issues in Adult Probation: Summary*, p. 35 (National Institute of Law Enforcement and Criminal Justice, Law Enforcement Assistance Administration, September 1979).

These summary descriptions illustrate many of the problems associated with attempting to assess probation effectiveness. The types of offenders constituting the samples (as represented by instant offenses) vary, as do the definitions used in each study to characterize failure. Four studies computed failure rates while the offenders were on probation, and the length of follow-up periods ranged from several months to many years.

Most of the studies reviewed here stated that their purpose was to assess "probation effectiveness"; however, unlike the five studies examined earlier, none of these studies defined a base (such as a failure rate for comparable parolees or offenders on summary probation) against which to compare findings in order to support a claim that probation is an effective alternative for rehabilitating offenders.

The review of these ten studies demonstrates that little progress has apparently been made over the past few years toward an adequate assessment of probation. The conclusions drawn by the authors of these studies, however, appear to suggest that there exists an unwritten agreement or rule of thumb that probation can be considered to be effective, and that a failure rate above 30 percent indicates it is not effective. This tendency is suggested by the comments in Table 12–3.

Probation Outcome and Statistics

In addition to measuring the effectiveness of probation, a number of studies have also attempted to isolate characteristics that could be related to offender rehabilitation. Table 12–4 presents a summary of the major factors

Table 12–3
Evaluations of Effectiveness of Probation

YEAR	AUTHOR	FAILURE RATE	COMMENT
1951	Caldwell	16.4%	". . . probation is an effective method of dealing with federal offenders."
1955	England	17.7%	"A reconviction rate of less than one-fifth or one-quarter . . . is an acceptable level of performance for a probation service."
1976	Missouri	30.3%	"Probation is an effective and efficient way of handling the majority of offenders in the state of Missouri."
1976	Comptroller General	55.0%	". . . probation systems we reviewed were achieving limited success in protecting society and rehabilitating offenders."
1977	Irish	29.6%	". . . supervision program is effectively accomplishing its objective."

that were found in each study to be statistically correlated with failure. Keeping in mind the methodological differences among the studies in terms of definition of failure and specification of follow-up period, it appears that the one characteristic most commonly found to be associated with failure is the probationer's previous criminal history. Other factors frequently cited are: the youthfulness of the probationer, marital status other than married, unemployment, and educational level below the eleventh grade.

Cost Effectiveness

While the public has demanded tougher sentences, it has become increasingly apparent that the costs associated with increased incarceration and prison construction are astronomical. Estimates place the cost of constructing a maximum security prison at approximately $70,000 per bed, with the cost of maintenance and housing inmates ranging between $10,000 and $15,000 per year (Allen and Latessa, 1983: 8). The acute shortage of prison space has made incarceration a scarce resource. Many states are faced with severe budget deficits, and legislators and the public are reluctant to vote for new prison construction. Yet there is also ample evidence that once prisons are built, they are filled. In addition, many states are under court order to reduce or limit their prison populations or the population in a specific prison. Because of the increasingly high costs associated with incarceration, researchers have begun to focus on the cost effectiveness of alternatives.

In light of these factors, and in addition to the research aimed at measuring effectiveness in terms of recidivism, there have been some attempts at demonstrating the cost effectiveness of probation. Typically with criminal justice agencies, costs are usually divided into three types: processing, program, and client-centered. Processing costs include monies spent in identifying and selecting individuals for a given program. Program costs are expenditures associated with the implementation and administration of the programs, as well as their operational expenses. Costs to the client that are generally associated with incarceration include direct costs, such as loss of earnings, and indirect costs, such as the psychological effects of alienation/prisonization, social stigma, and other detrimental effects upon the prisoner's marriage and family (Nelson, 1975).

Similarly, the benefits generated by probation could include savings to society through the use of diversion, wages and taxes generated by the participants, and reduced crime or recidivism rates (Vito and Latessa, 1979: 3). In addition, there are the costs associated with failure, such as the monetary loss and grief experienced by the victims.

Table 12–4
Studies Reporting Factors Related to Probationer Recidivism

Study	Previous Criminal History	Youth	Status Other Than Married	Not Employed	Low Income (Below $400)	Education Below 11th Grade	Abuse of Alcohol or Drugs	Property Offender	On-Probation Maladjustment	Imposition of Conditions
Caldwell (1951)	Significant correlation	Significant correlation	Significant correlation	Significant correlation	Significant correlation	Significant correlation		*		
England (1955)	Significant correlation	Significant correlation	Significant correlation	Significant correlation	Significant correlation	Significant correlation		*		Significant correlation
Davis (1955)	Significant correlation	Significant correlation						Significant correlation	Significant correlation	Significant correlation
Frease (1964)	Significant correlation		Significant correlation		†	Significant correlation	Significant correlation			
Landis (1969)	Significant correlation	Significant correlation	Significant correlation	Significant correlation	Significant correlation	Significant correlation	Significant correlation		Signification correlation	
Irish (1972)	Significant correlation	Significant correlation	Significant correlation	Significant correlation	Significant correlation	Significant correlation	Significant correlation	Significant correlation	*	
Missouri Division of Probation and Parole (1976)	Significant correlation	Significant correlation	Significant correlation	Significant correlation	‡	Significant correlation	Significant correlation	Significant correlation		
Kusuda (1976)		Significant correlation	Significant correlation	Significant correlation	†	Significant correlation	Significant correlation	*		
Comptroller General (1976)								*		
Irish (1977)	Signficant correlation							*	Significant correlation	

*In these studies, instant and postprobation offenses committed by probationers were predominately "property"; however, a correlation between property offenses and recidivism was not investigated.

†Correlation only with income between $100 and $400; those who make less than $400 and those who made above $400 both had an equal probability of success.

‡Correlation only with income between $100 and $700; those who made less than $100 or above $700 both had an equal probability of success.

Source: Harry E. Allen, et al., *Critical Issues in Adult Probation: Summary*, p. 35. National Institute of Law Enforcement and Criminal Justice, Law Enforcement Assistance Administration, September 1979.

The studies that provided the most thorough financial comparisons were those which treated the cost-benefit analysis as their primary focus, and considered direct and indirect costs and benefits.

In one of the most comprehensive studies of probation costs, Frazier (1973) attempted to develop realistic cost information on probation and incarceration for the purpose of comparison.

A number of estimates were used to compare the indirect costs associated with incarceration. These factors included the average wage and average months employed per year, the average taxes paid on gross wages, and the cost of welfare support for children whose wage-earning parent had been incarcerated. These figures were based upon data collected from a representative sample of 115 inmates, and were then extended to the entire inmate population in Texas for 1970. The total indirect cost of incarceration was estimated to be $5,938,447.

Frazier then combined the indirect with the direct cost of incarceration (defined as all costs included in the yearly budget of the Department of Corrections) to obtain a 1970 figure of $28,331,702. The savings generated by probation were then illustrated through the use of an example. If a felon were convicted, given a five-year sentence, incarcerated for three years, and then placed on parole for two years, the total costs would be $6,927. However, if the same felon were placed on probation, the costs would only equal $1,370—a savings of $5,557 over the five-year period. The authors concluded that if 3,000 inmates were diverted, a one-year savings of $5,715,000 could be generated.

In sum, the Texas study is an excellent example of the high quantity of information that can be generated by a cost-benefit analysis. The only apparent shortcoming is the failure to compare the costs of recidivism in the two systems. The recidivism rate of probationers versus parolees would take on more meaning under this type of comparison (Vito and Latessa, 1979: 16). There have been several other cost-benefit studies, however, that tend to include cost comparisons as part of a large research effort, and thus are plagued by errors of omission, and incomplete costs or benefit identifications.

Probation is the most widely selected correctional program, yet little is actually known about its true effectiveness. The research conducted to date has been hampered by many constraints and, as a result, is less than adequate. As with parole, the most important question essentially remains unanswered.

Summary

Despite the intensity of the current controversies surrounding parole and probation, one is struck by how little is actually known about the most crucial question: How effective is parole and probation?

Part of this dilemma rests with the concept of effectiveness. While, as noted above, most would agree that recidivism should be a primary performance measure, there is no consensus on its definition or the indicators to be used for its measurement. Other performance measures of effectiveness, especially those examining the management or supervisory aspects of parole and probation, are often ignored by researchers or given disproportionate emphasis by administrators. There is little systematic research of parole and probation concerning the most critical question of effectiveness.

Recent developments in the area of corrections further complicate assessing its effectiveness. While Caplan (1973), Finckenauer (1979), and Reckless and Allen (1979) agree that correctional programs and practices have been heavily impacted by conservative political philosophies, the fact remains that both liberal and conservative forces have coalesced in the critical questioning of parole and probation.

Liberals in particular question equitability in sentencing, procedural fairness, the indefiniteness of release dates, the medical model in corrections, and use of parole for the institutional control of inmates. Conservatives stress "just punishment," protection of the public, more severe punishment and increased prison terms, reductions of judicial leniency, incapacitation of "dangerous" offenders, and deterrence (Lipson and Peterson, 1980: 4).

The models proposed by such critics as Fogel, van den Haag, von Hirsch, Martinson, and others focus on "just deserts," doing justice, and longer prison sentences. The evidence for evaluating these models is not yet amassed. And while we seem to know little about the true effectiveness of parole, probation, and community supervision, we know even less about the effect and impact of abolishing parole, presumptive sentencing, and mandatory supervision periods. These are crucial areas for research, especially since twenty-three states revised their sentencing laws in 1979.

Notes

1. Much of this chapter was drawn from Edward J. Latessa and Harry E. Allen, *Parole Effectiveness: The State of the Art in Research*, unpublished draft (San Jose State University, San Jose, Calif.: San Jose Research Foundation, 1981).

2. Uniform Parole Reports, *Parole in the United States 1979* (U.S. Department of Justice, Bureau of Justice Statistics, 1979).

3. Part of the reason these studies are rarely conducted is that it is extremely difficult to determine "second-level" costs and benefits, such as lost income, social costs, and the costs associated with continued criminal behavior.

4. For a thorough discussion of this research see: David A. Pritchard, "Stable Predictors of Recidivism: A Summary," *Criminology* 17 (1979):15–21; and Michael R. Gottfredson, Susan D. Mitchell-Herzfeld, and Timothy J. Flanagan,

"Another Look at the Effectiveness of Parole Supervision," *Journal of Research in Crime and Delinquency* 19 (1982):277–98.

5. These states include Wisconsin, Michigan, Florida, Maryland, North Carolina, Massachusetts, Arizona, and California.

6. Most notably Arizona and California. For more detailed information, see S. Gettinger "Parole Contracts: A New Way Out," *Corrections Magazine* 1 (June 1975):3.

7. See *Uniform Parole Reports*, "A National Survey of Parole-Related Legislation Enacted During the 1979 Legislative Session." (U.S. Department of Justice, Bureau of Justice, 1979).

8. Presumptive sentences are fixed within the statutes for each class of offense. If a judge decides upon incarceration, the presumptive term must be imposed unless mitigating/aggravating factors are found. Determinate discretionary provides ranges of sentences. The judge can impose any prison term; however, that penalty is fixed and determinate. Under sentencing guidelines, a sentencing commission is established to set a narrowed range of penalties based upon severity of offense and prior record.

9. For a thorough discussion of this statute see Chapter 1.

10. The remainder of this section was drawn from Harry E. Allen, Eric W. Carlson, and Evalyn C. Parks, *Critical Issues in Adult Probation Summary* (National Institute of Law Enforcement and Criminal Justice, Law Enforcement Assistance Administration, U.S. Department of Justice, September 1979), pp. 29–37.

Study Guides

1. What performance indicators should be included in effectiveness studies?
2. What are the four primary constraints that hamper correctional research?
3. What do we know about parole effectiveness and the research that has been conducted to date?
4. What are some of the possible effects of abolishing parole?
5. What do we know about probation effectiveness and the research that has been conducted to date?
6. List the indirect and direct costs and benefits associated with probation.

Key Terms

"all or nothing" effectiveness indicators
cost-benefit analysis
data net

nothing works
presumptive sentencing
recidivism

References

Alaska Department of Health and Social Services. *Misdemeanant Probation Project.* Juneau, Alas.: Alaska Department of Health and Social Services, Division of Corrections, 1976.

ALLEN, HARRY E.; CARSON, ERIC W.; AND PARKS, EVALYN C. *Critical Issues in Adult Probation Summary*, pp. 35 and 37. National Institute of Law Enforcement and Criminal Justice, Law Enforcement Assistance Administration, U.S. Department of Justice, September 1979.

ALLEN, HARRY, AND LATESSA, EDWARD. "The Conservative Coup in Crime Policy and Corrections." Paper presented at the Academy of Criminal Justice Sciences, San Antonio, Tex., 1983.

_____. *Parole Effectiveness in the United States: An Assessment.* San Jose, Calif.: San Jose State University Research Foundation, 1980.

BABST, DEAN V., ET AL. "Relationships of Time Served to Parole Outcome for Different Classifications of Burglars Based on Males Paroled in 50 Jurisdictions in 1968 and 1969," *Journal of Research in Crime and Delinquency* 9 (1972): 99–116.

BABST, DEAN V., AND MANNERING, JOHN W. "Probation Versus Imprisonment for Similar Types of Offenders," *Journal of Research in Crime and Delinquency* 2 (1965):60–71.

BEASLEY, WILSON. "Unraveling the Process of Parole: An Analysis of the Effects of Parole Residency on Parole Outcome." Unpublished paper presented at the Annual Meeting of the American Society of Criminology, 1978.

BREWER, DAVID; BECKETT, GERALD; AND HOLT, NORMAN. "Determinate Sentencing in California: The First Years' Experience," *Journal of Research in Crime and Delinquency* 18 (1981):200–31.

CALDWELL, MORRIS G. "Review of a New Type of Probation Study Made in Alabama," *Federal Probation* 15 (1951):3–11.

California Department of Justice. *Superior Court Probation and/or Jail Sample: One Year Follow-Up for Selected Counties.* Sacramento, Calif.: California Department of Justice, Division of Law Enforcement, Bureau of Criminal Statistics, 1969.

CAPLAN, G. "Reflections on the Nationalization of Crime, 1964–68," *Law and the Social Order* 3 (1973):583–635.

Comptroller General of the United States. *State and County Probation: Systems in Crisis, Report to the Congress of the United States.* Washington, D.C.: Government Printing Office, 1976.

DAVIS, GEORGE F. "A Study of Adult Probation Violation Rates by Means of the Cohort Approach." *Journal of Criminal Law, Criminology and Police Science* 55 (March 1964):70–85.

EICHMAN, CHARLES. *The Impact of the Gideon Decision Upon Crime and Sentencing in Florida: A Study of Recidivism and Socio-cultural Change.* Unpublished master's thesis, Florida State University, 1965.

ENGLAND, RALPH W. "A Study of Postprobation Recidivism Among Five Hundred Federal Offenders," *Federal Probation* 19 (1955):10–16.

FINCKENAUER, JAMES. "Crime as a National Political Issue: 1964–1976," *Crime and Delinquency* 24 (1979):13–27.

Florida State Parole and Probation Commission. *Parole Success and the Female Parolee.* Tallahassee, Fla., 1976.

FRAZIER, ROBERT LEE. *Incarceration and Adult Felon Probation in Texas: A Cost Comparison.* Unpublished master's thesis, Institute of Contemporary Corrections and the Behavioral Sciences, Sam Houston State University, May 1972.

FREASE, DEAN E. *Factors Related to Probation Outcome.* Olympia, Wash.: Department of Institutions, Board of Prison Terms and Paroles, Section on Research and Program Analysis, 1964.

GLASER, DANIEL. "Effectiveness of the Federal Correctional System," *Federal Probation* 28 (1964):3–6.

GOTTFREDSON, DON. "Some Positive Changes in the Parole Process." Unpublished paper presented at the Annual Meeting of the American Society of Criminology, 1975.

GOTTFREDSON, DON; GOTTFREDSON, MICHAEL; AND GAROFALO, JAMES. "Time Served in Prison and Parolee Outcomes Among Parolee Risk Categories," *Journal of Criminal Justice* 5 (1977):1–12.

GOTTFREDSON, MICHAEL R.; MITCHELL-HERZFELD, SUSAN D.; AND FLANAGAN, TIMOTHY J. "Another Look At the Effectiveness of Parole Supervision," *Journal of Research in Crime and Delinquency* 19 (1982):277–98.

HOFFMAN, PETER, AND STONE-MEIERHOEFER, BARBARA. "Reporting Recidivism Rates: The Criterion and Follow-Up Issues," *Journal of Criminal Justice* 8 (1980):53–60.

HOLT, N. "Rational Risk Taking: Some Alternatives to Traditional Correctional Programs." In *Proceedings: Second National Workshop on Corrections and Parole Administration*, n.d.

IRISH, JAMES F. *Probation and Its Effect on Recidivism: An Evaluative Research Study of Probation in Nassau County, New York.* Mineola, N.Y.: Nassau County Probation Department, 1972.

———. *Probation and Recidivism.* Mineola, N.Y.: Nassau County Probation Department, 1977.

JACKSON, PATRICK G. *The Paradox of Control: Parole Supervision of Youthful Offenders.* New York: Praeger, 1983.

KRAMER, JOHN, AND KATKIN, DANIEL. "Assessing the Impact of Determinate Sentencing and Parole Sentencing and Parole Abolition in Maine." In *Determinate Sentencing and the Impact on Corrections.* California State University at Long Beach, 1979.

KUSUDA, PAUL H. *1974 Probation and Parole Terminations.* Madison, Wisc.: Division of Corrections, 1976.

LANDIS, JUDSON R.; MERCER, JAMES K.; AND WOLFF, CAROLE E. "Success and Failure of Adult Probationers in California," *Journal of Research in Crime and Delinquency* 6 (January 1969):34–40.

LIPSON, ALBERT, AND PETERSON, MARK. *California Justice Under Determinate Sentencing: A Review and Research Agenda.* Santa Monica, Calif.: Rand Corporation, 1980.

MARTINSON, ROBERT, AND WILKES, JUDITH. "Save Parole Supervision," *Federal Probation* 42 (1979):23–27.

Missouri Division of Probation and Parole. *Probation in Missouri, July 1, 1968 to June 30, 1970: Characteristics, Performance, and Criminal Reinvolvement.* Jefferson City, Mo.: Division of Probation and Parole, 1976.

NEITHERCUT, MARK. "Parole Violation Patterns and Commitment Offense," *Journal of Research in Crime and Delinquency* 9 (1972):87–98.

NELSON, CARL W. "Cost-Benefit Analysis and Alternatives to Incarceration," *Federal Probation* 39 (1975):45–50.

Pennsylvania Program for Women and Girl Offenders, Inc. *Report on Recidivism of Women Sentenced to State Probation and Released from SCI Muncy 1971–73.* Philadelphia, Penn.: Pennsylvania Program for Women and Girl Offenders, Inc., 1976.

RECKLESS, WALTER, AND ALLEN, HARRY. "Developing a National Crime Policy: The Impacts of Politics on Crime in America." In *Criminology: New Concerns*, edited by E. Sagarin, pp. 129–38. Beverly Hills, Calif.: Sage, 1979.

ROBISON, JOSEPH, AND SMITH, GERALD. "The Effectiveness of Correctional Programs," *Crime and Delinquency* 17 (1971):67–80.

RYAN, MARIE, AND PANNELL, WILLIAM. *Some Experience with Uniform Determinate Sentencing Act: July 1977–June 1978.* California Department of Corrections, 1979.

SYROTVIK, J. M. "The Relationship Between Birth Order and Parole Outcome," *Canadian Journal of Criminology* 29 (1978):456–58.

VAN ALSTYNE AND GOTTFREDSON, MICHAEL R. "A Multidimensional Contingency Table Analysis of Parole Outcome," *Journal of Research in Crime and Delinquency* 15 (1978):172–93.

VITO, GENNARO F. *Shock Probation in Ohio: A Comparison of Attributes and Outcome.* Unpublished doctoral dissertation, Ohio State University, 1978.

VITO, GENNARO F., AND LATESSA, EDWARD J. "Cost Analysis in Probation Research: An Evaluation Synthesis," *Journal of Contemporary Criminal Justice* 1 (October 1979):3–4.

VON HIRSCH, ANDREW, AND HANRAHAN, KATHLEEN. *The Question of Parole.* Cambridge, Mass.: Ballinger Publishing, 1979.

WALLER, I. *Men Released from Prison.* Toronto: University of Toronto Press, 1974.

Washington Department of Social and Health Sciences. *Who Returns? A Study of Recidivism for Adult Offenders in the State of Washington.* Olympia, Wash.: March 1976.

WILLIAMS, JAY, AND GOLD, MARTIN. "From Delinquent Behavior to Official Delinquency," *Social Problems* 20 (1972):209–29.

Wisconsin Division of Corrections. *A Comparison of the Effects of Using Probation Versus Incarcerations for Burglars with No Previous Felony Convictions.* Madison, Wisc.: Division of Corrections, 1965.

Recommended Readings

Allen, Harry; Carlson, Eric; and Parks, Evalyn. *Critical Issues in Adult Probation: Summary* (National Institute of Law Enforcement and Criminal Justice, Law Enforcement Assistance Administration, U.S. Department of Justice, Washington, D.C.: Government Printing Office, 1979). This publication presents an excellent summary of specific areas of probation effectiveness in the United States.

Comptroller General of the United States. *State and County Probation: Systems in Crisis, Report to the Congress* (Law Enforcement Assistance Administration, Department of Justice, 1976). As the title implies, this study by the Government Accounting Office portrays probation as being in a "state of crisis." It highlights the successes and failures of probation very well.

Palmer, Ted. "The 'Effectiveness' Issue Today: An Overview," *Federal Probation* 47 (1983):3–10. This article discusses the issue surrounding the "effectiveness" debate and offers some middle ground.

Waldo, Gordon. "Myths, Misconceptions and the Misuse of Statistics in Correctional Research," *Journal of Crime and Delinquency* 17 (January 1971):57–66. This article discusses the importance of evaluation research in the correctional system, and dispels many of the myths surrounding research.

13

Probation and Parole
at the Crossroads:
A Futuristic View

From 1945 until 1974, the major philosophical underpinnings of the correctional scene[1] have been postulated on the medical model of corrections. This model is now largely acknowledged as an idea whose time has passed. Its demise has coincided with and been in large part caused by widespread political, social, economic, and philosophical changes, creating some uncertainty in correctional areas, as well as a search for a coherent correctional ideology that would function to explain the present, predict the future, and focus public policy. No such consensus currently exists, although the punitive punishment and incapacitation model is on the rise and likely to expand in influence and use in defining correctional policy. Widespread effects on probation and parole can be seen.

Influences on the Futures of Probation and Parole

Former President Johnson is generally credited with legitimizing crime as a political issue and, since 1970, national politicians across the range of the political spectrum have advocated generally conservative policies for sentencing, objectives of corrections, prison expansion, punishment, and incapacitation. At least twenty-nine states have abandoned parole or shifted to some alternative to the indeterminate sentencing model. California, which shifted to determinate sentencing at the end of the 1970s, entered the seventies committing one in ten felons to prison, but ended it committing one in three. Our national prisons now hold the largest prison population in American history (1984: 454,000 offenders), and since 1973, the average annual rate of prison population growth has exceeded 12 percent. If current trends continue, the prison population could double every seven years. The United States already incarcerates proportionately more citizens (179) per 100,000 population than any other major Western nation.

It appears that the conservative approach for handling offenders has extensive public support, and current political forces are likely to generate demands for more habitual offender statutes, mandatory sentencing structures, further incapacitation, proportionately more prison commitments, longer prison sentences, and more frequent.imposition of the death penalty. If citizens' perception of the level of crime increases, there is a possibility of a Constitutional Convention, leading to restrictions of existing citizen rights, creating a presumption of guilt, abandoning the exclusionary rules of evidence, and an adulteration, if not outright abandonment, of citizen rights under the Fourth, Fifth, Sixth, Eighth, and even Fourteenth Amendments to the U.S Constitution. These are the bases of legal procedures within the criminal justice system.

Economic factors are also likely to influence corrections, especially probation. The economic jolts of the oil crisis caused by our energy dependency, particularly since 1974, are still working their ways through the economic system. Economic recession and business stagflation, while currently abating, are still possibly inseparably intermeshed, and failing innovative technological solutions to our long-term energy dependency, economic opportunity for the strata of population from which our "street criminals" are predominately drawn is likely to be further limited. The high unemployment rates (currently 7 percent nationally) have wreaked havoc on tax revenues, and there remains a public perception that employment is crucial to preventing recidivism among offenders. Tax revolts, perhaps best exemplified in the California example, pose issues that will plague probation and parole for at least the next decade.[2] In California, since the 1978 Proposition 13 impacts have come to be felt, some one in three probation officer positions no longer exist, and there is a movement toward further consolidation of adult and juvenile probation services and agencies. Personnel retrenchment of this dimension could lead to even larger caseloads, less supervision of and assistance to offenders in the community, and more recidivism. Punitiveness in the conservative approach, less personnel in the probation services, and increasing commitments to jails and prisons will mean less resources for the probation and parole components of corrections.

Social forces exist that compound the correctional scene. Migration results from "push and pull" factors that lead individuals and families to new locales and, hopefully, new opportunities. But migration is selective, both in terms of who might move (the socioeconomically disadvantaged, in particular) and which jurisdictions will receive them (particularly the Sun Belt of the United States). With few skills, drawn from rural backgrounds and orientations, frequently of minority composition, ill-prepared to exist (much less flourish) in an urban setting, many such migrants may form the "urban core" of street criminals. Juvenile gangs are reappearing; the second generation of recent migrants traditionally have higher juvenile delinquency rates, and arrest records compound corrections' roles, particularly in terms of economic employment opportunities.

Other Environmental Changes and Impacts

Both probation and parole have been influenced by these changes and forces. The effects on parole are evident in the moves toward the structuring of discretion and decision making in parole, in abandoning parole release in at least seven states, and in court-ordered reductions of prison populations (and other release alternatives) under the Fourteenth and Eighth amendments ("cruel and unusual punishment as defined by the emerging standards of human decency"). Parole has been assailed for a variety of faults, alleged and real, and may well be collaterally weakened by abandoning the medical model.

Probation has been impacted by these changes. The number of offenders placed on probation, the increase in caseloads, reduction in employment opportunities, recession, inflationary increases in prices and costs of living, unrealistic expectations and aspirations of becoming successful in a society requiring social skills and education, the judiciary's perception of public demands for punishment, and the lack of probation and parole service resources to manage offenders—all these (and other) factors have begun to force changes in offender control and supervision in the community. These factors and potential developments are listed in Table 13–1.

Management Strategies for Offender Control

It is obvious that state departments of corrections currently have little choice other than to accept court commitments, although some states (for example, Oregon) levy a charge on counties ("negative subsidy") for committing certain low-risk offenders to prison. But scarcity of prison beds,

Table 13-1
Trends and Potential Developments in Control of Offenders in the Community

Trends	Potential Developments
1. Crime volume increasing.	1. Reduction of probation and parole staffs.
2. Violent crime volume increasing.	2. Antiminority backlash develops.
3. Migration to Sun Belt increasing.	3. Contract probation implemented.
4. Migration to urban areas continuing.	4. Electronic monitoring of offenders begins.
5. Increased perception of crime by public.	5. Intrusive therapy with offenders begins.
6. Tax revolts and shortfalls increasing.	6. Issuing of national identity cards begins.
7. Shift to determinate sentencing.	7. Constitutional Convention reduces civil rights.
8. Extension of Eighth Amendment guarantees.	8. Restrictions on interstate migration begins.
9. Prison overcrowding continues.	9. Unification of correctional programs.
10. Inflation and rising costs of living.	10. Consolidation of correctional programs.
11. Prison gangs extend into the community.	11. Newer management models develop.
12. Citizens' fears of crime increasing.	12. Widespread prison construction.
13. Economic opportunity structures closing for the educationally disadvantaged.	13. Intensive probation and parole strategies are implemented.
14. Increasing shift of resources proportionately into institutional corrections.	14. Community resource management teams are extensively adopted.
15. Rising unemployment and erosion of traditional industrial base.	15. Death penalty resumes with more frequency.
	16. Economic incentives for stabilizing communities approved and implemented.
	17. Terrorism increases in frequency in country.
	18. "Risk Zones" identified in urban areas.

limited prison capacities, Eighth Amendment and Chapter 42 U.S. Code Section 1983 lawsuits, and even efforts to meet minimum standards underlying the ongoing accreditation movement may, in the future, force state departments of corrections to pursue alternative policy actions. These could be predicated on protecting prison capacities and populations, and would include certain defensive policies:

1. Using probation subsidies to strengthen community corrections
2. Using volunteers and paraprofessionals
3. Encouraging split sentences

4. Using community residential facilities
5. Encouraging shock probation, shock parole, and intensive supervision
6. Providing probation services on an "as requested" basis (as in Ohio)

These may slow, but probably will not abort, the crisis, since the sentencing judiciary can lower the correctional costs to local government by flushing local problems up to the state level through commitment to prison.

Over the next two decades and assuming current trends continue, state departments of corrections should consider implementing priority policies designed to unify and consolidate corrections. This may mean buying up local probation services, correctional centers, halfway houses, women's detention facilities, jails, workhouses, work-release and furlough centers, and other community-based correctional programs.

In terms of implementation, this could be done piecemeal. The first step could utilize purchase of services contracts and plans, and cost-sharing programs, possibly on a regional level. Further implementation could entail encouragement of planning commissions or consolidation. Other strategies could include setting and enforcing minimal correctional standards for jails, through seeking enabling legislation that would give jail inspection authority to departments of corrections. While there might be reference to local autonomy, the basic policy would remain to consolidate community corrections under state control.

During or, if necessary, after consolidation and unification, departments of corrections could implement caseload assignment models (the single-factor specialized caseload model or the more complex vertical model) that classify offenders by two or more factors or characteristics. Here, the different service delivery strategies detailed in Chapter 9 could be implemented. Brokerage as a service delivery strategy could also be encouraged; such an approach assesses the concrete needs of an offender and arranges for the probationer to receive services that directly address those needs by brokering resources and services already available from other agencies.

Single officer caseloads could give way to team supervision, which involves the assignment of an offender caseload to a team of officers in order to diversify the skills assembled in one team. This could make possible a broader range of expertise and skills, provide uninterrupted supervision and service provision to clients if a team member is absent, increase the likelihood of a client finding an officer with whom he or she feels comfortable, and place accountability for the caseload on the team as a whole.

Finally, in terms of service delivery strategies, supervision planning would be necessary. This includes the identification of problems and needs of an offender; identifying available resources and arranging for these; and evaluating the effectiveness of supervision activities. Each supervision plan would also require developing case-specific supervision objectives, case monitoring, and revision of supervision strategies and service as appropriate. The most coherent model for supervision planning is probably seen in the federal probation system (Administrative Office of the Courts, 1981).

Policy Options and Research Questions

There are five identifiable clusters of suggested future policy changes that could influence the evolution of correctional goals and the approaches to controlling offenders in the community. These obviously contain issues related to research and planning, budgeting, locus of authority, and management strategies.

The basic policy issue is whether to continue the status quo of large-scale imprisonment of offenders, or encourage the unification and consolidation of community offender control in the future. In prescriptive form and assuming the latter policy choice, these policies would be:

1. Slow the proportionate rate of prison commitments and population growth by:
   a. probation subsidies;
   b. negative subsidies in the form of charges to counties for their committing low-risk offenders to prison;
   c. developing specialized guidance and employment programs;
   d. continued development of community-based correctional program alternatives, such as restitution programs, deferred prosecution, shock probation and shock parole, regional rehabilitation councils, use of volunteers, the citizenization of corrections, etc.;
   e. intensive probation diversion programs, such as in Toledo, Ohio;
   f. structuring probation caseloads, to include summary probation as in Milwaukee (Romm, 1982);
   g. developing programs for early release from jails and prisons (work and educational furlough and release, prerelease centers, etc.).
2. Improve the classification, servicing, and control of offenders in the community by:
   a. implementing a coordination effort to develop residential treatment programs, probation hostels, day training centers, outreach centers, halfway houses, community treatment centers, etc.;
   b. developing and implementing routine needs assessments and supervision planning models to meet salient needs of offenders;

c. further developing and implementing risk-level classification instruments;

d. providing a mechanism or instrument to identify potentially dangerous offenders;

e. implementing safe and constitutional biomedical behavioral modification techniques, such as implants, electronic monitoring, aversive therapy, antabuse therapy, medical testing for marijuana and other illicit drugs, and so on.

3. Expand the scope and modify the role of the presentence investigation report to function as a probation contract.

4. Consolidate correctional services within jurisdictions, such as city and county, juvenile and adult, regionalization, or unification under a state agency.

5. Introduce newer management techniques in community correctional services and agencies, such as:

a. "quality circles" for problem identification and solutions (as in Japan and the automobile industry);

b. abandoning the traditional casework model;

c. adopting the team service, brokerage, community resource management team, and specialized caseload models;

d. implementing supervision planning models;

e. clarifying accountability by legal contracting with offenders and community service agents.

The research agenda suggested below does not necessarily represent an effort to integrate the issues in community control of offenders by means of long-range comprehensive or multiple-tier effort. Rather, it represents high priority research questions that need to be answered when making and pursuing the policy options. These are presented in the form of questions. As students entering the fields of probation and parole, you will find yourselves dealing with these questions in the next decade.

1. What is or should be the theoretical purpose(s) of community control: reintegration, public safety, incapacitation, or deterrence?

2. How should an information system be established that would provide both offender-based transactions as well as management information for planning, budgeting, accountability, and research?

3. Which biomedical behavioral modification techniques are constitutionally acceptable and effective and, if any, which will work with what types of offender needs and problems?

4. What should be the administrative locus of community control programs: the judiciary; or the local, county, or state executive?

5. How should offender control programs be financed: user fees, fines, cost-sharing across jurisdictions, local or state appropriations, or subsidies?

6. What are the cost-benefit ratios of the various program components or, assuming unified community correctional programs, of the service programs when controlling for offender type and characteristics?

7. What classification technique(s) can best be used in community corrections: risk, need, or a combination of both?

8. Which offenders are amenable to the use of volunteers and paraprofessionals in probation and parole?

9. What treatment intervention strategies are more useful in improving the community control of offenders and under what circumstances?

10. What community organizations and associations should be marshaled to assist in the political processes necessary for unification and consolidation of community corrections?

11. How can the fear of crime by citizens be reduced or made more realistic?

Summary

This chapter is an exercise in predicting the possible futures of probation and parole in the next decade in America. What may seem to be unlikely may become reality, and what may seem obvious may not happen for ten or twenty years, if ever. The exciting point is that you will experience the groping for answers, the search for solutions, the irritation of change. The next decade should prove to be a stimulating period.

We end with a leap of faith. Community-based corrections in general and probation in particular are and remain the wave of the future. The forms, practices, and programs will remain, but the service delivery mechanisms and delivery systems are likely to change. How rapid and extensive these changes will be remain open to question.

Notes

1. Portions of this chapter first appeared in Nick Gatz and Harry E. Allen, "Abandoning the Medical Model in Corrections: Some Implications and Alternatives," *The Prison Journal* 54 (1974):4–14.

2. See Jan Chaiken, Warren Walker, Anthony Jiga, and Sandra Polin. *The Impact of Fiscal Limitation on California's Criminal Justice System* (Santa Monica, Calif.: Rand Corporation, 1981).

References

Administrative Office of the United States Court Probation Division, Classification and Supervision Planning System (1981). Mimeo.

Gagnon v. Scarpelli, 411 U.S. 778 S. Ct. (1972).

GATZ, NICK, AND ALLEN, HARRY E. "Abandoning the Medical Model in Corrections: Some Implications and Alternatives," *The Prison Journal* 54 (1974): 4–14.

ROMM, JOSEPH. *Executive Summary, National Evaluation Program, Phase II: Intensive Evaluation of Probation.* Bethesda, Md.: System Sciences, Inc., 1982.

Recommended Readings

Allen, Harry E., and Latessa, Edward. "Corrections in America: 2000 A.D.," *Journal of Contemporary Criminal Justice* 1 (1980):1–3. This brief article projects current statistical changes and trends to the year 2000 and suggests policies for change.

Caplan, Gerald. "Reflections on the Nationalization of Crime: 1964–1968," *Law and the Social Order* 3 (1973):583–635. This article traces the impacts of the Goldwater-Johnson presidential race and details how political philosophies can influence and color correctional practices.

Ellickson, Phillis; Petersilia, Joan; Coggiano, M.; and Polin, Sandra. *Implementing New Ideas in Criminal Justice* (Santa Monica, Calif.: Rand Corporation, 1983). This stimulating monograph suggests major ways in which changes can be made in probation and parole, as well as identifying pitfalls when change is undertaken.

Glossary

This section is drawn from the *Dictionary of Criminal Justice Data Terminology* (U.S. Department of Justice, National Criminal Justice Information and Statistics Service, LEAA, Washington, D.C. 20531).

abscond (corrections): To depart from a geographical area or jurisdiction prescribed by the conditions of one's probation or parole, without authorization.

abscond (court): To intentionally absent or conceal oneself unlawfully in order to avoid a legal process.

acquittal: A judgment of a court, based either on the verdict of a jury or a judicial officer, that the defendant is not guilty of the offense(s) for which he or she has been tried.

adjudicated: Having been the subject of completed criminal or juvenile proceedings, and convicted, or adjudicated a delinquent, status offender, or dependent.

adjudication (criminal): The judicial decision terminating a criminal proceeding by a judgment of conviction or acquittal or by a dismissal of the case.

adjudication (juvenile): The juvenile court decision, terminating an adjudicatory hearing, that the juvenile is either a delinquent, status offender, or dependent, or that the allegations in the petition are not sustained.

adjudicatory hearing: In juvenile proceedings, the fact-finding process wherein the juvenile court determines whether or not there is sufficient evidence to sustain the allegations in a petition.

281

adult: A person who is within the original jurisdiction of a criminal, rather than a juvenile, court because his or her age at the time of an alleged criminal act was above a statutorily specified limit.

alias: Any name used for an official purpose that is different from a person's legal name.

alternative facility: An alternative place of limited confinement that may be an option for certain kinds of offenders. Such facilities may include treatment settings for drug-dependent offenders, minimum security facilities in the community that provide treatment and services as needed, work/study-release centers, and halfway houses or shelter-type facilities. All of these are less secure than the traditional jail, but offer a more stimulating environment for the individual.

appeal: A request by either the defense or the prosecution that a case be removed from a lower court to a higher court in order for a completed trial to be reviewed by the higher court.

appearance: The act of coming into a court and submitting to the authority of that court.

appearance, first (initial appearance): The first appearance of a juvenile or adult in the court that has jurisdiction over his or her case.

appellant: A person who initiates an appeal.

arraignment: The appearance of a person before a court in order that the court may inform the individual of the accusation(s) against him or her and enter his or her plea.

arrest: Taking a person into custody by authority of law for the purpose of charging him or her with a criminal offense or for the purpose of initiating juvenile proceedings, terminating with the recording of a specific offense.

arson: Any willful or malicious burning or attempt to burn, with or without intent to defraud, a dwelling, public building, motor vehicle or aircraft, personal property of another, etc.

assault: Unlawful intentional inflicting, or attempted or threatened inflicting, of injury upon another.

assault, aggravated: Unlawful intentional causing of serious bodily injury with or without a deadly weapon or unlawful intentional attempting or threatening of serious bodily injury or death with a deadly weapon.

assault, simple: Unlawful intentional threatening, attempted inflicting, or inflicting of less than serious bodily injury, in the absence of a deadly weapon.

assault with a deadly weapon: Unlawful intentional inflicting, or attempted or threatened inflicting, of injury or death with the use of a deadly weapon.

assigned counsel: An attorney, not regularly employed by a government agency, assigned by the court to represent a particular person(s) in a particular criminal proceeding.

attorney/lawyer/counsel: A person trained in the law, admitted to practice before the bar of a given jurisdiction, and authorized to advise, represent, and act for other persons in legal proceedings.

backlog: The number of pending cases that exceed the capacity of the court, in that they cannot be acted upon because the court is occupied in acting upon other cases.

bondsman-secured bail: Security service purchased by the defendant from a bail bondsman. The fee for this service ranges upward from 10 percent and is not refundable. The bail bondsman system, which permits a private entrepreneur to share with the court the decision on pretrial release, has been criticized for many years and is becoming obsolete in more progressive jurisdictions. (See RELEASE ON OWN RECOGNIZANCE.)

booking: A police administrative action officially recording an arrest and identifying the person, the place, the time, the arresting authority, and the reason for the arrest.

burglary: Unlawful entry of a structure, with or without force, with intent to commit a felony or larceny.

camp/ranch/farm: Any of several types of similar confinement facilities, usually in a rural location, that contain adults or juveniles committed after adjudication.

case: At the level of police or prosecutorial investigation, a set of circumstances under investigation involving one or more persons; at subsequent steps in criminal proceedings, a charging document alleging the commission of one or more crimes; a single defendant; in juvenile or correctional proceedings, a person who is the object of agency action.

case (court): A single charging document under the jurisdiction of a court; a single defendant.

caseload (corrections): The total number of clients registered with a correctional agency or agent during a specified time period, often divided into active and inactive, or supervised and unsupervised, thus distinguishing between clients with whom the agency or agent maintains contact and those with whom it does not.

caseload (court): The total number of cases filed in a given court or before a given judicial officer during a given period of time.

caseload, pending: The number of cases at any given time that have been filed in a given court, or are before a given judicial officer, but have not reached disposition.

cash bail: A cash payment for situations where the charge is not serious and scheduled bail is low. The defendant obtains release by paying in cash the full amount, which is recoverable after required court appearances are made.

CCH: An abbreviation for "computerized criminal history."

charge: A formal allegation that a specific person(s) has committed a specific offense(s).

charging document: A formal written accusation, filed in a court, alleging that a specified person(s) has committed a specific offense(s).

child abuse: Willful action or actions by a person causing physical harm to a child.

child neglect: Willful failure by the person(s) responsible for a child's well-being to provide for adequate food, clothing, shelter, education, and supervision.

citation (to appear): A written order issued by a law enforcement officer directing an alleged offender to appear in a specific court at a specified time in order to answer a criminal charge.

citizen dispute settlement: The settlement of interpersonal disputes by a third party or the courts. Charges arising from interpersonal disputes are mediated by a third party in an attempt to avoid prosecution. If an agreement between the parties cannot be reached and the complainant wishes to proceed with criminal processing, the case may be referred to court for settlement.

commitment: The action of a judicial officer ordering that an adjudicated and sentenced adult, or adjudicated delinquent or status offender who has been the subject of a juvenile court disposition hearing, be admitted into a correctional facility.

community facility (nonconfinement facility, adult or juvenile): A correctional facility from which residents are regularly permitted to depart, unaccompanied by any official, for the purpose of daily use of community resources, such as schools or treatment programs, and the seeking or the holding of employment.

community service: A period of service to the community as a substitute for, or in partial satisfaction of, a fine. This disposition is generally a condition of a suspended or partially suspended sentence or of probation. The offender volunteers his or her services to a community agency for a certain number of hours per week over a specified period of time. The total number of hours, often assessed at the legal minimum wage, is determined by the amount of the fine that would have been imposed or that portion of the fine that is suspended.

complaint: A formal written accusation made by any person, often a prosecutor, and filed in a court, alleging that a specified person(s) has committed a specific offense(s)

complaint denied: The decision by a prosecutor to decline a request that he or she seek an indictment or file an information or complaint against a specified person(s) for a specific offense(s).

complaint granted: The decision by a prosecutor to grant a request that he or she seek an indictment or file an information or complaint against a specified person(s) for a specific offense(s).

complaint requested (police): A request by a law enforcement agency that the prosecutor seek an indictment or file a complaint or information against a specified person(s) for a specific offense(s).

conditional diversion: At the pretrial stage, suspension of prosecution while specific conditions are met. If conditions are not satisfied during a specified time period, the case is referred for continued prosecution.

conditional release: The release of a defendant who agrees to meet specified conditions in addition to appearing in court. Such conditions may include remaining in a defined geographical area, maintaining steady employment, avoiding contact with the victim or with associates in the alleged crime, avoiding certain activities or places, participating in treatment, or accepting services. Conditional release is often used in conjunction with third-party or supervised release.

confinement facility: A correctional facility from which the inmates are not regularly permitted to depart each day unaccompanied.

convict: An adult who has been found guilty of a felony and who is confined in a federal or state confinement facility.

conviction: A judgment of a court, based either on the verdict of a jury or a judicial officer or on the guilty plea of the defendant, that the defendant is guilty of the offense(s) for which he or she has been accused.

correctional agency: A federal, state, or local criminal justice agency, under a single administrative authority, of which the principal functions are the investigation, intake screening, supervision, custody, confinement, or treatment of alleged or adjudicated adult offenders, delinquents, or status offenders.

correctional day program: A publicly financed and operated nonresidential educational or treatment program for persons required, by a judicial officer, to participate.

correctional facility: A building or part thereof, set of buildings, or area enclosing a set of buildings or structures operated by a government agency for the custody and/or treatment of adjudicated and committed persons, or persons subject to criminal or juvenile justice proceedings.

correctional institution: A generic name proposed in this terminology for those long-term adult confinement facilities often called "prisons," "federal or state correctional facilities," or "penitentiaries," and juvenile confinement facilities called "training schools," "reformatories," "boy's ranches," and the like.

correctional institution, adult: A confinement facility having custodial authority over adults sentenced to confinement for more than a year.

correctional institution, juvenile: A confinement facility having custodial authority over delinquents and status offenders committed to confinement after a juvenile disposition hearing.

corrections: A generic term that includes all government agencies, facilities, programs, procedures, personnel, and techniques concerned with the investigation, intake, custody, confinement, supervision, or treatment of alleged or adjudicated adult offenders, delinquents, or status offenders.

count: Each separate offense, attributed to one or more persons, as listed in a complaint, information, or indictment.

court: An agency of the judicial branch of government, authorized or established by statute or constitution, and consisting of one or more judicial officers, which has the authority to decide upon controversies in law and disputed matters of fact brought before it.

court of appellate jurisdiction: A court that does not try criminal cases, but which hears appeals.

court of general jurisdiction: Of criminal courts, a court that has jurisdiction to try all criminal offenses, including all felonies, and which may or may not hear appeals.

court of limited jurisdiction: Of criminal courts, a court of which the trial jurisdiction either includes no felonies or is limited to less than all felonies and which may or may not hear appeals.

crime (criminal offense): An act committed or omitted in violation of a law forbidding or commanding it for which an adult can be punished, upon conviction, by incarceration and other penalties or a corporation penalized, or for which a juvenile can be brought under the jurisdiction of a juvenile court and adjudicated a delinquent or transferred to adult court.

crime index offenses (index crimes): A UCR classification that includes all Part I offenses with the exception of involuntary (negligent) manslaughter.

crimes against businesses (business crimes, commercial crimes): A summary term used by the National Crime Panel reports, including burglary and robbery (against businesses).

crimes against households (household crimes): A summary term used by the National Crime Panel reports, including burglary (against households), household larceny, and motor vehicle theft.

crimes against persons: A summary term used by UCR and the National Crime Panel reports, but with different meanings:

UCR	National Crime Panel
Murder	Forcible rape
Nonnegligent (voluntary) manslaughter	Robbery (against persons)
	Aggravated assault
Negligent (involuntary)	Simple assault
Forcible rape	Personal larceny
Aggravated assault	

crimes against property (property crime): A summary term used by UCR, both as a subclass of the Part I offenses and as a subclass of Crime Index offenses, but with different meanings:

As a subset of UCR Part I offenses	As a subset of UCR Crime Index offenses
Robbery	Burglary
Burglary	Larceny—theft
Larceny—theft	Motor vehicle theft
Motor vehicle theft	

crimes of violence (violent crime): A summary term used by UCR and the National Crime Panel, but with different meanings:

As a subset of UCR Index Crimes	As a subset of National Crime Panel crimes against persons
Murder	Forcible rape
Nonnegligent (voluntary) manslaughter	Robbery (against persons)
	Aggravated assault
Forcible rape	Simple assault
Robbery	
Aggravated assault	

criminal history record information: Information collected by criminal justice agencies on individuals, consisting of identifiable descriptions and notations of arrests, detentions, indictments, informations, or other formal criminal charges, and any disposition(s) arising therefrom, including sentencing, correctional supervision, and releases.

criminal justice agency: Any court with criminal jurisdiction and any other government agency or subunit that defends indigents, or of which the principal functions or activities consist of the prevention, detection, and investigation of crime; the apprehension, detention, and prosecution of alleged offenders; the confinement or official correctional supervision of accused or convicted persons; or the administrative or technical support of the above functions.

criminal proceedings: Proceedings in a court of law undertaken to determine the guilt or innocence of an adult accused of a crime.

defendant: A person against whom a criminal proceeding is pending.

defense attorney: An attorney who represents the defendant in a legal proceeding.

disposition: The action by a criminal or juvenile justice agency that signifies that a portion of the justice process is complete and jurisdiction is relinquished or transferred to another agency, or that signifies that a decision has been reached on one aspect of a case and a different aspect comes under consideration, requiring a different kind of decision.

disposition (court): The final judicial decision that terminates a criminal proceeding by a judgment of acquittal or dismissal, or that states the specific sentence in the case of a conviction.

disposition (juvenile court): The decision of a juvenile court, concluding a disposition hearing, that a juvenile be committed to a correctional facility, or placed in a care or treatment program, or required to meet certain standards of conduct, or released.

disposition hearing: A hearing in juvenile court, conducted after an adjudicatory hearing and subsequent receipt of the report of any predisposition investigation, to determine the most appropriate disposition of a juvenile who has been adjudicated a delinquent, a status offender, or a dependent.

diversion: The official halting or suspension, at any legally prescribed processing point after a recorded justice system entry, of formal criminal or juvenile justice proceedings against an alleged offender, and referral of that person to a treatment or care program administered by a nonjustice agency or a private agency, or no referral.

driving under the influence, alcohol (drunk driving): The operation of any vehicle after having consumed a quantity of alcohol sufficient to potentially interfere with the ability to maintain safe operation.

driving under the influence, drugs: The operation of any vehicle while attention or ability is impaired through the intake of a narcotic or an incapacitating quantity of another drug.

drug law violation: The unlawful sale, transport, manufacture, cultivation, possession, or use of a controlled or prohibited drug.

early release: Release from confinement before the sentence has been completed. Early release to supervision means less jail time and, with more rapid turnover, lower jail populations and capacity requirements. Early release may come about through parole, time off for good behavior or work performed, or modification of the sentence by the court. The last procedure is usually associated with sentences to jail with a period of probation to follow. Although there are some objections to its use, "probation with jail" is a very common disposition in some jurisdictions. More often than not these sentences are in lieu of a state prison term.

embezzlement: The misappropriation, misapplication, or illegal disposal of legally entrusted property with intent to defraud the legal owner or intended beneficiary.

escape: The unlawful departure of a lawfully confined person from a confinement facility, or from custody while being transported.

expunge: The sealing or purging of arrest, criminal, or juvenile record information.

extortion: Unlawful obtaining of or attempting to eventually obtain the property of another by the threat of eventual injury or harm to that person, or the person's property, or another person.

felony: A criminal offense punishable by death, or by incarceration in a state or federal confinement facility for a period of which the lower limit is prescribed by statute in a given jurisdiction, typically one year or more.

field citation: Citation and release in the field by police as an alternative to booking and pretrial detention. This practice reduces law enforcement costs as well as jail costs.

filing: The commencement of criminal proceedings by entering a charging document into the official record of a court.

finding: The official determination of a judicial officer or administrative body regarding a disputed matter of fact or law.

fine: The penalty imposed upon a convicted person by a court requiring that he or she pay a specified sum of money. The fine is a cash payment of a dollar amount assessed by the judge in an individual case or determined by a published schedule of penalties. Fines may be paid in installments in many jurisdictions.

fugitive: A person who has concealed himself or fled a given jurisdiction in order to avoid prosecution or confinement.

group home: A nonconfining residential facility for adjudicated adults or juveniles, or those subject to criminal or juvenile proceedings, intended to reproduce as closely as possible the circumstances of family life, and at minimum providing access to community activities and resources.

Recommended conditions of use: Classify government facilities fitting this definition as *community facilities.*

Annotation: Group home is variously defined in different jurisdictions. Most of the facilities known by this name are privately operated, though they may be financed mainly by government funds. Classification problems unique to private facilities have not been dealt with in this terminology, although most recommended standard descriptors for publicly operated facilities are also applicable to the private sector. See CORRECTIONAL FACILITY for recommended standard descriptors. The data collection questionnaire for the LEAA series "Children in Custody" defines *group home* as, "Allows juveniles extensive contact with the community, such as through jobs and schools, but none or less than half are placed there on probation or aftercare/parole." It is distinguished from *halfway house* in this series by the percent of residents on probation or parole.

halfway house: A nonconfining residential facility for adjudicated adults or juveniles, or those subject to criminal or juvenile proceedings, intended to provide an alternative to confinement for persons not suitable for probation, or needing a period of readjustment to the community after confinement.

Recommended conditions of use: Classify government facilities fitting this definition as *community facilities.*

Annotation: Halfway house is variously defined in different jurisdictions. Most of the facilities known by this name are privately operated, though they may be financed mainly by government funds. Classification problems unique to private facilities have not been dealt with in this terminology, although most recommended standard descriptors for publicly operated facilities are also applicable to the private sector. See CORRECTIONAL FACILITY for recommended standard descriptors. The data collection questionnaire for the LEAA series "Children in Custody" defines *halfway house* as, "Has 50 percent or more juveniles on probation or aftercare/parole, allowing them extensive contact with the community, such as through jobs and schools." It is distinguished from *group home* in this series by the percent of residents on probation or parole.

hearing: A proceeding in which arguments, evidence, or witnesses are heard by a judicial officer or administrative body.

hearing, probable cause: A proceeding before a judicial officer in which arguments, evidence, or witnesses are presented and in which it is determined whether there is sufficient cause to hold the accused for trial or whether the case should be dismissed.

homicide: Any killing of one person by another.

homicide, criminal: The causing of the death of another person without justification or excuse.

UCR term (for police-reporting level)	*Dictionary entry term*
Criminal homicide	Criminal homicide
Murder (often used as cover term for murder and nonnegligent manslaughter)	Murder
Nonnegligent manslaughter	Voluntary manslaughter
Negligent manslaughter	Involuntary manslaughter
(Included in negligent manslaughter)	Vehicular manslaughter

homicide, excusable: The intentional but justifiable causing of the death of another or the unintentional causing of the death of another by accident or misadventure, without gross negligence. Not a crime.

homicide, justifiable: The intentional causing of the death of another in the legal performance of an official duty or in circumstances defined by law as constituting legal justification. Not a crime.

homicide, willful: The intentional causing of the death of another person, with or without legal justification.

indictment: A formal written accusation made by a grand jury and filed in a court, alleging that a specified person(s) has committed a specific offense(s).

infraction: An offense punishable by fine or other penalty, but not by incarceration.

inmate: A person in custody in a confinement facility.

institutional capacity: The officially stated number of inmates or residents that a correctional facility is designed to house, exclusive of extraordinary arrangements to accommodate overcrowded conditions.

intake: The process during which a juvenile referral is received and a decision is made by an intake unit either to file a petition in juvenile court, to release the juvenile, to place the juvenile under supervision, or to refer the juvenile elsewhere.

intake unit: A government agency or agency subunit that receives juvenile referrals from police, other government agencies, private agencies, or persons and screens them, resulting in closing of the case, referral to care or supervision, or filing of a petition in juvenile court.

jail: A confinement facility, usually administered by a local law enforcement agency, intended for adults but sometimes also containing juveniles, that holds persons detained pending adjudication and/or persons committed after adjudication for sentences of a year or less.

jail (sentence): The penalty of commitment to the jurisdiction of a confinement facility system for adults, of which the custodial authority is limited to persons sentenced to a year or less of confinement.

judge: A judicial officer who has been elected or appointed to preside over a court of law, whose position has been created by statute or by constitution, and whose decisions in criminal and juvenile cases may only be reviewed by a judge or a higher court and may not be reviewed *de novo*.

judgment: The statement of the decision of a court that the defendant is convicted or acquitted of the offense(s) charged.

judicial officer: Any person exercising judicial powers in a court of law.

jurisdiction: The territory, subject matter, or person over which lawful authority may be exercised.

jurisdiction, original: The lawful authority of a court or an administrative agency to hear or act upon a case from its beginning and to pass judgment on it.

jury, grand: A body of persons who have been selected and sworn to investigate criminal activity and the conduct of public officials and to hear the evidence against an accused person(s) to determine whether there is sufficient evidence to bring that person(s) to trial.

jury, trial (jury, petit; jury): A statutorily defined number of persons selected according to law and sworn to determine certain matters of fact in a criminal action and to render a verdict of guilty or not guilty.

juvenile: A person subject to juvenile court proceedings because a statutorily defined event was alleged to have occurred while his or her age was below the statutorily specified limit of original jurisdiction of a juvenile court.

Annotation: Jurisdiction is determined by age at the time of the event, not at the time of judicial proceedings, and continues until the case is terminated. Thus a person may be described in a given data system as a juvenile because he or she is still subject to *juvenile court* proceedings even though his or her actual age may be several years over the limit. Conversely, criminal process data systems may include juveniles if the juvenile court has waived jurisdiction.

Although the age limit varies in different states, it is most often the eighteenth birthday. The variation is small enough to permit nationally aggregated data to be meaningful, although individual states should note their age limit in communications with other states.

UCR defines a juvenile as anyone under eighteen years of age.

See YOUTHFUL OFFENDER.

juvenile court: A cover term for courts that have original jurisdiction over persons statutorily defined as juveniles and alleged to be delinquents, status offenders, or dependents.

juvenile justice agency: A government agency, or subunit thereof, of which the functions are the investigation, supervision, adjudiction, care, or confinement of juveniles whose conduct or condition has brought or could bring them within the jurisdiction of a juvenile court.

juvenile record: An official record containing, at a minimum, summary information pertaining to an identified juvenile concerning juvenile court proceedings and, if applicable, detention and correctional processes.

larceny (larceny-theft): Unlawful taking or attempted taking of property, other than a motor vehicle, from the possession of another.

law enforcement agency: A federal, state, or local criminal justice agency of which the principal functions are the prevention, detection, and investigation of crime, and the apprehension of alleged offenders.

law enforcement agency, federal: A law enforcement agency that is an organizational unit, or subunit, of the federal government.

law enforcement agency, local: A law enforcement agency that is an organizational unit, or subunit, of local government.

law enforcement agency, state: A law enforcement agency that is an organizational unit, or subunit, of state government.

law enforcement officer (peace officer, policeman): An employee of a law enforcement agency who is an officer sworn to carry out law enforcement duties, or a sworn employee of a prosecutorial agency who primarily performs investigative duties.

law enforcement officer, federal: An employee of a federal law enforcement agency who is an officer sworn to carry out law enforcement duties, or a sworn employee of a federal prosecutorial agency who primarily performs investigative duties.

law enforcement officer, local: An employee of a local law enforcement agency who is an officer sworn to carry out law enforcement duties, or a sworn employee of a local prosecutorial agency who primarily performs investigative duties.

law enforcement officer, state: An employee of a state law enforcement agency who is an officer sworn to carry out law enforcement duties, or a sworn employee of a state prosecutorial agency who primarily performs investigative duties.

level of government: The federal, state, regional, or local county or city location of administrative and major funding responsibility of a given agency.

manslaughter, involuntary (negligent manslaughter): Causing the death of another by recklessness or gross negligence.

manslaughter, vehicular: Causing the death of another by grossly negligent operation of a motor vehicle.

manslaughter, voluntary (nonnegligent manslaughter): Intentionally causing the death of another with reasonable provocation.

misdemeanor: An offense usually punishable by incarceration in a local confinement facility for a period of which the upper limit is prescribed by statute in a given jurisdiction, typically limited to a year or less.

Model Penal Code: A generalized modern codification of that which is considered basic to criminal law, published by the American Law Institute in 1962.

monitored release: Recognizance release with the addition of minimal supervision or service; that is, the defendant may be required to keep a pretrial services agency informed of his or her whereabouts while the agency reminds the defendant of court dates and verifies the defendant's appearance.

motion: An oral or written request made by a party to an action, before, during, or after a trial, that a court issue a rule to order.

motor vehicle theft: Unlawful taking, or attempted taking, of a motor vehicle owned by another with the intent to deprive the owner of it permanently or temporarily.

murder: Intentionally causing the death of another without reasonable provocation or legal justification, or causing the death of another while committing or attempting to commit another crime.

nolo contendere: A defendant's formal answer in court to the charges in a complaint, information, or indictment in which the defendant states that he or she does not contest the charges, and which, while not an admission of guilt, subjects the defendant to the same legal consequences as a plea of guilty.

offender (criminal): An adult who has been convicted of a criminal offense.

offender, alleged: A person who has been charged with a specific criminal offense(s) by a law enforcement agency or court, but has not been convicted.

offense: An act committed or omitted in violation of a law forbidding or commanding it.

offenses, Part I: A class of offenses selected for use in UCR, consisting of those crimes that are most likely to be reported, that occur with sufficient frequency to provide an adequate basis for comparison, and that are serious crimes by nature and/or volume.

Annotation: The Part I offenses are:

1. Criminal homicide
   a. murder and nonnegligent (voluntary) manslaughter
   b. manslaughter by negligence (involuntary manslaughter)
2. Forcible rape
   a. rape by force
   b. attempted rape
3. Robbery
   a. firearm
   b. knife or cutting instrument
   c. other dangerous weapon
   d. strongarm

4. Aggravated assault
   a. firearm
   b. knife or cutting instrument
   c. other dangerous weapon
   d. hands, fist, feet, etc.—aggravated injury
5. Burglary
   a. forcible entry
   b. unlawful entry—no force
   c. attempted forcible entry
6. Larceny—theft (larceny)
7. Motor vehicle theft
   a. autos
   b. trucks and buses
   c. other vehicles

offenses, Part II: A class of offenses selected for use in UCR, consisting of specific offenses and types of offenses that do not meet the criteria of frequency and/ or seriousness necessary for Part I offenses.

Annotation: The Part II offenses are:

Other assaults (simple,* nonaggravated)
Forgery and counterfeiting
Fraud
Embezzlement*
Stolen property—buying, receiving, possessing
Vandalism
Weapons—carrying, possessing, etc.
Prostitution and commercialized vice
Sex offenses (except forcible rape, prostitution, and commercialized vice)
Narcotic drug law violations
Gambling
Offenses against the family and children
Driving under the influence*

Liquor law violations
Drunkenness
Disorderly conduct
Vagrancy
All other offenses (excepting traffic law violations)
Suspicion*
Curfew and loitering law violations (juvenile violations)
Runaway* (juveniles)

Terms marked with an asterisk (*) are defined in this glossary, though not necessarily in accord with UCR usage. UCR does not collect reports of Part II offenses. Arrest data concerning such offenses, however, are collected and published.

parole: The status of an offender conditionally released from a confinement facility prior to the expiration of his or her sentence, and placed under the supervision of a parole agency.

parole agency: A correctional agency, which may or may not include a parole authority, and of which the principal functions are the supervision of adults or juveniles placed on parole.

parole authority: A person or a correctional agency that has the authority to release on parole adults or juveniles committed to confinement facilities, to revoke parole, and to discharge from parole.

parolee: A person who has been conditionally released from a correctional institution prior to the expiration of his or her sentence, and who has been placed under the supervision of a parole agency.

parole violation: An act or a failure to act by a parolee that does not conform to the conditions of his or her parole.

partial confinement: An alternative to the traditional jail sentence, consisting of "weekend" sentences, which permit offenders to spend the work week in the community, with their families, and at their jobs; furloughs, which enable offenders to leave the jail for a period of a few hours to a few days for specified purposes—to seek employment, take care of personal matters or family obligations, or engage in community service; or work/study release under which offenders work or attend school during the day and return to the detention facility at night and on weekends.

penalty: The punishment annexed by law or judicial decision to the commission of a particular offense, which may be death, imprisonment, fine, or loss of civil privileges.

percentage bail: A publicly managed bail service arrangement that requires the defendant to deposit a percentage (typically 10 percent) of the amount of bail with the court clerk. The deposit is returned to the defendant after scheduled court appearances are made, although a charge (usually 1 percent) may be deducted to help defray program costs.

person: A human being, or a group of human beings considered a legal unit, who has the lawful capacity to defend rights, incur obligations, prosecute claims, or who can be prosecuted or adjudicated.

personally secured bail: Security that is put up by the defendant or the defendant's family. This arrangement is generally out of reach of the less affluent defendant.

petition (juvenile): A document filed in juvenile court alleging that a juvenile is a delinquent, a status offender, or a dependent, and asking that the court assume jurisdiction over the juvenile, or asking that the juvenile be transferred to a criminal court for prosecution as an adult.

petition not sustained: The finding by a juvenile court in an adjudicatory hearing that there is not sufficient evidence to sustain an allegation that a juvenile is a delinquent, status offender, or dependent.

plea: A defendant's formal answer in court to the charges brought against him or her in a complaint, information, or indictment.

plea, final: The last plea to a given charge, entered in a court record by or for a defendant.

plea, guilty: A defendant's formal answer in court to the charges in a complaint, information, or indictment, in which the defendant states that the charges are true and that he or she has committed the offense as charged.

plea, initial: The first plea to a given charge, entered in a court record by or for a defendant.

plea, not guilty: A defendant's formal answer in court to the charges in a complaint, information, or indictment, in which the defendant states that he or she is not guilty.

plea bargaining: The exchange of prosecutorial and/or judicial concessions, commonly a lesser charge, the dismissal of other pending charges, a recommendation by the prosecutor for a reduced sentence, or a combination thereof, in return for a plea of guilty.

police department: A local law enforcement agency directed by a chief of police or a commissioner.

police officer: A local law enforcement officer employed by a police department.

population movement: Entries and exits of adjudicated persons, or persons subject to judicial proceedings, into or from correctional facilities or programs.

predisposition report: The document resulting from an investigation undertaken by a probation agency or other designated authority, which has been requested by a juvenile court, into the past behavior, family background, and personality of a juvenile who has been adjudicated a delinquent, a status offender, or a dependent, in order to assist the court in determining the most appropriate disposition.

presentence report: The document resulting from an investigation undertaken by a probation agency or other designated authority, at the request of a criminal court, into the past behavior, family circumstances, and personality of an adult who has been convicted of a crime, in order to assist the court in determining the most appropriate sentence.

prior record: Criminal history record information concerning any law enforcement, court, or correctional proceedings that have occurred before the current investigation of, or proceedings against, a person; or statistical descriptions of the criminal histories of a set of persons.

prison: A confinement facility having custodial authority over adults sentenced to confinement for more than a year.

prison (sentence): The penalty of commitment to the jurisdiction of a confinement facility system for adults, of which the custodial authority extends to persons sentenced to more than a year of confinement.

prisoner: A person in custody in a confinement facility, or in the personal custody of a criminal justice official while being transported to or between confinement facilities.

privately secured bail: An arrangement similar to the bail bondsman system except that bail is provided without cost to the defendant. A private organization provides bail for indigent arrestees who meet its eligibility requirements.

probable cause: A set of facts and circumstances that would induce a reasonably intelligent and prudent person to believe that an accused person had committed a specific crime.

probation: The conditional freedom granted by a judicial officer to an alleged offender, or adjudicated adult or juvenile, as long as the person meets certain conditions of behavior. One requirement is to report to a designated person or agency over some specified period of time. Probation may involve special conditions as discussed in the definition of suspended sentence. Probation often involves a suspended sentence, but may be used in association with suspension of final judgment or deferral of sentencing.

probation (sentence): A court requirement that a person fulfill certain conditions of behavior and accept the supervision of a probation agency, usually in lieu of a sentence to confinement but sometimes including a jail sentence.

probation agency (probation department): A correctional agency of which the principal functions are juvenile intake, the supervision of adults and juveniles placed on probation status, and the investigation of adults or juveniles for the purpose of preparing presentence or predisposition reports to assist the court in determining the proper sentence or juvenile court disposition.

probationer: A person required by a court or probation agency to meet certain conditions of behavior, who may or may not be placed under the supervision of a probation agency.

probation officer: An employee of a probation agency whose primary duties include one or more of the probation agency functions.

probation violation: An act or a failure to act by a probationer that does not conform to the conditions of his or her probation.

pro se (in propria persona): Acting as one's own defense attorney in criminal proceedings; representing oneself.

prosecutor: An attorney employed by a government agency or subunit whose official duty is to initiate and maintain criminal proceedings on behalf of the government against persons accused of committing criminal offenses.

prosecutorial agency: A federal, state, or local criminal justice agency of which the principal function is the prosecution of alleged offenders.

public defender: An attorney employed by a government agency or subdivision, whose official duty is to represent defendants unable to hire private counsel.

public defender's office: A federal, state, or local criminal justice agency or subunit of which the principal function is to represent defendants unable to hire private counsel.

purge (record): The complete removal of arrest, criminal, or juvenile record information from a given records system.

rape: Unlawful sexual intercourse with a female, by force or without legal or factual consent.

rape, forcible: Sexual intercourse with a female against her will, by force or threat of force.

rape, statutory: Sexual intercourse with a female who has consented in fact but is deemed, because of age, to be legally incapable of consent.

rape without force or consent: Sexual intercourse with a female legally of the age of consent, but who is unconscious, or whose ability to judge or control her conduct is inherently impaired by mental defect, or impaired by intoxicating substances.

recidivism: The repetition of criminal behavior; habitual criminality.

Annotation: In statistical practice, a recidivism rate may be any of a number of possible counts of instances of arrest, conviction, correctional commitment, and correctional status changes, related to counts of repetitions of these events within a given period of time.

Efforts to arrive at a single standard statistical description of recidivism have been hampered by the fact that the correct referent of the term is the actual repeated criminal or delinquent behavior of a given person or group, yet the only available statistical indicators of that behavior are records of such system events as rearrests, reconvictions, and probation or parole violations or revocations. It is recognized that these data reflect agency decisions about events and may or may not closely correspond with actual criminal behavior. Different conclusions about degrees of correspondence between system decisions and actual behavior consequently produce different definitions of recidivism, that is, different judgments of which system event repetition rates best measure actual recidivism rates. This is an empirical question, and not one of definition to be resolved solely by analysis of language usage and system logic.

Resolution has also been delayed by the limited capacities of most criminal justice statistical systems, which do not routinely make available the standardized offender-based transaction data (OBTD) that may be needed for the best measurement of recidivism.

Pending the adoption of a statistical description of recidivism, and the ability to implement it, it is recommended that recidivism analyses include the widest possible range of system events that can correspond with actual recidivism, and that sufficient detail on offenses charged be included to enable discrimination between degrees of gravity of offenses. The units of count should be clearly identified and the length of community exposure time of the subject population stated.

The National Advisory Commission on Criminal Justice Standards and Goals recommends a standard definition of recidivism in its volume *Corrections* (1973): "Recidivism is measured by (1) criminal acts that resulted in a conviction by a court, when committed by individuals who are under correctional supervision or who have been released from correctional supervision within the previous three years, and by (2) technical violations of probation or parole in which a sentencing or paroling authority took action that resulted in an adverse change in the offender's legal status." Neither of these formulations is endorsed as adequate for all purposes. Both limit the measure and concept of recidivism to populations that are or have been under correctional supervision. Yet the ultimate significance of data concerning the repetition of criminal behavior often depends upon the comparison of the behavior of unconfined or unsupervised offenders with the behavior of those with correctional experience.

referral to intake: In juvenile proceedings, a request by the police, parents, or other agency or person that a juvenile intake unit take appropriate action concerning a juvenile alleged to have committed a delinquent act or status offense, or be dependent.

release from detention: The authorized exit from detention of a person subject to criminal or juvenile justice proceedings.

release from prison: A cover term for all unlawful exits from federal or state confinement facilities primarily intended for adults serving sentences of more than a year, including all conditional and unconditional releases, deaths, and transfers to other jurisdictions, excluding escapes.

Release on parole/	Release while still under jurisdiction of correc-
Conditional release	tional agency, before expiration of sentence
Discretionary	Release date determined by parole authority

Mandatory	Release date determined by statute
Discharge from prison	Release ending all agency jurisdiction
Unconditional release	
Discretionary	Pardon, commutation of sentence
Mandatory	Expiration of sentence
Temporary release	Authorized, unaccompanied temporary departure for educational, employment, or other authorized purposes
Transfer of jurisdiction	Transfer to jurisdiction of another correctional agency or a court
Death	Death from homicide, suicide, or natural causes
Execution	Execution of sentence of death

In some systems, "release on parole" represents only discretionary conditional release. It is recommended that mandatory conditional releases be included, as both types describe conditional releases with subsequent parole status.

release on bail: The release, by a judicial officer, of an accused person who has been taken into custody, upon the accused's promise to pay a certain sum of money or property if he or she fails to appear in court as required, which promise may or may not be secured by the deposit of an actual sum of money or property.

release on own recognizance: The release, by a judicial officer, of an accused person who has been taken into custody, upon the accused's promise to appear in court as required for criminal proceedings. (See BONDSMAN-SECURED BAIL).

release, pretrial: A procedure whereby an accused person who has been taken into custody is allowed to be free before and during his or her trial.

release to third party: The release, by a judicial officer, of an accused person who has been taken into custody, to a third party who promises to return the accused to court for criminal proceedings.

residential treatment center: A government facility that serves juveniles whose behavior does not necessitate the strict confinement of a training school, often allowing them greater contact with the community.

restitution: Usually a cash payment by the offender to the victim of an amount considered to offset the loss incurred by the victim or the community. The amount of the payment may be scaled down to the earning capacity of the offender and/or payments may be made in installments. Sometimes services directly or indirectly benefiting the victim may be substituted for cash payment.

retained counsel: An attorney, not employed or compensated by a government agency or subunit, nor assigned by the court, who is privately hired to represent a person(s) in a criminal proceeding.

revocation: An administrative act performed by a parole authority removing a person from parole, or a judicial order by a court removing a person from parole or probation, in response to a violation on the part of the parolee or probationer.

revocation hearing: An administrative and/or judicial hearing on the question of whether or not a person's probation or parole status should be revoked.

rights of defendant: Those powers and privileges that are constitutionally guaranteed to every defendant.

robbery: The unlawful taking or attempted taking of property that is in the immediate possession of another, by force or the threat of force.

robbery, armed: The unlawful taking or attempted taking of property that is in the immediate possession of another, by the use or threatened use of a deadly or dangerous weapon.

robbery, strongarm: The unlawful taking or attempted taking of property that is in the immediate possession of another by the use or threatened use of force, without the use of a weapon.

runaway: A juvenile who has been adjudicated by a judicial officer of a juvenile court as having committed the status offense of leaving the custody and home of his or her parents, guardians, or custodians without permission and failing to return within a reasonable length of time.

seal (record): The removal, for the benefit of the subject, of arrest, criminal, or juvenile record information from routinely available status to a status requiring special procedures for access.

security: The degree of restriction of inmate movement within a correctional facility, usually divided into maximum, medium, and minimum levels.

security and privacy standards: A set of principles and procedures developed to ensure the security and confidentiality of criminal or juvenile record information in order to protect the privacy of the persons identified in such records.

sentence: The penalty imposed by a court upon a convicted person, or the court decision to suspend imposition or execution of the penalty.

sentence, indeterminate: A statutory provision for a type of sentence to imprisonment where, after the court has determined that the convicted person shall be imprisoned, the exact length of imprisonment and parole supervision is afterward fixed within statutory limits by a parole authority.

sentence, mandatory: A statutory requirement that a certain penalty shall be imposed and executed upon certain convicted offenders.

sentence, suspended: The court decision postponing the pronouncement of sentence upon a convicted person, or postponing the execution of a sentence that has been pronounced by the court.

sentence, suspended execution: The court decision setting a penalty but postponing its execution.

sentence, suspended imposition: The court decision postponing the setting of a penalty.

shelter: A confinement or community facility for the care of juveniles, usually those held pending adjudication.

speedy trial: The right of the defendant to have a prompt trial.

stationhouse citation: An alternative to pretrial detention, whereby the arrestee is escorted to the precinct police station or headquarters rather than the pretrial detention facility. Release, which may occur before or after booking, is contingent upon the written promise of the defendant to appear in court as specified on the release form.

status offender: A juvenile who has been adjudicated by a judicial officer of a juvenile court as having committed a status offense, which is an act or conduct that is an offense only when committed or engaged in by a juvenile.

status offense: An act or conduct that is declared by statute to be an offense, but only when committed or engaged in by a juvenile, and which can be adjudicated only by a juvenile court.

subjudicial officer: A judicial officer who is invested with certain judicial powers and functions, but whose decisions in criminal and juvenile cases are subject to *de novo* review by a judge.

subpoena: A written order issued by a judicial officer requiring a specified person to appear in a designated court at a specified time in order to serve as a witness in a case under the jurisdiction of that court, or to bring material to that court.

summons: A written order issued by a judicial officer requiring a person accused of a criminal offense to appear in a designated court at a specified time to answer the charge(s). The summons is a request or instruction to appear in court to face an accusation. As an alternative to the arrest warrant, it is used in cases where complaints are registered with the magistrate or prosecutor's office.

supervised release: A type of release involving more frequent contact than monitored release. Typically, various conditions are imposed and supervision is aimed at enforcement of these conditions and provision of services as needed. Some form of monetary bail also may be attached as a condition of supervised release, especially in high-risk cases.

suspect: A person, adult or juvenile, considered by a criminal justice agency to be one who may have committed a specific criminal offense, but who has not been arrested or charged.

suspended sentence: Essentially a threat to take more drastic action if the offender again commits a crime during some specified time period. Where no special conditions are attached, it is assumed that the ends of justice have been satisfied by conviction and no further action is required as long as the offender refrains from involvement in new offenses. Suspended sentences may be conditioned on various limitations as to mobility, associates, or activities or on requirements to make reparations or participate in some rehabilitation program.

suspicion: Belief that a person has committed a criminal offense, based on facts and circumstances that are not sufficient to constitute probable cause.

theft: Larceny, or in some legal classifications the group of offenses including larceny, and robbery, burglary, extortion, fraudulent offenses, hijacking, and other offenses sharing the element of larceny.

third-party release: A release extending to another person the responsibility for ensuring the defendant's appearance in court. This may be a person known to the defendant or a designated volunteer. Third-party release may be a condition of unsecured bail, with the third party as a cosigner.

time served: The total time spent in confinement by a convicted adult before and after sentencing, or only the time spent in confinement after a sentence of commitment to a confinement facility.

training school: A correctional institution for juveniles adjudicated to be delinquents or status offenders and committed to confinement by a judicial officer.

transfer to adult court: The decision by a juvenile court, resulting from a transfer hearing, that jurisdiction over an alleged delinquent will be waived and that he or she should be prosecuted as an adult in a criminal court.

transfer hearing: A preadjudicatory hearing in juvenile court for the purpose of determining whether juvenile court jurisdiction should be retained or waived over a juvenile alleged to have committed a delinquent act(s), and whether he or she should be transferred to criminal court for prosecution as an adult.

trial: The examination of issues of fact and law in a case or controversy, beginning when the jury has been selected in a jury trial, or when the first witness is sworn, or the first evidence is introduced in a court trial, and concluding when a verdict is reached or the case is dismissed.

trial, court (trial, judge): A trial in which there is no jury, and in which a judicial officer determines the issues of fact and law in a case.

trial, jury: A trial in which a jury determines the issues of fact in a case.

UCR: An abbreviation for the Federal Bureau of Investigation's uniform crime reporting program.

unconditional discharge: As a post-trial disposition, essentially the same as unconditional diversion. No savings are obtained in criminal justice processing costs, but jail populations may be reduced; conditions of release are imposed for an offense in which the defendant's involvement has been established.

unconditional diversion: The cessation of criminal processing at any point short of adjudication with no continuing threat of prosecution. This type of diversion may involve the voluntary referral to a social service agency or program dealing with a problem underlying the offense.

unsecured bail: A form of release differing from release on recognizance only in that the defendant is subject to paying the amount of bail if he or she defaults. Unsecured bail permits release without deposit or purchase of a bondsman's services.

venue: The geographical area from which the jury is drawn in which trial is held in a criminal action.

verdict: In criminal proceedings, the decision made by a jury in a jury trial, or by a judicial officer in a court trial, that a defendant is either guilty or not guilty of the offense(s) for which he or she has been tried.

verdict, guilty: In criminal proceedings, the decision made by a jury in a jury trial, or by a judicial officer in a court trial, that the defendant is guilty of the offense(s) for which he or she has been tried.

verdict, not guilty: In criminal proceedings, the decision made by a jury in a jury trial, or by a judicial officer in a court trial, that the defendant is not guilty of the offense(s) for which he or she has been tried.

victim: A person who has suffered death, physical or mental suffering, or loss of property as the result of an actual or attempted criminal offense committed by another person.

warrant, arrest: A document issued by a judicial officer that directs a law enforcement officer to arrest a person who has been accused of an offense.

warrant, bench: A document issued by a judicial officer directing that a person who has failed to obey an order or notice to appear be brought before the court.

warrant, search: A document issued by a judicial officer that directs a law enforcement officer to conduct a search for specified property or persons at a specific location, to seize the property or persons, if found, and to account for the results of the search to the issuing judicial officer.

witness: A person who directly perceives an event or thing, or who has expert knowledge relevant to a case.

youthful offender: A person, adjudicated in criminal court, who may be above the statutory age limit for juveniles but is below a specified upper age limit, for whom special correctional commitments and special record sealing procedures are made available by statute.

Index

303